TRUE STORIES OF THE PARANORMAL

THE COMPLETE COLLECTION

By

Cindy Parmiter

Copyright: July 2017

Prologue

We have all experienced brushes with the paranormal in our lives, whether we realize it or not. It gives one pause that, perhaps, we have-at one time or another-been within arms-reach of a portal to another dimension and been blissfully unaware. Maybe, we have stood beside the ghost of a lost child and not allowed ourselves to see him for fear of the repercussions. Perhaps that creaking sound wasn't simply a worn out floorboard or the house settling, but rather something unseen that resides beyond our safe and comfortable existence.

The spirit world is a strange and mysterious place. Just as we here on this side deal with love, loss, jealousy and even vengeance, so do those who have passed on to whatever awaits the living once they leave the earthly world behind. Most continue on; as they are meant to do. They reflect upon what they learned in this life as they prepare to move on to a higher plane. Others are more stubborn. They cannot forget the life they once possessed and make it their mission to return to what they once knew.

Whatever the circumstances, they all have stories to tell. This book is the combined volumes of my "True Stories of the Paranormal" series. The stories contained within these pages range from simple encounters with friendly spirits to terrifying experiences real people have had with true evil that originated beyond this world.

As you sit in your home, safe and sound, keep in mind that the thin veil between what we know and what we think we know to be real is a fragile one. It can drop at any moment revealing things we can only imagine in our dreams or, in some cases, our worst nightmares.

Parmiter/ Paranormal Collection / 4

Chapter 1
Our Dream House

My husband Larry and I married in August, 2000. At the time, we were living in a dingy apartment with no air conditioning and a refrigerator that kept food lukewarm at best. We needed to find a more suitable place, but it was slim pickings on our meager income. This is where my darling mother stepped in to help.

At the time, she was working as a caregiver for an elderly woman who just happened to have a rental property that had recently been vacated. The house was located in Parkersburg, West Virginia. My mother had worked for this lady for years and was also a casual friend of the previous tenant of the rental house.

The rent was dirt cheap and my mom's employer was willing to let us move in without a deposit since she knew and trusted my mother. It sounded like a dream come true and we jumped at the chance. It was summertime and steaming hot when we drove over to take a look at what would become our new home.

The sight of it left something to be desired. It was a two-story house with paint peeling from every angle. It wasn't pretty on the outside, but the neighborhood was pleasant and quiet and we would be close to my jobs. When we entered the house, I was flabbergasted. It was as quaint and lovely inside as it was dirty and decrepit on the outside.

Cold air from the window air conditioning unit greeted us like a welcoming friend as we entered the living room.

As for the interior, the rooms were spacious and clean. There was a fireplace with a mantel in the living room. The house had a big floor furnace between the living room and the dining room. The kitchen was neat and just the right size for an on-the-go cook such as myself. There were two bedrooms upstairs, both of which boasted walk-in closets. A small bathroom rounded out the living area of the home. We were eager to start a family and this looked like the perfect place for us.

The house also had a large basement where the washer and dryer were located. It was a bit musty, but that was more or less to be expected. It was obvious by the homemade workbench that someone had spent a lot of time down there. They had also, by the look of things, never thrown anything away. Old doors and windows were stored meticulously on shelving which seemed to have been built for that very purpose. I came across some rat poison which put me off a little bit, but the landlady assured me that the rodent problem had been taken care of long ago. Someone had, apparently, forgotten to remove the boxes of poison.

The bottom line was that we loved the house. The rent was unbeatable. The landlady was nice. She said we could bring our two cats. She loved animals and didn't have a problem with us adopting a dog if we wanted one in the future. She did tell us that repairs would be our responsibility since we weren't paying much rent. That sounded fair and we sealed the deal with handshakes and hugs. As for my husband and I, we were thrilled to start our life together in our new house. We began moving in the very next day.

My brother and a family friend were recruited to help us move. We were completely out of the apartment and into our new house in a day or so. Things couldn't have been better. I had a refrigerator that worked like a charm. The house was as cool as a cucumber. We were happy and content in our dream house. The only thing missing from our happy lives was a baby.

We had been married for a year when we decided to start seriously trying to conceive. Contrary to what I had been told in high school, it's not always that easy. We tried for months with no luck. Every month I would get my hopes up only to have them dashed by Mother Nature. Finally, we saw a specialist who ran all sorts of tests and informed us that a child might not be in the cards for us. Fertility treatments were an option. He suggested we go home and think it over.

This was crushing news. We stayed up all night talking and trying to decide which road to take. After much back and forth, we decided to let nature take its course. If we conceived naturally, great, if not--then we would adopt. The pressure was off.

That was on a Friday. On Monday morning I woke up with the strangest feeling, I can't explain it, I just felt as though something was different. I began to wonder and hope that maybe, just maybe, I would have a miracle. I always kept pregnancy tests on hand so I opened one up and gave it a shot. Amazingly, I had two pink lines for the first time after so many months of one line and the dreaded "not pregnant." Little did we know that, even as the doctor was explaining to us that we might never conceive, I was already expecting.

When I finally saw a positive test result, I woke my sleeping husband to tell him the good news. He was elated that we were finally going to be parents. I phoned my doctor's office as soon as they opened to schedule an appointment. I wanted an expert to confirm what my home test was telling me. I had heard that the tests could be faulty and wasn't taking any chances.

My doctor squeezed me in that afternoon. The nurse gave me a pregnancy test. I did the usual routine and handed it back to her. She said she'd be right back. She was as excited as I was when she poked her head into the room a short time later and announced with a big smile "You're pregnant!"

My pregnancy, I'll have to say, was the easiest pregnancy I could have asked for. Everything went smoothly with no complications. Nine months flew by and in August of 2002 my beautiful baby girl was born via C-section.

The first few months with our new baby were rocky. She absolutely refused to sleep in the nursery we had so carefully decorated and child-proofed for her. She would wail like the world was coming to an end anytime we laid her in her crib. Strangely, even though it was a beautiful room, neither one of our cats would set foot in it. It seemed odd, but I didn't give it too much thought. Cats can be fickle sometimes.

It was around this time that we began to experience some strange phenomena. For one thing, the lightbulbs in the overhead fixture in our dining room started to blow out. I don't mean burn out, as lightbulbs do. These would literally shatter, sending shards of glass raining down on the table and floor. All that would be left in the socket would be the metal ring. This happened more times than I could count no matter what wattage of bulbs we used. We even had an electrician take a look at the wiring. He could find no fault in our electrical system. There was no obvious reason for the bizarre phenomena.

Another thing that we noticed was that all of our electrical equipment began to malfunction. The air conditioner had to be repaired on numerous occasions. The television set would go on the blink regularly. We would have to replace VCRs and DVD players every time we turned around. The refrigerator stopped working, forcing us to purchase a new one at our own expense. The list goes on and on. If it ran on an electrical current--we ended up having to buy a new one or fix the old one. Again, the electrician could find no explanation. The wiring was sound. It just became an annoying thing we learned to put up with. We didn't read anything sinister into it at the time.

For the first year of our daughter's life, she slept in the bed with me and my husband. We really had no choice; it was either that or listen to her blood curdling screams all night long. Again, I didn't read too much into this; I was a first time mom and assumed that perhaps all babies behaved this way.

Unfortunately, having a one-year old in our bed was wreaking havoc on us emotionally. One or the other of us would wake up nearly every night in a panic, certain that we had crushed the baby in our sleep. It had to stop. She was going to have to sleep in her room and that was that.

Night after night, for longer than I would like to admit, our baby girl cried herself to sleep in her beautiful pink bedroom that was supposed to be her sanctuary. She didn't get used to it, as we had hoped she would. Every morning when I would go in to get her up for breakfast, she would be standing in her crib, arms outstretched, tears running down her cheeks, face as red as a beet. I would pick her up and she would cling to me as though she would never let me go. Something was wrong, but I didn't know what was going on and she couldn't tell me, not yet anyway.

When she began to talk, everything changed. One morning, in the midst of the usual crying, she said that someone had been shaking her crib all night. She didn't say it in those exact words, since she was barely two years old, but that was the gist of it and I understood her perfectly. I was scared and so was she.

As her vocabulary grew, she eventually told me that there were two men in her room. Sometimes they stood by the door, at other times by the window. They watched over her constantly, at least when she was in her room. Sometimes they would shake the crib while she was in it. Most of the time, they simply stood and stared at her.

I told my husband what she said and he was livid. He stormed up the stairs and yelled into the room. "I don't know who you are or why you're here, but if you hurt my kid, I'll fucking kill you!" Neither my husband nor I ever doubted for one moment what she was telling us. Other things had begun to happen in the house that we couldn't explain. We started to think that someone was there with us and they weren't at all happy about sharing the house.

The first incident that I remember happened one day when we were all in the living room watching television. My daughter and I were in the rocking chair and Larry was sitting on the floor. As we sat minding our own business the peacefulness was shattered by the sound of something crashing to the floor in the kitchen.

Larry jumped up and ran to see what had happened with our daughter and me right behind him. "Holy shit!" was all he could manage to say. Our toaster oven, which had been sitting on the counter top against the wall, was lying in pieces all over the floor. Now, you have to understand that these counters were at least two and a half to three feet wide and the oven was nowhere near the edge. No possible way had it slid off. The countertops were level. Nothing had jarred the house. No earthquakes or big trucks had thundered passed the house. It had been a quiet day like any other. The appliance hadn't simply fallen off of the counter; it had been smashed into oblivion. Literally, there were pieces of it from one end of the kitchen to the other as though someone had lifted it over their head and heaved it to the floor.

Larry and I just stared at each other in silence. Finally, I told him to take our daughter back into the living room while I cleaned up the mess. The whole time I was picking up the remnants of what had once been our toaster oven, I was trying to come up with a logical explanation for what had just happened. There was none. I convinced myself that it was just a fluke, sometimes things happen with no rhyme or reason. There was nothing to do except to forget about it. Little did we know at the time, but this was only the beginning.

Smashed toaster ovens aside, the most pressing matter at that time was what to do about our child's night terrors. She couldn't stay in her room alone and our bedroom wasn't big enough to sleep three. So, I decided that, at least for the time being, I would sleep on the floor beside her crib. From that night on, until we moved out of the house, I slept in my daughter's room. She was immediately at ease. The crying fits that had gone on for so long ceased, literally, overnight. The reason would soon be clear when the whirlwind of activity in the room seemed to settle upon me.

In order to explain what began happening to me in my daughter's bedroom, I have to take you back to when I was a child. My maternal grandmother lived in a house that absolutely terrified me. I based my novel "Fox Holler" on that house. My sister and I have talked many times about that house and how scared we were when we had to stay there on our summer visits to Grandma's.

The incident I remember most clearly happened when I was around eight or nine. I was sleeping in the back bedroom with my mom and dad. The room was pitch dark and I was sound asleep. All at once I was awakened by swirling images all around me. I don't know how else to explain it except to say that it looked like a fireworks show going off in my head. There were lights flashing everywhere and balls of light whizzing by me. Everything was moving so fast and I remember the feeling of dizziness and falling even though I hadn't moved.

I screamed for my mom, "They're after me! They're after me!!" I was trembling and terrified. My mom held me and told me that there was nothing there. I cried and shook uncontrollably. She assured me that it was only a nightmare. She told me to go back to sleep and that I would be alright. There was nothing to be afraid of. I knew that she was wrong. There was something in that house that I was very afraid of. I did, however, go back to sleep. I never forgot the terror of that night. It was repeated almost every time I stayed at that house.

Sleeping on the floor in my daughter's room that first night was like reliving those nights at my grandma's all over again. As I closed my eyes and attempted to drift off to sleep, my senses were suddenly assaulted by a barrage of flashing lights and whirling balls that seemed to fly right by my head. My eyes were closed, but I felt like they were open. It was almost an exact repeat of what I had seen all those years ago. The light show was dizzying. I felt like everything was spinning even though I was lying down. I can't describe the feeling, it's just this hive of activity that I seemed to be in the middle of. I liken it to being chased by something that has found its way into your psyche. It would go on for so long that I wanted to scream and then, just like that, it would stop. Blackness would return and everything would go back to normal.

This happened night after night. I dreaded it, but somehow I knew that if I didn't stay in the room and experience this terrifying routine, whatever it was would once again turn its attention to my daughter. I've never understood exactly what was going on and I've never heard anyone else say they experienced such a thing. I do know that it's very real and it comes from somewhere not of this plane.

Not too long after the toaster oven incident we had almost an exact replay, except this time it was the tea kettle. The kettle was on the back burner of the stove, as it always was, when we once again heard a crash coming from the kitchen. We ran in only to discover that our nice red tea kettle with the fancy spout was now in pieces all over the floor. The spout was in one place, the lid another, the handle another. Every bit of it that could be broken off was.

Again, Larry and I stood staring at each other in disbelief. No way had that tea kettle just leapt off of the stove. It was a flat surface. The house wasn't on a hill. The stove didn't pitch forward. All we knew was that it was, inexplicably, smashed to smithereens. We joked that someone or something really didn't like our kitchen appliances. We would lose our sense of humor soon enough.

Weeks would go by and we would have no inkling that anything in the house was amiss, except for my nightly fireworks show. One afternoon while were sitting at our dining room table having a leisurely lunch, we heard a crash in the basement. This time, I was the one who went to see what had happened.

In the basement, it looked like a hurricane had passed through. All of the panes of glass that had been so carefully stored in their own little cubbies were lying smashed into a million pieces on the floor. The boards and doors that had been stored there were in splinters. I yelled for my husband to come take a look. Neither of us knew what to say or do. Those window panes and doors had been lying flat on shelving that had been made specifically to hold them. It was as if the house had just tipped them out onto the floor. I wanted to cry, not only because of the mess I would now have to tend to but, also, because someone or something was wrecking our house. We wondered what it was they wanted from us. It wouldn't be long before we would have our answer.

The basement of our house was the room I disliked the most. It was the only room that gave me a horrible feeling anytime I went down there. Unfortunately for me, that was where the laundry room was so I spent more time there than I would care to remember. It's difficult to describe the vibe that the basement gave off. It was cloying and claustrophobic even though it was an oversized room. I always felt as though someone was down there with me, urging me to hurry and go back upstairs. I'm not ashamed to admit that there were several times when I would throw the laundry in the washing machine and then run up the stairs, too scared to look behind me. I know there probably wasn't anything there, but the hairs would stand up on the back of my neck. Again, this is a room that our cats hated. They were miserable anytime they went down there.

One episode I will share might embarrass my husband, but it happened and I will relate it to you as he related it to me. One summer's night when our air conditioner was on the blink, my daughter and I decided to sleep over at my mother's house. Larry stayed behind, eager to have the house to himself. He settled in to watch a movie that was a little racier than we would normally watch when his plans were thwarted by the sound of an avalanche in the dining room.

There was an area in the corner behind the refrigerator that we used for storage. When he went to investigate the noise, he found that all of the items that we had stored back there had managed to come crashing down all over the place. Not a thing was left undisturbed. He was so spooked by the event that he turned off the television and ran upstairs to bed. Apparently, someone didn't approve of his choice of movies.

Something else about our house that was creepy, but explainable, was a constant scratching in the walls upstairs. We heard it all day, every day. Eventually, we found out what the culprits were when one of our cats caught a bat in our house in the middle of the night. It made the most awful "whirring" noise as our big Maine Coon grabbed it by its wing. We captured it and released it outside. Our cats were vaccinated against rabies so we didn't give it much thought. At least, now we knew what was scratching inside our walls. This would not be our last encounter with these uninvited guests, the next time would be much more frightening and we would pay dearly for our kindness.

Larry worked, at that time, as a karaoke host which meant that he was usually out until the wee small hours of the morning. On one such night, I had accidentally fallen asleep on the couch watching television. Our daughter was upstairs in her bedroom. I was abruptly awakened by the same whirring sound that I had heard on the night that our cat caught the bat upstairs. As my eyes focused, I could see the little brown bat frantically flying around our living room. There was no telling how long he had been there or what he might have gotten into.

I jumped up from the couch and did the first thing that came to mind--I phoned my sister. She worked the night shift at a local grocery store so I knew she would be up. I told her about the bat and she said she would leave work and be right over. I could always depend on her when I was in a jam. Within a half hour she was at my door holding a fishing net. She cornered the bat in the dining room and captured him in the net.

She asked me what I wanted her to do with him, turn him loose or keep him to have him tested for rabies. Kindhearted and sometimes foolish me, I said turn him loose. She released him as she left to go back to work. I went upstairs to settle in beside my daughter's crib. Stopping off in the bathroom I noticed that there was blood all over the place. The bat had somehow managed to squeeze in through a tiny hole over the shower. He had then banged into the walls, I'm assuming while he was trying to find a way out. I noticed also that I had two small marks on my ankle. They were tiny, just little pinpricks. I turned off the light and lay down to try to get some sleep. My mind kept nudging me back to the little red marks on my ankle. I decided that I should read up on bat bites just to be on the safe side.

Unable to sleep, I went downstairs and searched online for any information I could find about the bats that were native to our area. Turns out, the species of bat that was found locally had been found to carry rabies. Alarmingly, a bat's teeth are so fine that it is possible to be bitten and not realize it. And, since rabies is carried in the saliva, a person didn't even have to be bitten to be exposed. Rabies is rare and it was a pretty good bet that our bat didn't have it, but even though the disease is easily preventable, it is fatal once symptoms appeared. After weighing all the possibilities, I decided to call our doctor the following morning.

He confirmed what I had most feared. Any exposure to a bat should be regarded as dangerous. Since my daughter's room did not have a door on it, there was no way of knowing whether or not the bat had gone into her room before he made his way downstairs. We would both have to go through the rabies vaccinations as a precautionary measure. Better safe than sorry. Had we kept the bat, the Health Department could have determined if he, in fact, carried the rabies virus. We had turned him loose so it would be us who would suffer. Numerous trips to the hospital for shots and several thousands of dollars later, we were in the clear. Lesson learned.

Our dream house was taking a toll on us in more ways than one. By the time my daughter was four, she had already had to go through the pain of rabies shots. She had been terrorized in her bedroom by two men who gave her no peace. She had also seen one of her cats killed by a sudden onslaught of sand fleas which had converged on our basement seemingly overnight. Our cats never set foot outside and yet one of them had died from an infestation so severe that it had claimed her in a matter of hours. We called in exterminators to no avail. And then, as quickly as the infestation had begun, it was over. Our other cats (by this time we had three) somehow managed to survive the ordeal. I had begun to truly hate that house.

Something that my daughter was the first to notice was the constant sound of running water in the house. If we were downstairs in the living room, we would hear water running upstairs. If we were upstairs in the bedrooms, we would hear water running in the kitchen. It ran day and night. It became a game to us after a while. We would run to see if we could catch the culprit who was turning the water on, but the sound would stop immediately as soon as we got close to the source. This was just one more annoyance that we learned to live with.

The final straw that convinced us that we weren't meant for that house, and certainly weren't welcome there, came one cold night in February 2008. Larry was upstairs in the bathroom. Our daughter was in bed and I was turning off the television, getting ready to turn in for the night. As I walked up the stairs that led to the bedrooms, the whole house shook as something behind me made a thunderous crashing sound.

I ran towards the dining room only to find that our floor furnace had fallen into the basement. I didn't even know such a thing was possible. Larry came running down the stairs in response to the sonic boom that had rocked the house. He stopped short when he saw the gaping hole in the floor where our furnace had once been. He raced downstairs to shut off the pilot light while I called 911.

I phoned the emergency number and explained what had happened. The operator said that he would send the Fire Department as soon as possible. He gave no further instructions as I hung up the phone. My husband came back upstairs and said that the pilot light was off, everything would be okay. We were completely ignorant of the danger we were in. I called 911 again and told the operator that my husband had turned off the pilot light. The operator said that was a good idea. Again, he gave no further instructions and didn't seem too worried about the whole situation.

Larry and I sat waiting patiently for the firemen, although we weren't sure why they were even needed. After all, there was no fire. Watching from our living room window, we could see the whole street suddenly light up with fire trucks. Sirens were blaring and lights were flashing. There were people scrambling everywhere.

There was a knock on the door and we opened it to find a parade of emergency personnel anxious to get into our house. They were no nonsense and straight to the point. They informed us, in no uncertain terms, that we had to get out of the house immediately. I explained to one fireman that I had to get my daughter. He yelled "Do it now!" I ran up the stairs and grabbed her and a blanket. She was groggy and didn't understand what was going on. As I ran back down the stairs with my daughter in my arms, I asked the same fireman I had spoken to earlier if I could go find my cats. I was scared that the commotion would spook them and they would run outside. In no uncertain terms, he informed me that our lives were in danger and that we needed to get out and not worry about the cats.

I didn't realize until I stepped out onto the street that they had cordoned off our whole neighborhood. People were standing in their bathrobes all around us staring at our house and the commotion it was causing. As it turns out, turning off the pilot light to the furnace didn't do much good. The gas was still on and we had a water heater with a pilot light that was still burning.

After what seemed like hours, the firemen slowly began streaming out of the house. The one I had spoken with earlier approached us. He told my husband that he wanted to shake his hand. He said that we were the luckiest people he had ever met. The fireman went on to explain that when the furnace fell it had landed on a makeshift blower that the people who lived there before us had installed. This had prevented the furnace from going all the way to the basement floor which would have severed the gas line thereby causing, in all likelihood, the house to explode.

The fireman told us that in reality, the whole block should have been burning at this point. He said that we had a better chance of winning the lottery than walking away, unscathed, from something like this. We had been lucky indeed. And, he added as a side note, our cats were safe. He red tagged the furnace and told us to call the gas company in the morning. Other than that, we were free to go back inside.

I phoned my sister and had her take my daughter for the night. She had been through enough. Larry and I stayed in the house, albeit with no heat, and pondered what had happened and what it all meant.

Someone wanted us out of the house and we knew it. I know that some people will say that floor furnaces fall in for no reason every day. They will also say that amateurishly installed blowers keep said furnaces from causing explosions by preventing the gas line from severing. Well, I was there. This wasn't normal. Our thoughts were that someone coveted the house and we were intruding on their territory. They didn't want to harm us. They just wanted us to leave and they had escalated their efforts to get us out. When scaring our daughter and smashing our belongings didn't prove effective, they resorted to something that would get everyone's attention. Well, it worked. We began house hunting the very next day. If they wanted the house that badly, they could have it. Since they were upping the ante, we didn't want to wait around to see what they would do next.

After all was said and done, we had spent five years in that house. The first year or so were uneventful. Everything changed after our daughter was born. I have always heard that the energy a baby brings to a house can stir up past energies, long at rest. Maybe that's true. Perhaps it was just a coincidence.

Always curious about whom it was that wanted us to leave the house, I finally broke down and told my mom what we had been experiencing there over the years. By this time, we had closed on our new house and I needed to put our demons to rest. My mother is deeply religious and doesn't like to speak of anything supernatural. This is why I never mentioned anything to her before about the entity that was in the house that she had helped secure for us. As is turned out, she knew more than I ever could have imagined.

The family who had lived in the rental house before us had been there for decades. They consisted of an older couple and the woman's father, who had been bedridden for years in the room that would later be our nursery. He had passed away in the house and the couple had continued to live there until the husband also passed away, in the same room. His widow went on to live there for many years after her husband's death before retiring to a senior living facility. Two men had died in that house. Two men--sound familiar?

When I told my mom all of the things that had plagued us in the house, especially the part about the two men who had terrorized her beloved granddaughter, she was shocked. She had known the men in life and couldn't believe they would do such things. "They were such nice people," she said, "Such nice people."

Update In the summer of 2019, I received a message from a man who informed me that he had recently retired from the Parkersburg Police Department after twenty-five years of service.

The gentleman had just read the story of our haunted house and wondered where exactly it had been located. When I told him, he added yet another interesting piece to the puzzle.

He said that he couldn't be certain, but he was pretty sure that he had been called to that address one night to investigate a disturbance. The woman who phoned the emergency number was frantic. According to her, voices were coming out of her telephone even though the receiver was resting in its cradle.

When the officer arrived, he could find nothing wrong with the device. Although he hadn't heard the voices himself, the agitated state of the family members convinced him that they had not been imagining things.

The retired lawman believes, to this day, that the call was not a hoax. The family was distraught and beside themselves when he arrived. He could sense that something strange was going on inside that house, but he had been powerless to do anything about it. And so, apparently, the saga continued long after our departure.

Chapter 2:
The Lost Soul

My husband's Aunt Shirleyanne and her family shared their home with an entity that at first was playful and harmless, but eventually terrorized the family to the point of them calling in help to rid their home of this wayward spirit.

The home that Shirleyanne and her husband chose to raise their young family in was located in West Allis, Wisconsin. It was spacious and the kids had plenty of room to run around and enjoy being kids. The family was happy there and didn't really notice anything was amiss until objects began disappearing and reappearing even though no one in the house would admit to taking them. It became a game to find the shoes and hair barrettes that would be in a closet or on a dresser one minute and then not be seen again for weeks only to turn up exactly where they belonged without explanation.

The lights in the house also began acting up. A light in the kitchen might turn itself on and off while the family was eating dinner. Or the bedroom lights might suddenly turn on in the middle of the night waking whoever might be sleeping. The constant flickering of lights was a nuisance, but it didn't hurt anyone and the family eventually got used to it even though they knew it wasn't normal.

When the time came to do some home renovations, they started in the kitchen. Shirleyanne was so thrilled to be getting rid of the old, dilapidated sink. She had picked out a new modern looking basin which would complement her countertops. When the delivery truck brought the sink, it was cracked and unusable so they ordered another one which upon delivery was also cracked. This happened on six different occasions. The sink would leave the store intact and arrive at the home cracked. The delivery people handled it with kid gloves to no avail. The basins were always cracked when the time came to install them.

Shirleyanne finally gave up on the sink she wanted and ordered another one that wasn't as nice, but would serve the purpose. When that sink arrived and they took the old sink out they were surprised to discover the original manual that had come with the old sink. The second sink that Shirleyanne had chosen was the exact same make as the one they were taking out. It wasn't cracked and was installed with no trouble whatsoever.

Shirleyanne had no interest in antiques; she had never collected them and didn't find them particularly appealing. That is until she moved into this house. Now, she began surrounding herself and her family in antiques. She found herself at antique malls and estate sales, always on the lookout for some item from a bygone era that she could add to her growing collection. She didn't fully understand her sudden interest in antiques, collecting them was just something she felt compelled to do.

Another item in the house that began giving the family headaches was an alarm clock that went off even though no alarm was set. The family would deliberately make a point of checking the clock before bedtime to be sure the alarm wasn't set, but it would blare in the middle of the night and wake them from a sound sleep. Eventually, Shirleyanne unplugged the clock so they could get some rest. The clock alarmed anyway. She finally threw it out, deciding that enough was enough.

Lights flickering on and off and objects being moved around the house were annoying, but not frightening. The family had a feeling that they weren't alone in their house, but whatever had taken up residence there seemed harmless so they didn't pay it much mind. That is until it began to frantically search for something it apparently couldn't find.

The family would be awakened in the middle of the night by the sound of someone running through the house. That would be followed by the sound of the washer and dryer doors being opened and slammed shut. Drawers would be pulled out and violently shut as if someone was looking for something. This would go on for hours. On at least one occasion, Shirleyanne actually saw a dark figure moving through the house. She was sure that it was a young woman. Even though Shirleyanne could see the woman, the woman didn't seem to see Shirleyanne.

Shirleyanne watched as the shadowy figure ran madly throughout the house as though in a panic. She had clearly lost something very dear to her. After that night, the family decided to do some research and get to the bottom of just who it was who was haunting their house.

By researching public records, Shirleyanne found the names of the people who had owned the house prior to them. There had been more than one previous owner, but they were able to narrow the probable spirit down to one possibility.

A young couple had lived in the house years before Shirleyanne and her family moved in. Shirleyanne managed to track down some of the woman's relatives in hopes that they could shed some light on why she might be earthbound and tied to their home. The woman's family agreed to help in any way that they could.

Her family explained that she and her husband had lived in the house only a short time before the woman became pregnant. She had been overjoyed with the prospect of motherhood and reveled in her pregnancy. The couple was elated when the baby came into their lives. Everything seemed perfect until the infant took ill and passed away unexpectedly.

The grief stricken woman was heartbroken and died shortly after losing the baby. Their theory was that perhaps her nighttime frantic searches were her way of looking for her lost baby.

They told Shirleyanne that they would come to the house and talk to her. Perhaps they could convince her to move on. Shirleyanne and her family were willing to try anything at this point.

The young woman's family was familiar with the house. They had been there many times while the woman was still living. They walked through the hallways and rooms and talked to the woman's spirit as you would talk to any relative you missed and still loved.

They told her that it was time for her to move on and that someone else now lived in the house. They explained to her that her baby had already departed and that all she had to do in order to join her child was to step into the light. Feeling that they could do no more, her family wished her well on her journey and said a final goodbye before leaving. Shirleyanne thanked them for their trouble and waited to see what would happen next.

As simple as this solution seems, it apparently worked. Shirleyanne and her family had no more nightly visits from the lost woman. The lights stopped flickering on and off and the phantom footsteps ceased. At last, they had their house back. In the end, the love of a mother for her child knows no boundaries--in this life or the next.

Spirit Animals

My love of animals is one thing I pride myself on. I have always adored cats and dogs and any other animal I was lucky enough to have had wander through my life. This chapter focuses on encounters that I have had with animal apparitions as well as stories that have been related to me by others. Anyone out there who doubts that animals have souls might just change their mind after reading some of the following stories.

Chapter 3:
Tabitha

When I was in my twenties, my sister rescued a tiny little tabby kitten from a freeway underpass. The kitten would have surely been hit by a car had Sue not stopped traffic to save her. I fell in love with this soft bundle of sweetness and knew that I would have to keep her. I named her Tabitha and she was a loyal and treasured pet for eight wonderful years.

After many happy years together, Tabitha developed diabetes and it ravaged her body in a very short amount of time. Nothing seemed to slow the progress of this terrible disease. We couldn't get her blood sugar regulated and she died of cardiac arrest. I was devastated. We buried her in a pet cemetery and I visited her gravesite and placed flowers on her stone marker for many years after she passed. She had been a very special cat indeed and I missed her terribly.

Tabitha had always slept with me. I would settle in under the covers and she would jump up on the bed and nestle in the crook of my legs. This was our nightly ritual for many years. It was a few weeks after she had died when I first noticed the telltale signs that my sweet kitty might still be with me in spirit.

I would find toys that I had bought for Tabitha lying in the middle of the floor even though I had no cats at the time. She was always losing her toys, they would end up under the sofa or the bed or they would just disappear never to be seen again. Some of the toys that were turning up were ones that I hadn't seen in years. I wanted to believe that this was a sign from Tabitha, but I didn't want to read too much into it.

That was until she started jumping up on the bed. I would climb in bed, as I always did, settle in under the covers, turn on my side and then I would feel the bed move as something jumped up beside me and curled up in the crook of my legs. I would immediately reach down and feel for Tabitha, but she wasn't there. Nothing was there. This happened night after night for months. I never saw a cat or anything else jump onto the bed, but I felt the phantom cat's presence and it became a great comfort to me. And then it stopped.

I imagine now that maybe this was my much loved cat's way of telling me that she was okay now. Everything was fine. She missed her life, but it was time for her to move on. It was time for me to move on as well. I'm still glad that she gave me that reassurance that love never dies, it just turns into something else, a warm place in your heart where lost love can rest for eternity.

Chapter 4:
A Cat's Warning

I worked as a real estate agent on and off from 2000-2005. The following story was told to me by a fellow realtor. She had worked at an Ohio real estate office in the late 1990s and this event involved a co-worker in that office.

My agent friend did not know the name of the woman who experienced this unusual brush with the unexplained, so I will call her "Jane" in the retelling. This encounter was with an animal spirit that Jane did not have a personal connection with. Sometimes, our guardian angels come with whiskers instead of wings.

Jane had been house hunting for weeks and had been shown many perfectly lovely homes, but none of them were suited for her. She just wanted to walk into a house and feel like she was home and that hadn't happened yet. Her realtor called her with a house that had everything she was looking for: three bedrooms, two baths, a backyard garden and a fenced-in yard. She was excited to see it for herself. Her agent set up a viewing and Jane waited anxiously to get a look at what might very well be her new home.

When Jane arrived to view the house, her real estate agent was already inside. As they walked through the house, Jane knew that her mind was pretty much made up, she wanted this place. It had been freshly painted and the carpets looked new. Each room was more beautiful than the last. She was sold.

The realtor told Jane to go ahead up to the second level and check out the upstairs bath and bedrooms for herself while she made a quick phone call. Jane walked up the stairs and became her own hostess as she toured the rooms. She found one bedroom that she knew right away would become her home office. The view from the window in that room was breathtaking. She wanted the house. This would be her new home.

As she stood at the window admiring the view, Jane felt something brush gently against her legs. She looked down to find a perfectly lovely white cat circling in and out between her ankles. She bent down and picked the cat up. The animal was friendly and well taken care of…this was obviously someone's pet. Her first thought was that the cat must belong to the realtor. She put it back down on the floor and continued walking through the upstairs rooms. The cat followed her everywhere she went, meowing the whole time.

Jane took an instant liking to the cat and decided that if the cat didn't have an owner, she would keep it. Then, for no reason, the cat began to hiss at Jane. The entire atmosphere in the room changed when the cat became aggressive. Jane began to feel so nauseated that she had to run into the bathroom, afraid that she was going to vomit.

After the sick feeling had passed, Jane went back downstairs to talk to the realtor. She found her agent still on the phone and waited for her to finish so she could have her full attention. When the realtor was done, Jane asked her about the cat, was it hers? No, the realtor didn't bring a cat with her and there shouldn't be a cat in the house. Jane began to lead the realtor up the stairs to search for the cat. She stopped before reaching the second level and couldn't go any further.

There was such a malevolent feeling as they approached the upstairs of the house that Jane felt instantly ill once again. She told her agent that she couldn't go back up there. The agent went alone while Jane waited downstairs. The realtor came back down the stairs and told Jane that she could find no cat. Jane assured her that there was a cat in the house. They searched downstairs and the realtor made another sweep of the upstairs, but they never found any evidence of the cat.

Jane told her realtor that she would have to think about the house, she would let her know. She went home and thought about everything that had happened that day. She loved the house at first but, something about that cat had changed her mind. She had a bad feeling about the house and never wanted to set foot in it again. She called her realtor with the bad news; they would have to keep looking.

Months went by and Jane did eventually find a house that was just what she was looking for. It was her dream home and she was happy there. Not long after settling into her new home, she would receive an unexpected phone call from her realtor with some news that would make her truly thankful for her chance encounter with the mysterious cat.

Her realtor asked her if she had been following a story in the newspaper. Jane didn't know what story the realtor was referring to. It seems that a couple had been murdered in their home. It had been a home invasion, apparently random, and the young husband and wife had been taken upstairs, tied to chairs and bludgeoned to death. Jane was saddened by the news of this tragedy, but wasn't sure why her real estate agent felt the need to share this news with her. It was the location of the house that she thought might interest Jane, it had occurred at the home the agent had shown her months prior, the home where Jane had seen the disappearing cat.

Jane had replayed the events of that fateful day over and over in her mind after learning of the tragic events that had taken place in what could have been her house. If she hadn't encountered the cat upstairs, she would surely have bought the house. The cat had deterred her from making the purchase, thereby saving her from the fate suffered by the unfortunate couple who did buy the house. Was it all just a coincidence or was Jane's guardian angel watching over her that day in the form of a mysterious white feline?

Chapter 5:
Rowdy

The next unexplained animal encounter happened to someone very close to me, my sister, Sue. Ever since I can remember, she has been an animal rescuer. Whether it was an injured bird or a stray cat, she would do whatever she could to help an animal in need. On a summer's day in 2005, someone called her up with an animal emergency, a baby squirrel had been found, it was barely alive and the woman was in a panic. Sue, being Sue, raced to the aid of this animal in need.

The baby squirrel was barely clinging to life when Sue arrived. She took it home and began the arduous task of trying to save this tiny newborn. She bottle fed the squirrel around the clock and made sure it stayed warm on a heating pad. Eventually, after much tender loving care, the baby squirrel rallied. He would live, and what a life he would have.

After a few weeks of being spoiled and pampered, the little squirrel was thriving. Unfortunately, he had never been exposed to the harsh realities of the outside world. He had been handled by a human since shortly after his birth. Sue was afraid that he wouldn't stand a chance if she turned him loose to fend for himself. She made the difficult decision to keep him. She hadn't really wanted a pet squirrel, but it seemed like the only logical solution.

Sue kept the squirrel, who she named "Rowdy", for nearly ten years. He led the life of a pampered Poodle. She bought him the most expensive produce and nuts. He feasted on strawberries, cashews and avocados. He ran freely through the house jumping onto Sue's shoulders whenever she walked by. They became nearly inseparable.

When Rowdy was around nine years old, he began to have trouble eating. Sue took him to the veterinarian and was told that his teeth were overgrown. It was a simple procedure to clip down the teeth. There was another problem. The doctor also discovered a tumor on Rowdy's tongue. She removed a bit to have biopsied. It was probably nothing she assured Sue, but it never hurt to check these things out.

Sue took Rowdy home and waited to hear the results of the biopsy. In the meantime, Rowdy was still not eating well. He wasn't energetic. He just wanted to sleep. By the time the veterinarian phoned Sue to tell her that Rowdy had cancer, she already knew.

The decision to have Rowdy humanely euthanized was a difficult one. Sue had raised him almost since his birth. She had taken him in and nursed him back to health and now she had to end that very life she had saved. It was heartbreaking for her and she was inconsolable.

She decided to bury Rowdy's remains in her back yard under a big oak tree. It was peaceful and other squirrels played underneath the tree all summer long. It was a beautiful place to spend eternity. As she was walking away from his final resting place after saying a tearful goodbye, she saw that there lay one perfectly formed red leaf at the foot of the tree. All of the other leaves were green except for this one. She said that it was so perfect that she picked it up thinking it was artificial, but it was a real leaf. She kept it as a reminder of Rowdy. He wasn't like all of the other squirrels who ran around under the tree. He was her one and only.

Days turned into weeks and Sue couldn't seem to shake the grief she was trying so hard to escape. She went to work every day trying to stay busy to take her mind off of Rowdy. She was self-employed and her jobs required quite a bit of driving from one client's home to another. She enjoyed the scenery and adored her clients, but her heart was heavy as she made her rounds.

On one particularly dreary day she was feeling more downtrodden than usual. She just wanted to finish up with her last client of the day and go home. As she was about to ring the doorbell at her last stop, something lying in front of the door caught her eye. She bent down and picked up the object, an immediate feeling of peace washing over her. It was a perfectly formed red leaf, so perfect in fact that she thought it must be artificial. It was a real leaf, identical to the one she had found at Rowdy's gravesite. There were no other leaves on the sidewalk or stoop except for that one.

Sue couldn't wait to get home to make sure that the other leaf was still there. It was right where she always kept it: beside a framed photo of Rowdy. She picked up the leaf which had stayed red and vibrant and compared it to the leaf she had found at her client's house; they were perfect matches. She placed both leaves on the mantel beside the picture of the little animal she had saved and nurtured. Everything was going to be alright now. Life would go on.

Chapter 6:
Midnight

This last encounter with an animal spirit involves Larry, Ashlyn and myself. When we moved into our very own home, we knew we would be adopting at least one dog to add to our family. We still had our two rescue cats that were both over fifteen-years old and still going strong. Our first addition was a male Shih-Tzu named Gizmo. Katie, our mixed breed rescue dog, came next followed closely by Buscemi, our Rat Terrier.

We decided that five pets were enough. We were finished adopting for a while. That is until my sister phoned me with the news that my Aunt Theresa had passed away. She left behind an eleven year old cat and a fourteen year old dog. My mother and sister were taking the cat, but there were no takers for the poor dog. We'll take her escaped my lips before I could stop myself.

My aunt's house was nearly two hundred miles from ours so my sister agreed to bring the dog to us after my aunt's funeral. We waited anxiously to meet the newest member of our family. After a couple of days, I finally got the call we had been waiting for. They were in town and I could pick up the dog. Ashlyn and I were out the door and in the van in record time.

My first impression of the dog was not a good one. She was a black Lab mix, dirty, grossly overweight and so arthritic she could barely walk. Her name was "Midnight". I learned a valuable lesson on this one--first impressions can be deceiving. In time, I would build a strong bond with this amazing dog.

Midnight had never, in her fourteen years of life, set foot inside of a house. She had lived on my aunt's front porch through scorching hot summers and brutally cold winters. My aunt didn't believe in having dogs inside of the house. I didn't know how Midnight would react to being inside. As it turned out, she loved it.

It was October when Midnight came to live with us and it was already getting chilly. She would lie in front of the fireplace heater on her big overstuffed dog bed and revel in all of the attention she was getting.

Our other dogs didn't pay too much attention to the new arrival. They sniffed her and went about their business. They would grow to love her just as we did. The first order of business was to get her weight down so she could move around with a bit more ease. She had lain on the concrete porch for so long that her elbows were cracked and bloody, all of the fur had long ago been worn off. We put salve on her dry cracked skin and massaged her stiff joints.

In a matter of two months, Midnight had begun to transform into the dog she could have been all along. She would run through our back yard with the other dogs. Considering that when she first came to us she could barely stand up, this was quite a feat. She never barked, but she would greet me every morning with an excited series of whimpers and whines all while she was leaping in the air anticipating her homemade chicken and rice breakfast. She was happy and healthy and full of life, and then it all came crashing down.

I always let the dogs out before bedtime and rewarded them with a bedtime dog biscuit before settling them in for the night. Midnight loved this routine and would grab the biscuit out of my hand without fail, until the night of July 2, 2014. On that night, she just turned her head away and lay down on her dog bed. I didn't think too much of it at the time, we all have our moments when we're a little under the weather. I patted her head and went to bed. She would eat in the morning.

The next morning, Midnight didn't want to get up to go outside. She didn't greet me with the usual whining and jumping around. She was very lethargic. Worse yet, even though she had eaten her breakfast, she seemed to choke it down. Something was wrong. I would give her until the veterinarian's office opened and go from there.

It was all downhill from there. I let her outside and she walked very slowly out to our big popcorn tree and lay down underneath it. I went out to see how she was and she wouldn't even acknowledge that I was there. I yelled for my husband to come pick her up for me. We had to get her to the vet's office immediately.

The vet ran some x-rays and did some blood work. The news was not good. Midnight had a football sized cancerous tumor on her spleen. At her advanced age, the doctor advised against surgery. Midnight was bleeding internally. We had to do the right thing for her.

As we sat on the floor saying our goodbyes to our sweet Midnight, we all felt cheated. She was just beginning to enjoy the good life and it was all being taken away. She was euthanized and we arranged to have her cremated. I picked her ashes up a few days later at a local funeral home. She had been in our lives only eight short months.

Life went on, but we had a very sad house for a while. There was something missing and we all felt it. That is until one night, about two months after Midnight had passed, when my husband made his usual nighttime raid on the kitchen. I was curled up on the couch with our other three dogs. They were sleeping soundly as I watched whatever scary movie we had chosen for that night's entertainment.

After Larry had made his sandwich, he came back into the living room and stood staring at me and our dogs, all still sound asleep. "Which dog was in the kitchen with me?" he asked. I was a bit confused by the question. "What are you talking about?" I asked. "One of the dogs was in the kitchen with me just now," he informed me. "The dogs haven't moved," I told him.

We went back and forth arguing about this for a few minutes. He swore up and down that there had been a dog in the kitchen with him. He had bumped into it several times while he was preparing his snack. He hadn't paid attention to which dog it was because he was so used to a dog following him into the kitchen to sneak a bite of whatever he inevitably dropped on the floor. He never turned on the kitchen light since it was close to the living room; he just used the light from the television as his guide.

This whole incident got me thinking, maybe Midnight wasn't quite finished with us yet. Not long after the phantom dog was in the kitchen, Ashlyn and I both heard a dog walking through our hallway. The floor is linoleum and the dog's toenails make a distinctive "clickety-click" sound when they walk on it. Our three dogs were outside at the time. I heard the noise first and asked Ashlyn which dog didn't go out with the others. She assured me that they were all outside.

We sat quietly for a moment and sure enough, there it was again, a dog was walking through the hallway. We both darted in there hoping to catch a glimpse of the culprit, but there was no dog. We both knew what we heard. It was dog. We had heard that sound hundreds of times. Again, we chalked it up to our Midnight paying us a visit to let us know that she was still enjoying her life indoors, even though she had hated that linoleum floor when she was living, she was terrified to walk on it because her feet would slip out from under her. I guess everything changes in the afterlife--even a dog's fear of linoleum.

We have had several similar brushes with Midnight over the past year. One of us will see the shadow of a dog going around a corner into one of the bedrooms even though all of our dogs are accounted for. The phantom toenail clicking has occurred on several occasions, as well. And, sometimes, it's just her scent that reminds me that Midnight is still around. She had a distinctive doggie odor that our other dogs don't have. It was strong and no amount of bathing could get rid of it. On occasion, I have walked into a room and recognized that smell, it only lasts for a short time but, it is unmistakable. We were blessed to have spent time with this very special dog in life. Just how special she really was is evident in that she continues to grace us, on occasion, with her sweet presence.

Bewitched Objects

Before I get started with this segment I need to clarify a few things. My first book, Three Haunted Tales, featured a short story entitled "Breathe". Even though the story was fiction, I borrowed parts of it from the real life experiences of my mother and my aunt. The following stories are theirs. If you read my book and recognize a few of these incidents you'll know why. They happened to my family members before they happened to my character in "Breathe". Also, my husband's name is Larry, but I also had a cousin named Larry whom you will be introduced to soon. I just want to clarify that they are two completely different people.

Chapter 7:
The Chiming Clock

My mother Jerry, as I have mentioned before, is a very religious no-nonsense woman. She doesn't believe in the occult or the supernatural. That being said, she is the owner of a possessed object. She doesn't like to talk about it and it was like pulling teeth to get any information out of her regarding this object. There is much more to this story than I can share, but I will tell you what she has told me. It all started with a Christmas present I purchased for her at a local retail store.

Ever since I can remember, my mother has loved chiming clocks. My daughter and I were shopping in a local chain store a few weeks before Christmas in 2012 when I spied something I knew my mom would have to have. It was a big wall clock with a swinging pendulum. The clock was silver in color and it chimed on the hour. She would love it! It wasn't expensive or anything, but I knew it would be something she would cherish and I was right. What I didn't know at the time was that there was something very unusual about this clock. According to my mom, it spoke to her.

You have to understand that my mother is a senior citizen. She is not, however, senile in any way. She is as sharp as a tack and still works five days a week; rain or shine. She drives herself wherever she wants to go. She is non-stop from the minute her feet hit the floor until she goes to bed at night. She's a firecracker and always has been. She would be the first one to tell you that clocks don't talk. Except, of course, for the one I bought her for Christmas.

The clock had been on the wall in my mother's bedroom for months without incident. It was just a normal, everyday, chiming wall clock, until one night when my mom was jolted from her sleep by the sound of a whispering voice. "You're not pretty!" "Put your boots on!"

She bolted upright and grabbed the flashlight she keeps beside her bed. She shone the light around the room; there was no one there. She turned the light off and lay back down, perhaps she had been dreaming. The voice spoke again. "You're not pretty!" "Put your boots on!" She sat up again and switched on the light. The voice was coming from the clock. This time it didn't stop. It kept on repeating the same things over and over "You're not pretty!" "Put your boots on!" The words were nonsense and had no significance to her.

Now most people would have gotten out of that room, or better yet, ditched that clock. Not my mom. She turned off the light, told the clock to shut up, and covered her ears with her pillow. This became a nightly ritual for her. The clock said the same things almost every night. If anyone else told me this story I would laugh and tell them they were imagining things. The thing is, I know my mom. She would never, ever make this up. If she says the clock talks then it talks.

My sister and I both told her to throw the clock away...my sister even bought her a new chiming clock that is much more expensive. My mom wouldn't hear of it. She loves that clock and she's keeping it. My biggest problem with this whole scenario is that the clock says other things that my mom refuses to repeat. All she will say is that the other things are far darker and more sinister and she doesn't want us to know lest we be harmed in some way by whatever is the source of the voice. It sounds strange, but she is deadly serious about this. She will risk her own well-being, but not ours.

She has the clock to this day and, to my knowledge, it is still terrorizing her. Stranger still, she isn't the only person in the family who has had a clock which was used as a conduit by some other worldly force.

Chapter 8:
The Apartment

My Aunt Theresa, the one who had been Midnight's first owner, was always a great source of ghost stories for me. She had lived in a haunted apartment when she was first married. Later, towards the end of her life, she had been the owner of a cuckoo clock that spoke to her every night at three o'clock on the dot. I'll start with the story of her apartment.

When my aunt was newly married, she and my uncle moved into a small apartment in the town of Hinton, West Virginia. It was the 1960s and life was just beginning for them. The apartment was nothing fancy, but it was their first home together and they loved it, at least, in the beginning.

Aunt Theresa had always been connected to the spirit world. She and my grandmother both spoke in tongues when they were overcome by the Holy Spirit. It was actually quite frightening to see when I was a child, but they assured me that it was a good thing. Even though my aunt was Fundamentalist Christian, she also believed in ghosts and the supernatural. Strange events seemed to follow her everywhere she went. It didn't frighten her until she moved into the apartment in Hinton.

My aunt's first inkling that something wasn't quite right in her new apartment was the uneasy feeling she had that she was being watched. She told me many times that no matter where she went in the apartment or what she was doing, someone was watching her. Unseen eyes bore into her twenty-four hours a day. She got to the point of staying away from home as much as possible when my uncle was at work so she could have some peace.

The longer they lived there, the worse things got. They began fighting constantly. They had always gotten along well and enjoyed being together, but that all changed once they were in the apartment. My uncle worked long hours and made a point of staying gone even on his days off. My aunt would go to my grandmother's house rather than be at home alone.

One day while she was washing her hair in the kitchen sink, she said that she had such a gut-churning feeling of doom come over her that she nearly passed out. The room filled with a putrid odor and she felt someone's breath on the back of her neck. She was too terrified to turn around, afraid of what she might see, so she threw the shampoo bottle behind her in a desperate attempt to hit whatever was in the room with her.

The putrid smell lifted and the cloistering feeling in the room faded. She turned around only to find an empty apartment and shampoo spilled all over the floor. When my uncle returned home that evening she told him what had happened, he laughed at her. He hated the apartment and knew that something wasn't right there, but he didn't believe her. She wanted to move out right then, but she had nowhere to go.

Incidents like the one in the kitchen began to happen regularly. Nothing happened when my uncle was around. Everything seemed to center around my aunt. She would be performing some mundane task like folding laundry when all at once the room would be enveloped in the smell of rotting garbage. She would choke on the foul odor and usually flee to my grandma's house. She didn't know the source of the smell, but she did know that it was not good and that it was not of this world.

The overwhelming feeling of being constantly watched took a toll both mentally and physically on my aunt. She never felt safe in her home. Even while taking a bath to relax, she would be reminded that she was not alone. She would close the bathroom door and submerge herself in the warm soapy water only to have the door fly open even though she was supposedly the only one home.

My mother was a witness to the evil presence that had settled in my aunt's apartment. She had spent some time there while my father was in the military. My mom said that even though she didn't smell the horrible decaying stench that haunted my aunt, she did have the overwhelming feeling that someone was watching them at all times. My mother was so uncomfortable there that she cut her stay short and opted to spend the remaining time with my grandmother. My aunt begged her to stay, but she couldn't bring herself to spend any more time in that apartment.

My mom wasn't the only visitor to my aunt's apartment who felt the presence of something sinister. My cousin Larry would come to stay with them occasionally when he was in town. When he stayed there he slept on the living room couch. He said that he would be awakened in the middle of the night by the sounds of whispering. He would see shadowy figures sitting on the chairs which sat adjacent to the couch. The figures would be pointing at him and whispering. After one particularly harrowing encounter with the night whisperers, he cut his visit short and checked into a motel for the remainder of his stay.

It took one undeniable act to finally convince my uncle that it was time to move. My aunt and uncle were sleeping soundly one night when they were awakened by loud pounding on the door. My uncle, furious at having been jolted out of a sound sleep, stormed to the door and flung it open; there was no one there. He slammed the door and bolted the lock before returning to bed.

He had no more than lay under the covers when the banging on the door started again. He jumped up and ran to catch the prankster who was keeping him from his much needed sleep. He opened the door only to find the hallway vacant. There was no one stirring in any of the other apartments. The building was quiet.

Puzzled and still fuming, he decided to sit up in the living room. If they knocked again, he would catch them. He sat facing the door. A few minutes passed and the pounding started again. He not only heard it this time, he also witnessed it. My uncle could see the entire door moving as he stood up to confront whoever was on the other side. As he approached it, the door flung open with such force that it knocked a hole in the wall.

My uncle was in shock at this point. There was not a soul to be seen except for my terrified aunt who had heard the crash and now stood trembling in the hallway. Whatever had been banging on the door was nowhere to be seen. Thoroughly shaken by the experience, they moved out the next day. My uncle never once spoke to me of that incident or any others involving the apartment. He put it behind him and pretended it never happened. The memories of it never left my aunt. She spoke of it until the time of her death.

Chapter 9:
The Witching Hour

Many years later, after my uncle had long since passed away, my Aunt Theresa was living in a farmhouse in Alderson, West Virginia. This house was not haunted, to my knowledge. My aunt lived there for decades without incident. She was, however, a collector of antiques and unusual objects. One such object was an antique cuckoo clock. I'm not sure how or where she acquired the clock. It could have been at an auction or tag sale, there's really no way to know at this point. I do know one thing--after she passed it was the one item that no one would touch.

My mother and aunt spoke almost every night on the telephone before they went to bed. They lived nearly two hundred miles apart and liked to stay in touch as much as possible. They were alike in many ways. They both loved animals. Both were deeply religious and would gossip like schoolgirls. They differed in one very distinct way, although my mother shunned any talk of ghosts and the supernatural, my aunt embraced it.

During one of their nightly telephone hen sessions, my aunt casually mentioned to my mom that her cuckoo clock had been stopping every night at three o'clock on the dot. The little bird would come out and cuckoo on every other hour except for that one. Instead, a voice would speak to her through the clock. It wasn't anything as simple as "Put your boots on". My aunt's clock was a harbinger of doom.

My aunt said that the clock would warn her of impending deaths in the family. It would also chide her for her beliefs. Strangely, like my mother, she didn't get rid of the clock. These clocks held a fascination for them that I don't think even they understood. They feared them, dreaded nighttime when they would be alone with them, and yet, they wouldn't burn them or throw them in the trash. My aunt, for one, believed that once a presence had invaded your home, it was there forever whether or not you removed the object in which it seemed to dwell. I think my mom just liked her clock too much to get rid of it.

Weeks turned into months with no let up from the nightly barrage of hateful banter and dark predictions which spewed forth from my aunt's cuckoo clock. At one point she did stop winding it in the hope that it would just stay dormant, but it didn't work out that way. The clock no longer released the cuckoo on the hour, but the voice continued to assault her at three o'clock just like always.

After so many months of hearing terrible things emanating from this clock, most of which had not come to pass, she was at her wit's end. No longer wishing to have the clock inside of her house, she banished it to the storage shed in the backyard. There's no way of knowing if the voice continued after that since no one would have been able to hear it. The voice apparently did need the clock in order to communicate with my aunt because once it was out of the house the three o'clock visitations ceased. My aunt fell in her driveway not long after that and died from unexpected complications. She had been active and in good health so her death came as quite a shock to those who knew her.

My mother never told my aunt about her experiences with her talking clock. She never likes to make a fuss. When my relatives descended upon my aunt's house to go through her hoard of collectibles and antiques no one that I'm aware of laid claim to the clock. We had all heard about it and no one wanted to take a chance on bringing a dark spirit into their home. I don't know what became of it. Perhaps it was hauled away with the trash. Maybe a neighbor who didn't know its history picked it up. I'll never know and I'm sort of glad I don't.

Chapter 10:
Little Alice

One of the strangest objects I have ever encountered was a doll that my husband's Grandma Audrey gave us shortly before her death. Audrey was a tough as nails, feisty woman in her eighties who loved nothing better than to shop at auctions and flea markets. The doll she gave us was a find from one of her endeavors and what a find it was.

This doll actually came with a name--Little Alice. It was a large doll, at least two feet tall, and it talked. Don't get me wrong, it was supposed to talk but, some of the things it said were what threw us for a loop.

Little Alice had blonde curly hair and an innocent face. She wore a lacy dress and a white bonnet. She was quite lovely and extremely odd. At first, the things she said made perfect sense. "My name's Little Alice" and "We are going to be friends". All of that was normal and good and we were fine with it but, some of the other things were clear out of left field.

I was holding Little Alice one day and making her talk. She said the usual innocent things and then she said: "You need professional help." I had never heard a talking doll say such a thing and I was floored. I tried for hours to get her to say it again, but she wouldn't. In fact, that was the one and only time she ever said it even though she repeated everything else over and over again.

Little Alice telling me that I needed professional help became a source of great ridicule for me for years. My husband loved to bring that up to anyone and everyone who would listen. Unfortunately, other things that she said weren't as amusing.

We were sitting outside one day on our porch swing with Little Alice when in the midst of the usual "We are going to be friends" she began reciting what sounded like court documents. There was mention of concentration camps and, strangely enough, a dinner of peas and carrots. Her speech went on and on uninterrupted for several minutes…and she spoke with a heavy German accent the whole time.

When she finally fell silent, my husband and I tried in vain to get her to say it again. She never did. Anytime she said something completely off the wall it only happened once.

Unlike my mother and my aunt, I had no problem getting rid of Little Alice. That doll was strange and she had spooked us for the last time. I don't know if she was possessed or manufactured to say those strange things one time and one time only but, I wasn't keeping her around to find out.

We banished her to the storage shed in our yard, but even there, she still gave me the creeps. I ended up throwing her out with the trash so I wouldn't have to see those eyes staring blankly at me any time we were in need of a garden ho or rake.

Months went by and when the time came to clean out the shed I found a reminder of Little Alice. Her blond curly hair was lying on a shelf behind some old paint cans. Why it wasn't under her bonnet when I threw her away I don't know. It was just another question mark in the saga of our strange talking doll.

Chapter 11:
Parasites

I'm giving my cousin Larry a segment in this book all his own. He was a remarkable person who, for whatever reason, courted disaster everywhere he went. He was also a magnet for supernatural phenomena. Spirits followed him around like the Pied Piper. He was haunted and tormented by voices and shadows who would allow him no peace.

The following are just a few of the many stories I've heard which involved my dear cousin Larry.

Larry was well into his teens when I was born. I remember from an early age hearing my relatives speak in hushed tones of the dark shadows which seemed to follow him everywhere he went. He had been raised mostly by my maternal grandmother first in a house in the woods that was undoubtedly inhabited by restless spirits, this was the house in which I experienced my night terrors, and then in a house in the small town of Alderson, West Virginia.

Larry had moved away from West Virginia for a while, setting up residence in a small apartment in North Carolina. It was there that the entities that would forever terrorize him began their assault. He spoke often of the endless havoc they would wreak. Doors would slam in the middle of the night, lights would turn themselves on and off and, at times, the burners on the stovetop would suddenly blaze bright red for no reason.

It was at this point that my fragile cousin began to drink heavily. Make no mistake, he didn't see demons because he drank, rather, he drank because he saw demons. The spirits in his apartment would not allow him to sleep. He would no more than doze off before a door would slam or heavy footsteps running on the stairs would wake him. He never knew what they would do next.

He had already made up his mind to move back to West Virginia when the spirits let him know that they weren't finished quite yet. He was moving his belongings out to his car when unseen hands pushed him down a flight of stairs. I heard him tell this story many times and he never wavered. He was the only person on the stairs. No one was behind him when he felt hands grip his shoulders and shove him forward sending him headfirst down the steps to the landing.

He was bruised and stoved up, but otherwise unharmed physically. He was scarred mentally, however. He seemed to gloss over the other events when he related them but, not this one. For the first time, I believe he realized that something was trying to warn him that if they wanted to they could hurt him or worse.

On returning to West Virginia, Larry took a job at the famous Greenbrier Hotel. He loved working there and was a valued employee. He still lived with my grandma part of the time, even though he had a room at the Greenbrier any time he wanted one. He and my grandma had a close bond and I think he felt a sense of safety and security with this woman who was unshakeable in her devotion and faith in God.

It was at my grandmother's house in Alderson that the spirits returned to torment Larry. He would lie in bed at night, drifting off to sleep, when shadows would appear at his second floor bedroom window. He could see them floating and hear them as they beckoned to him. "Come out, Larry. Come out tonight." This would go on for hours and it became an almost nightly ritual.

When he told my grandmother about the voices and the shadows that tried to lure him into the night, she told him that they were demons attempting to entice him into the darkness, to take him with them to a purgatory from which he would never escape. She warned him to ignore them.

Never acknowledge that they were there and never, ever confront them.

Larry kept his job at the hotel and tried to lead a normal life, but the nightly visitations were again taking a toll on him and he was drinking to numb his fear and anxiety. Some people might attribute some of his problems to his drinking, which is possible. That doesn't explain why others besides Larry experienced strange phenomena at my grandmother's house and in my aunt's haunted apartment.

The difference between what other relatives, including myself, experienced and what Larry experienced in all of the same places was that he was the only one who could actually see the spirits. We all had encounters in which we felt that some unseen force was terrorizing us, but he could see what we could only sense. That would be enough to drive anyone to drink.

Sadly, we'll never know for sure what occurred in the final hours of Larry's short life. He was staying at my grandmother's house in Alderson at the time. The two of them had stayed up talking until the time when Larry excused himself to go to bed. Nothing was out of the ordinary. He seemed fine and in good spirits.

The next morning, my grandmother knocked on Larry's bedroom door and told him that breakfast was ready. He didn't respond. She opened the door and found him lying in bed, seemingly in a deep sleep. She left him for a while and went about her daily chores. When she checked on him later, she knew something was wrong. He hadn't moved. She felt his cheek. It was as cold as ice. My dear tormented cousin had died sometime during the night of a massive heart attack. He was barely forty years old.

Chapter 12:
The House In The Hollow

One of the most terrifying places I have ever had the misfortune to visit was my maternal grandmother's house in a hollow of Greenbrier County, West Virginia. The property was set deep in the woods, accessible only by travelling a windy, heavily rutted road that cut a pathway through the mountains. I based the house in my novel, "Fox Holler," on my grandma's home in the woods.

My parents would take us to stay at my grandma's house every summer for a week or so. I dreaded it with a passion. The home itself was pleasant enough. It was white with a big front porch that sported a swing and rocking chairs. There was a chicken coop in the backyard that, from time to time, actually housed chickens. The front yard was spacious and fenced-in with gates located in the front and on the side.

My grandma didn't have indoor plumbing so we had to use an outhouse when we stayed with her. This was something kids today can't imagine. Creeping out into the night with a flashlight to answer the call of nature in a little wooden shack with all sorts of night creatures belching and howling was not anyone's idea of fun, especially not a child like me who possessed a vivid imagination and a great fear of the boogeyman. Holding it until morning became my goal in life.

Being that the house was in the middle of the woods, when night fell, it literally fell. The sun would go down and it was as if someone had thrown a blanket over my grandma's house. The term "pitch black" is a pretty accurate description. Whoever said that there is nothing in the darkness that isn't there in the light never slept over at my grandma's house in the holler.

I told my story of being besieged by nightmares while staying in this house earlier in this collection. The light show and dizzying feeling of something chasing me through my own mind is something that haunts me to this day. The fear is indescribable. It might not sound like much, but, the dread enveloped me as my mother can attest to. This was no normal nightmare, this was pure terror. I screamed that "they" were after me as my mom tried to quiet her hysterical young daughter. Little did I know at the time, but I wasn't the only one who had experienced such things in this house.

My sister, Sue, slept in what was referred to as the "back bedroom" when we stayed with my grandma. She's a tough cookie and never mentioned anything strange happening to her there until I told her I was writing this book. When I asked her if she had any paranormal encounters she would like to share she immediately piped up with, "Sure, mostly the things that happened at grandma's house." I knew then that I was not alone.

It seems that the back bedroom had a reputation for being the one room in the house that no one liked to sleep in. It was my Cousin Larry's room when he stayed with my grandma and he, too, experienced many unexplainable events within its four walls.

Those who had slept in the room all claimed that just as they were dozing off someone, or something, would hit the foot of the bed and snap them wide awake. They each described the experience the same way. Just as they settled in and were drifting off to sleep, two hands on either side of their feet would slap the bed. Whoever was occupying the room would be jolted back into consciousness with a start. Of course, they would find themselves alone, in spite of what had just happened. This made for a very uncomfortable night's sleep.

Another experience that everyone who slept in the back bedroom shared was the feeling that someone was watching them as they slept. My sister lay awake most nights as unseen eyes bored into her. She loved our grandma dearly, but dreaded staying at her house.

Nighttime was never pleasant at the house in the woods. Even though the house was well off the beaten path, if you had never been there it was nearly impossible to find, phantom knocks on the door in the middle of the night were common place. My grandmother, who didn't believe in the supernatural, told us many times of being awakened by loud banging on her front door in the wee hours of the morning. Her dog would howl and she would peek out the curtain only to find the porch vacant, even though she could clearly hear the boards creaking as if someone were pacing back and forth. She never saw a soul and she had never opened the door to investigate further.

My grandmother's dogs hadn't fared well at the old house. One by one, they would disappear. Sometimes, they would vanish and no sign of them was ever found. On other occasions, bones and teeth would eventually turn up in the yard which she assumed were the last remnants of one or more of her dogs. She never knew what happened to them. Maybe they met their fate by tangling with coyotes or some other woodland creature, or perhaps the night visitors who crept onto the porch and knocked on the door in the middle of the night had silenced them. I guess we'll never know.

When my grandfather was living, he had installed spring action locks on the front and side gates which led into my grandma's yard. This way, the wind couldn't blow the gates open, they had to physically be unlatched and then they would snap closed with a bang. This kept the chickens and dogs in the yard. The problem was, it couldn't keep unwanted visitors out.

My grandma, uncle, mother and just about everyone else in the family had heard the gate open and then slam shut when there was no one else around. They would be sitting on the porch, deep in conversation or just sipping on sun tea and enjoying the quiet day, when the gate would creak open and then seconds later snap shut. No one entered the yard. This happened countless times in broad daylight. My uncle swore up and down that he had seen the gate open on several occasions and then close again as if someone had walked through and then shut the gate behind them, although there was never anyone there.

This story always struck me as particularly strange due to the obvious fact that spirits wouldn't need to open the gate in order to gain access to the yard. That being said, enough people saw it happen that I have no doubt that it did occur. Perhaps it was an event from the past being replayed time and again by whatever energies remained. Or, more likely, the ghostly beings that haunted the area wanted to make sure that the living knew they were present.

My mother doesn't like to talk about anything supernatural. Her fear is that talking about the unexplained or occult might open you up to some very bad things that are best left unspoken. She did, however, relate a story that had haunted her as a child and still gives her a bad feeling to this day.

This did not occur at the same house, but at another house in another hollow. This would have been my mother's childhood home. The family had no running water and relied on a spring which ran down the mountainside for their drinking and cooking water. My mom recalled the sinking feeling she would get in the pit of her stomach when the time came to trek up the clearing which cut through the mountain and led to the spring.

She described the area as an overgrown field that led up the hill. It was surrounded on both sides by deep forest. My mother said that everything would be fine until she and her brothers and sisters reached the foot of the hill and then something would begin stirring in the treetops that led the way up the mountain.

They would start out walking every time, but end up running until they reached the spring at which time the rustling in the treetops would stop. In the hundreds of trips they made up that mountainside to fetch water, they never once saw anything unusual in the woods that led the way to the spring. That being said, they were followed every single time. They could see the trees moving and hear the leaves rustling and branches breaking, but there was no sign of what was causing all of the ruckus.

She did know that whatever it was, it gave them all a terrible feeling and made them run as fast as their legs would carry them to get away from whatever it was. The faster they would move, the faster it would make its way through the trees. This went on for years from the time they were small children until they were grown and moved out on their own. It only stopped because they left the house. These many decades later, my no nonsense mother still doesn't feel comfortable talking about the thing in the woods that made innocent trips to a mountain spring such a nightmare for her and her family.

My grandma's house in the holler eventually became more of a burden for her than it was worth. She ended up moving into the town of Alderson, West Virginia. There, she rented a small house with indoor plumbing and all of the amenities most of us are accustomed to. Nothing out of the ordinary happened to anyone in that house, except for my cousin Larry who was a magnet for spirits wherever he went. Many of his experiences, as you know, are chronicled in this collection.

Chapter 13:
The Red-Faced Man

My great grandmother had lived on a house located on a hill above the one that my mother grew up in. It was a country home and my mom and her sisters spent a lot of time at the house when they were younger. Something wasn't right about the house. They didn't like staying there, but they were kids and had no choice. It was a place of little joy and much terror for them.

My aunt remembered, as does my mom, many times when the girls would wash up the dishes and put them away only to have the kitchen come alive as soon as they left the room. They would hear silverware rattling around and go back into the kitchen to find nothing out of place. This happened on many occasions.

The sound of phantom footsteps was commonplace in the old house. The girls would be tucked in for the night when the sound of heavy footfalls would break the silence. The sound would start downstairs and make its way up the steps and into the girl's bedroom. They would hear the heavy boots walk up to the foot of their bed and then the room would get quiet. All of a sudden, the blankets would be thrown off of them and onto the floor. They would scream and their grandma would rush in and shush them. Again, this wasn't a onetime event; it was repeated almost every time they slept there. They never actually saw anyone, the room was pitch black, but they heard him.

As frightening as the nightly visits from the figure who pulled the covers off of the bed were, the real terror came from who or whatever peered through the bedroom window at them. They called him the "red-faced man". They would hear the sounds of a horse whinnying and then they would see a red face looking at them through the window. This is made all the more bizarre because the room they slept in was on the second floor of the house.

There was never any explanation for the events at the house. All three girls had the exact same experiences. They saw and heard the same footsteps, the same horse whinnying, and the same red face peeking in the window. Their grandmother never seemed to be bothered by any of it, maybe for good reason.

There was talk at the time that some of the local women were dabbling in witchcraft and my great-grandmother had been a suspect. This was, of course, all rumor and conjecture, but it could account for some of the unusual claims from people who had the misfortune of spending a night at her house on the hill.

Chapter 14:
The Cemetery

My cousin, Larry, was someone who courted spirits throughout his life, whether he wanted to or not. When he was staying with his sister in North Carolina in the late

1970s, he had an experience no one involved would ever forget.

One morning as Larry's sister, Donna, was getting ready for work, her brother burst into the house and ran up the stairs yelling her name. He had something very important to show her outside.

It was seven o'clock in the morning, Donna was running late and she was in no mood for nonsense. She told him it would have to wait until later. He would have none of it. Larry insisted that she come outside. He was bursting with nervous energy.

Curious, Donna finally relented and followed her excitable brother down the stairs and outside to the driveway where he began pointing out something on his car. When Donna saw what her brother was so anxious about, she understood why he had been adamant that she come have a look. Bewildered, she asked her brother what on Earth had happened to the car.

Larry explained to his sister that he and three friends had been bored the day before and had driven to Virginia to explore a purportedly haunted cemetery. When they arrived at their destination, it was already dark and they had backed their car in next to the front gate. It was locked and they couldn't enter, so they sat in the car and pondered their next move.

As they were talking, someone began to bang on the trunk of the car. Before they knew it, whoever it was, attempted to open the back passenger side door. They all hit their door locks and started yelling for Larry to drive away.

As he put the car in gear and prepared to pull away from the gate, the back end of the car lifted completely up off of the ground. Everyone in the car was screaming for him to drive, but the car wouldn't move. Finally, whoever was terrorizing them dropped the car back down to the ground and they sped off into the night.

Shaken, Larry and his friends drove straight back to North Carolina. In the first light of morning, they saw something that chilled them to the bone. This was what Larry had wanted his sister to be witness to.

Whoever, or whatever, had been at the cemetery gate that night had left evidence of its presence. There, on the lid of the car's trunk, were two bloody hand prints. The bloody prints were also on the door handle. Larry and his friends had made a narrow escape that night, but from what? Wisely, they never returned to find out.

Chapter 15:
The Anniversary

My best friend while I was growing up was a girl who lived a couple of streets over from me. Her name was Roberta O'Neal.

Robbie and I met when we were both in the first grade and we remained close friends until we were well into our twenties. Somehow, we drifted apart, but I still think of her often.

She is the friend who I spent many summers with, sitting under a big tree reading ghost stories aloud to each other. Those childhood memories will forever be dear to me as will Roberta.

Robbie came from a big Irish/American family. She was the youngest of seven girls. Her father had been left to raise his daughters alone after his wife died of cancer when Roberta was only three years old.

My friend had not had the chance to get to know her mom. She had vague memories of a woman who had held her and taken care of her who she thought was her mother, but it could have been wishful thinking on her part.

The sisters were so far apart in age that Robbie always thought of her eldest sister as a mother figure. She even told the other kids at school that her sister was her mother.

Even though Roberta had no real recollection of the woman who had died when her daughter was just a toddler, she did feel her presence every year on the anniversary of her passing.

For whatever reason, the family didn't celebrate what would have been their mother's birthday. They did, however, commemorate the day of her passing. It was an important day for them and I was witness to this year after year. They didn't celebrate her passing; they celebrated her return.

Roberta knew a lot about her mother from stories that her father and sisters would relate to her. She knew what her mother had liked to eat, drink, watch on television and listen to on the radio. She also knew what kind of perfume she had worn.

Every year, on the anniversary of her passing, the scent of their mother's favorite fragrance would waft through the air, drifting from room to room as though she were following her children around all day.

They also reported hearing her soft laughter coming from the bedroom first thing every morning on the anniversary. Their father still slept in the same room he had shared with his wife and the lilting sound of his dead wife's amused giggles would awaken him every year.

As strange as it sounds, this tight knit family were comforted by these yearly visits from their beloved lost wife and mother. They looked forward to them.

Roberta would talk about it for days leading up to the event and then continue reliving whatever happened on that day for weeks afterwards.

Some years, there would only be the laughter and the perfume, those were a given. On other years one or more family member would claim that they had felt an unseen hand stroke their hair or touch their arm.

Each person in the O'Neal household was touched in some way on the anniversary of their loved one's passing, whether it be physically or emotionally. They all felt her presence on that day and they took great comfort in it.

The older we got, the less I heard about the yearly visits from her mother, but I think they were still happening. With age came the realization that not everyone would share their enthusiasm for this very special occurrence in their lives. It was something they wanted to keep close to them. They feared ridicule and I don't blame them.

Whatever happened every year on that somber anniversary had turned a tragic loss for any family into something that gave them a sense of peace and, it was a reminder that love never dies it only changes form.

Chapter 16:
When It Rains

You've all heard the old expression "When it rains, it pours," well, this story gives that adage a whole new meaning. My dear friend, Janet, and her husband, Mike, lived for many years in a house just outside of Charleston, West Virginia. They had purchased the house through a rent to own contract with her husband's grandparents. It was an older home and a definite fixer upper but, it was theirs and they loved it.

Not long after moving in, Jan began to notice that on overcast or rainy days, whether it be winter or summer, the house would become so drafty that she would have to wear a sweater or huddle up in a blanket to keep warm. She wasn't the only one who noticed this phenomenon. Visitors to her home would comment on how cold it was even in the middle of a scorching summer. They would ask her to turn the air conditioning off which she would assure them wasn't running. There was usually no need.

A drafty house on inclement days wasn't a big deal even if it was just a little bit strange. Other things, however, were more disturbing. On rainy days, Jan would experience excruciating migraine headaches. She knew that headaches could be weather related, but they had never affected her before moving into the house. At times, she would be bedridden until the rain past along with her headaches.

Another odd thing that would occur only on rainy days was that brown water would run from the spigots in the sinks and shower. She learned that she couldn't do laundry on rainy days. The water would stain the clothing and it would be ruined. They could neither bathe nor wash dishes in the water; it smelled putrid and they feared that it was possibly toxic. This was several years ago and the idea of having the water analyzed didn't occur to them. It was an old house with a lot of quirks. They would deal with it in their own way, which was to not use the water when rain was in the forecast.

The most bizarre event that happened to Jan in the house occurred one evening when Mike was out bowling with his league and she was home alone. She had settled in to watch television when her peaceful evening was interrupted by the sound of water hitting the floor in the spare bedroom.

Jan jumped up off of the couch and ran to the bedroom to investigate. When she opened the door, water was dripping in a steady stream from the ceiling. The steady streams of water were coming from more than one place in the room. The floor and bedding were soaked and Jan was in a panic.

It was not raining outside, so she needed to find the source of the water leak. She didn't know how to shut off the water main. She did turn off the valves in the kitchen and bath to no avail, water continued to rain down from the ceiling. She would have to wait for Mike. He would know what to do.

After what seemed like hours, the water stopped dripping. Jan laid bath towels on the floor in an attempt to soak up some of the water before it ruined the wood flooring. There wasn't a dry spot in the room. No other room in the house was wet except for this one.

Mike finally arrived home to find his wife on her hands and knees mopping up water with rags and a plastic bucket. She told him what had happened and he set out to find the source of the leak. Mike was no plumber, but he checked the pipes that he could find. No obvious leaks were present. He would have to call a real plumber in the morning. They turned in, bewildered and none too happy. This might turn out to be a very expensive problem for the couple.

The plumber was at their house by late in the afternoon on the following day. He inspected the pipes inside and out. The house had its issues, but he could find no leaks that would have resulted in the flooding that had taken place in the spare bedroom. He chalked it up to a one time freak event and left them with a hefty bill. Jan and Mike were beginning to wonder why their house and water had such a strange, and hazardous, relationship.

One of the worst effects that rain had on their household was the way her husband's behavior changed with the weather. This man, who at any other time was funny and a pleasure to know and keep company with, would become sullen and withdrawn as soon as rain clouds moved in. He would snap at Jan over absolutely nothing.

He would fly into rages over things as insignificant as a dirty spoon in the silverware drawer or the cat getting hair on his jacket. She would say that she didn't even recognize him when he stood inches from her face and yelled at her. His face would contort into a mask of hatred. This was not the man she loved. This was a bully who berated her mercilessly over nothing.

And then, just as quickly as the storm had come, it would be gone. The sun would shine and he would, literally, change back into the man she knew and loved. She begged him to get help with his temper. He would swear up and down that he had no recollection of the events she would relate to him of his hostile, borderline violent, behavior. All he could do was apologize, he honestly didn't remember and Jan knew he was telling the truth.

The turmoil in their house was beginning to take a toll on the once happy couple. Standing alone, none of the events seemed like much to worry about, but all together, they were destroying Jan and her husband.

She began to dread the rain more than ever. The raging husband, the putrid water, the cold chill that permeated the house, it was more that she could bear. The final straw came when her parents came from Pennsylvania to spend the weekend at the house. It was summertime and they had planned to spend two lazy days barbecuing in the back yard, playing croquet, and enjoying one and other's company.

Her parents arrived on Friday afternoon and things couldn't have been more perfect. They went out to dinner and the couples spent a pleasant evening catching up before returning to Jan's house. This was the first time that her parents had visited since she and Mike had bought the house and she wanted them to like it as much as she did, or at least used to.

She showed her mom the garden she had planted near the back patio while Jan's father sat in the living room with Mike talking about guy things. Jan's mom seemed to sense that something wasn't quite right and she asked her daughter if everything was okay. Jan says that her first instinct was to lie and say that everything was great, couldn't be better, but she knew that her mom would see right through the ruse. Her mom was very intuitive. She considered herself somewhat psychic, but rarely talked about her ability, with good reason.

When Jan's mother was a little girl, she began to have regular visits from an older couple who would sit with her in her room and tell her stories about their children who were grown up and lived far away. The lady would brush the little girl's hair and tell her that she looked just like her own daughter when she was a child.

The older couple were always kind to Jan's mother, spending countless hours playing with her in the yard, having tea parties in her room, and telling her stories until she slipped into a peaceful sleep. The only problem was that no one else could see them.

When the little girl told her mom about the nice couple who spent so much time with her; her mother chastised her for making up stories. Her mother would hear her daughter talking to the couple when she was supposed to be asleep and she would storm into the room and demand that her daughter stop being foolish and close her eyes.

The little girl, who would grow up to be Jan's mother, didn't understand why her own mother wouldn't let her be friends with the old couple, but she did as she was told. She began ignoring the couple when they came to play. She told them to go away and that she wasn't allowed to be friends with them anymore. Eventually, the old couple stopped coming to her, but she never forgot how sad they looked the last time she saw them. They told her they loved her, but she turned her back to them, they didn't exist, her mom said so.

Years later while thumbing through an old photo album, Jan's mom, who by this time was a teenager, saw a picture of a couple with a little girl. They were standing outside on a sunny day. They were squinting and the man was holding the child in his arms. Jan's mom immediately recognized the couple; they had been her playmates all those years ago when she was just a child.

She showed the picture to her mother and asked who they were. "That's my mom and dad," her mother replied, "and that was me when I was a little girl."

She went on to explain that they had died not long after that photo had been taken. Their truck had been run off the road one night and they crashed into a ravine. They were both killed instantly. She had been raised by her paternal grandparents.

Jan's mother told her mom that this was the couple who used to visit her. Their daughter that she reminded them of was her own mother. Both of them wept as they remembered the couple they had both loved, one of them in life, the other from the afterlife.

Jan's mother had experienced other psychic phenomena throughout her life. She chose, most of the time, to ignore it. She had always felt horrible about sending the couple, her grandparents, away. She feared for them. Had she sent them to purgatory? She would never know. It was better to suppress her ability that way no one could get hurt.

Now, however, Jan was in trouble, her mom sensed it. She told Jan that she didn't want to interfere, but she sensed that something horrible had happened in that house and she wanted to help. She asked her daughter if that would be alright with her and Jan nodded her head, things were bad and getting worse, she needed to know what had happened in her house and how rain played a role in it.

Jan's mother told her daughter not to tell her anything that had been going on in the house until she did a walk thru for herself. She wanted to get a sense of the house without having any information about the events that had been plaguing her daughter and son-in-law.

As she walked quietly through the rooms, Jan watched as her mom would stop periodically and wrap her arms around herself as if she had gotten a sudden chill. She passed by Mike and Jan's father in the living room and they stared at her, unsure of what was going on. When her mother stood by the kitchen sink and then turned the faucet on and off again, Jan knew that her mom was on to something.

When her mom had completed her psychic tour of the house, she took Jan by the hand and led her into the master bedroom. They sat on the edge of the bed and were silent for a moment. Jan's mother finally broke the silence by telling her daughter that the house was tainted. It was a "sick house" and Jan would never be happy there.

Jan didn't know what to say. She knew that her mom was right, something was very wrong with the house, but she wasn't quite ready to give up on it and she told her mom so. Jan's mother was adamant, the house was doomed and so was anyone who lived there. She then told Jan what brought her to that conclusion.

Jan's mother had felt a wave of dread pass over her as soon as she stepped into her daughter's house. There had been a death there, at least one, and it had been by violence. The more time she spent in the house, the more pronounced the feeling became. After walking through all of the rooms, she had pieced together her theory of the tragic events that turned the house into what it was today.

She told Jan that she had a strong feeling that a woman had gone mad in the house many years before Jan and Mike had moved in. The woman suffered from black depressions that worsened when the days were dark or when the weather was bad.

On one rainy night when she could take the emotional pain no longer, the woman had filled the bathtub that adjoined the spare bedroom with water and crawled in. She then proceeded to slit her wrists. She had bled to death alone in the tub on that dark rainy night. No one knew and Jan's mom sensed that the woman's body had remained in the house for a long time before anyone missed her.

Jan shuddered as she listened to the story. It was hard to believe and yet made perfect sense. It would explain the connection that water seemed to have to the house and the dark events that continued to take place there. Jan's mother explained that the woman was tied to the house and she didn't have any intention of ever leaving. She would drive Jan and Mike mad if they stayed.

Jan and her mother stayed up well into the night talking about the house. They were joined by Jan's father and Mike. They all sat around debating what to do. How could they sell a house that was obviously haunted? Would they have to tell any prospective buyers what they knew? How could they afford to leave everything and move?

After much worry and brainstorming, they came up with a solution. They wouldn't hide the fact that the house was tainted. They would market the house for what it was: a possibly haunted house, take it or leave it, buyer beware-- literally. It worked. They sold the house at a price well below what they were asking, but they were rid of it and their lives could get back to normal.

They ended up moving to a small town called Belle, West Virginia where they lived happily for several years before Mike was transferred to Utah where they now reside. They didn't keep in touch with the people who bought their old house, but Jan says that she heard years ago that the house had been destroyed in a fire. She didn't know if the same people had the house when the fire occurred or if they, too, had passed it on to someone else.

There is a certain irony to the fact that a house so closely tied to water would ultimately be destroyed by fire; poetic justice indeed.

Premonitions of Death

We are so closely connected with worlds just beyond our sensibilities that sometimes, something from those other worlds reaches out to warn us that something bad has, or will, happen. Harbingers of doom are common in folklore. Encounters with unusual white animals are said to be forewarnings of death. Beware, if a bird flies into your home and lands on a certain chair or bed, the person who normally rests there might be in for a visit from the Grim Reaper. Rocking an empty chair will bring death to the person who normally sits there. It seems that everything has hidden meaning if you talk to mountain folks. It could be silly superstition, or maybe there's more to it that we would like to admit.

Chapter 17:
The Light

When my mother was pregnant with me, her father suffered a stroke. My grandparents lived in Fort Springs, West Virginia at the time, which was a good four hour drive from my parents' house. That was no matter for them and they immediately packed up my seven year old sister and made the trip to Fort Springs.

When they arrived, they were told that my grandpa was being transferred to the Veteran's Hospital in Beckley, West Virginia which was a couple of hours away. They would have to wait to see him. My mother decided to stay the night with her family at my grandparents' house. They would all drive to Beckley in the morning. My father, who was never one to let an opportunity to fish pass him by, phoned his brother-in-law and made arrangements to pick him up to go jitterbug fishing.

It was already dark by the time my dad and uncle started out on the road to White Sulphur Springs to do some fishing. People deal with crises in their own ways. My dad's way was to get his mind on something else, which in this case was going fishing. It didn't matter that it was night fishing; he loved the tranquility of the forest.

They stayed out until the wee small hours of the morning and then packed up their fishing gear and loaded up my dad's car for the trip back into town. My dad was planning on staying over with his sister and brother-in-law before joining my mom later in the morning for the drive to

Beckley. They headed out onto the dark back country roads that led back into civilization.

No other cars were on the dark mountain road, just the two brothers-in-law regaling each other with tall tales about who was the better fisherman. It was the middle of the night and all was quiet. With no warning, the night was suddenly split by a blinding light which forced my father to slam on the brakes lest he lose control of the car.

As he describes it, the entire road and woods surrounding it were enveloped in a white light so bright that he and my uncle were temporarily blinded. They could see nothing but the bright light that seemed to have swallowed up not only the two men, but everything around them. There was absolute quiet. No cars passing by. No aircraft of any kind. Dead silence. It lasted for only a few seconds and then was gone. The light lifted and darkness fell over them just as it had before. The road ahead was dark once again. No other cars and no signs of life except for my dad and uncle who were, by this time, quite rattled by what they had just seen.

They sat for a while in the car trying to find a logical explanation for what had just happened. Nothing made sense. It hadn't been a passing car, they were both sure of it. This was like no light either of them had ever seen before. My father glanced at his watch. The time was just after 3:00am. They shrugged off the bewildering incident and headed towards my uncle's house, eager to be off the road as soon as possible.

Later that morning, my father drove to Fort Springs and picked up my mother to take her to Beckley to see her dad in the hospital. It was over an hour's drive which was not the least bit pleasant for my eight months pregnant mother who was worried sick about her father. My dad didn't mention the strange light he and my uncle had seen on the road only a few hours earlier. It didn't seem significant to him at the time. He would soon have a change of heart.

When they reached the hospital, my mother's siblings were already there waiting for her. The news wasn't good. My grandfather, whom I would never know, had already passed away. The massive stroke he had suffered had taken him during the night.

My mother was beside herself. She hadn't been able to tell him goodbye or spend time with him in his final hours and she was heartbroken. One of the nurses spoke up as she ushered the grieving family into a private room where they could console each other without an audience. There was nothing you could have done, she told them, I was with him and he went peacefully in his sleep. "What time did he die?" One of them asked out of curiosity. "Around 3:00am," she answered.

This information meant nothing to any of them except for my dad. He felt a lump in his throat. He then told the grieving family of his experience on the road. He told them of the blinding light that had flooded over them and halted their progress at 3:00am. My mom and her family took some comfort in knowing that my grandpa had sent a message to them, in a way, that he was passing over to the other side. He was a bright light and then he was gone.

Chapter 18:
A Sister's Goodbye

My father-in-law was very close to his only sibling, his sister Rose. They had a close bond that, even though they were grown and lived a thousand miles apart, was unshakeable. Rose had been in fragile health for most of her adult life and her brother had tried his best to be there for her when she needed him. They always hated having to say goodbye when he had to pack up and head home after a visit.

When I first met my husband, Rose was in the battle of her life with systemic lupus. Sadly, she lost the fight and passed away in her fifties, leaving behind three grown children as well as her grief stricken older brother. She had taken time, in the moment of her passing from this world to the next, to say her final goodbyes in a most unusual way.

At the time, my father-in-law was dividing his time between a home in Ohio and one in Florida. He was at his Florida home when he got word that his sister's health was failing and that he should make plans to travel back to Ohio as soon as possible.

He and his wife had been preparing to travel to Ohio by trailer, setting up camp at rest areas along the way. My father-in-law spoke with his sister on the telephone and asked her if that would be alright with her and she told him that it wasn't a problem. My in laws were on the road the following day.

At one of the rest stops along the way, my father-in-law was sitting in the camper reading a magazine when he saw something that resembled a comet come through the wall that was in front of him.

As the comet got closer to him, it turned into a fully formed figure of a woman. A five foot long black trail followed behind her. Her hair was swept back as if by a strong wind. As she got closer to him, her mouth opened and she bared her teeth and began to snarl.

The snarling woman hovered in front of my father-in-law's face for a few seconds and then floated passed him and out the opposite wall from which it had entered. He checked the time. It was 1:00 o'clock in the morning.

Just over an hour later, he received the call informing him that his sister had passed away. She had died at 1:45. He had known that Rose was gone before hearing the news. The snarling figure that had burst into his trailer had been wearing her face.

My father-in-law later spoke to a Catholic priest and told him of the strange visit just before his sister's death. The priest wasn't surprised by the story. He told him that death appears to some as a black apparition. He felt that Rose was upset that her brother hadn't been there in her final hours and had lashed out at him in spirit. Her body had still been living at the time of the visit, but her soul had already departed.

Phantom Noises

I have heard from many people who, although they wouldn't go so far as to say their homes were haunted, would say that they were being harassed by noises they couldn't explain. They came in different forms: babies crying, cat's meowing, unexplained footsteps, doors slamming by themselves and mysterious laughter just to name a few. These are a few of their stories.

Chapter 19:
Hush Little Baby

This story was related to me by the aunt of a young woman who had a strange and possibly supernatural tale to tell. I was given permission to share her story with the agreement that I would change her last name to protect her privacy. All other details are accurate.

Michelle Sams rented a small efficiency apartment in the town of Fairmont, West Virginia while she was attending classes at Fairmont State University. Her parents allowed her just enough of a monthly stipend that she didn't need a roommate. Money was tight, however, and she had to watch every penny.

The apartment was part of a small complex, Michelle's unit being the middle apartment on the second floor. She didn't know any of her neighbors, yet, but she had spoken to a couple of them briefly when she was in the process of moving in. They seemed nice and she looked forward to getting to know them better.

On her very first night in her new apartment, Michelle was awakened in the early hours of the morning by the shrill sounds of a baby crying. The child's wailing went on unabated for what seemed to her like hours. Where were the baby's parents, she wondered. Why didn't they quiet their child? She thought it very inconsiderate, but there wasn't much she could do except to turn on her radio and try to drown the crying out so that she could get some sleep.

The next morning, a tired Michelle decided to go shopping at some local flea markets for household goods and furnishings. She wanted to spruce up her tiny abode as best she could with what little money she had.

As she was walking to her car, she happened to see the next door neighbor bringing out a bag of trash. As politely as she could, Michelle approached the man and reintroduced herself to him. He remembered her from when she was moving in boxes a few days prior. He was friendly and they made small talk for a few minutes before Michelle decided to mention the fact that his baby had kept her up all night with its incessant wailing.

She asked the man if everything was alright with his baby, she had heard the child crying and was worried that it might be ill. The man shook his head. She had the wrong guy, he didn't have any children. He lived with his girlfriend and a cat. There was no baby.

Michelle didn't know the man, but she did know that the sound of crying had been coming from the direction of his apartment. His was the unit on the end. There were no other apartments on that side. Perhaps it was coming from the apartment below his, she theorized. She then asked him if the baby had disturbed him or his girlfriend. He hadn't heard any crying and his girlfriend hadn't mentioned anything about a baby crying.

She didn't want any bad blood with her neighbors so she decided to let the subject drop. Maybe they were heavy sleepers. It wasn't a big deal anyway. They chatted a bit more and then she hopped in her car and proceeded to run her errands. The matter was soon forgotten.

That night, as Michelle was watching television and reviewing her upcoming class schedule, she heard it again. A baby's piercing cries cut through the night. The sound was definitely coming from the apartment to the left of hers, she could hear it as clear as a bell. The neighbor had been lying for some reason. It was his baby that was sobbing uncontrollably. She decided to confront him then and there when he wouldn't be able to deny it.

Michelle marched next door, the baby's cries still ringing in the air. She knocked on her neighbor's door and waited. A young woman, presumably the girlfriend, answered the door. The apartment was quiet except for the sound of the television in the background.

Michelle explained that she had just moved into the apartment next door. They briefly exchanged pleasantries and then Michelle told the woman her reason for the visit. She explained that their baby's crying was getting to be a bit disturbing and she wondered if there was anything she could do to help them out.

The woman gave Michelle the same puzzled look that her boyfriend had given her earlier in the day. She informed her that she didn't have a baby. She didn't know what Michelle was talking about. Growing tired of the ruse, Michelle adopted a firmer approach. She explained to the woman, as patiently as she could, that she knew there was a baby and she didn't want to play games. She went on to tell her neighbor that she didn't want to get the landlord involved so, please, try to keep the baby quiet at night.

The woman more or less told Michelle that she was crazy before shutting the door in her face. This was not the relationship that Michelle had hoped to have with the people she had to live next door to. The ear splitting crying was bad enough, but the lying about it was even more upsetting. She did notice, however, that the crying had ceased when the woman came to the door. Maybe they got the message.

It wasn't to be. Michelle had no more than settled into bed that night and closed her weary eyes before the silence was shattered by the familiar wails of the neighbor's baby. The crying went on all night and stopped just before dawn. Michelle had had enough. She would call the landlord and report the neighbors. She didn't want to cause trouble, but school would be starting in a matter of days and she couldn't make it through her classes on no sleep.

As soon as nine o'clock rolled around, she was on the phone with the man who had rented her the apartment. She told him all about the crying baby and the neighbors who wouldn't do anything about it. He was as flummoxed as they had been. Her neighbors weren't lying, they didn't have a baby. In fact, none of the tenants who currently lived in the complex had babies.

He explained to Michelle that he catered to college students and they rarely had children. Michelle was adamant, maybe someone with an infant was visiting them, she didn't know but, she was going to break her lease and move out if he didn't do something about the noise. She reminded him that he had assured her that the complex was quiet and that it would be the perfect place for her.

The landlord told Michelle that he would have a talk with her neighbors, all of the neighbors in fact, and would get to the bottom of the noise complaint. He prided himself on his tenants comfort. He would take care of the problem. Michelle was satisfied with his response. She looked forward to finally getting a night's sleep.

Later that afternoon, as she was leaving to have lunch with a friend, Michelle bumped into her next door neighbor at the communal mailboxes. He gave her a frosty glare, but didn't say a word. Michelle assumed the landlord must have spoken to him about the complaint she had made. Oh, well, she thought, he should have owned up to his responsibility.

That evening, Michelle received a call from her landlord. He had spoken to every tenant. No one had a baby and there hadn't been any recent guests with babies. Maybe Michelle had been hearing noise from someone's television, or cat's fighting. At any rate, he had asked them all to keep the noise down. That was all he could do.

Michelle wanted to argue that she knew the difference between sounds from a television and the wailing of an infant, but what was the point? Hopefully, the neighbors had gotten the message and they would keep their baby quiet. She would wait and see.

She didn't have to wait long for her answer. That night, just as it had done every night since she moved in, the baby began to scream and cry uncontrollably into the early hours of the morning. Michelle glanced at the clock on her bedside table, it read 2 o'clock. The crying continued for several hours until it finally stopped.

Michelle was so exhausted that she could hardly think for herself. She hadn't slept more than two or three hours since she moved in. Why did the baby only cry at night? It never made so much as a whimper all day and then wailed all night long. This routine went on night after night for weeks. She would try one last tactic to try to get something done about it.

She visited all of her neighbors, except for the ones next door with the crying baby, and asked them if they would file a complaint against them for the noise violation. Not one of Michelle's neighbors had ever heard a baby crying in the complex or, if they had, they wouldn't admit it.

Michelle couldn't believe it and she tried arguing her point. How could they not hear it? The crying was incredibly loud and went on all night long, every night. Sorry, they would say, we can't help you.

Michelle phoned her parents that evening and asked them if she could move back in. The apartment wasn't working out. Her mom was hesitant. They had rented the apartment for their daughter for a reason. She was uncontrollable. She had been a handful as a teenager: rebellious, angry and promiscuous. After some counseling and a strong dose of tough love, she had shaped up by the time she was twenty and had finally showed some interest in going to school and getting her life on track.

What Michelle's parents didn't know about their daughter, was that she had become pregnant on three separate occasions by three different boys. Her aunt, who shared this story with me, helped her niece pay for the abortions. It was when her aunt threatened to tell Michelle's parents about the pregnancies, that Michelle decided to straighten up and turn her life around.

As much as they loved their daughter, Michelle's parents were afraid that moving back home would be a step backwards for her and that she would revert back to her old ways. Her mother told her that they would help her find a new apartment, but she couldn't come home. It would be the best solution for everyone involved.

Michelle didn't agree with her parent's decision, but she went along with it. As long as she didn't have to listen to the baby crying every night, she would live anywhere. Michelle's father went with her when she confronted the landlord and told him she was moving lease or no lease.

Her father threatened legal action on the grounds that the landlord had misrepresented the building when they signed the lease. After some wrangling back and forth, they agreed to let the landlord keep the security and cleaning deposits as well as the last month's rent even though Michelle had only lived in the apartment for a few weeks.

Michelle's parents helped her find another place across town. It was further from campus, but the neighborhood was nice and this was a small rental house. She wouldn't have to worry about sounds coming through the walls. She could study and sleep in peace.

Her parents and a few friends helped move all of her belongings from the noisy apartment into her new house. They were exhausted after a hard day's work and Michelle's father ordered pizza for everyone as a thank you.

After everyone had gone home, Michelle took her first opportunity to relax at her new place. She took a long, hot bath and curled up on the sofa in front of the television. It wasn't long before she dozed off.

She hadn't been asleep long when the peace and quiet was shattered by a sound that was, by now, familiar to her-- the desperate wailing of an infant. She could tell at once that the forlorn crying was coming from inside her house. It sounded like it was all around her, in the walls and the ceiling. It echoed and pounded in her ears.

There would be no confronting neighbors or complaining to the landlord this time. Michelle made an appointment the next day to see her therapist. She had stopped her sessions months earlier because there didn't seem to be a need. Now, she wasn't so sure.

She later explained to her aunt that the therapist felt that the phantom crying was a manifestation of her regret over having had the abortions. Michelle doubted his theory. She felt that she had done the best thing she could do at the time. She wasn't proud of her behavior, but neither was she wracked with guilt.

At any rate, he prescribed medications to help her sleep and to calm her psyche. Eventually, the nightly visits from the crying baby became more erratic and eventually ceased altogether. Was the phantom crying a reminder from somewhere beyond Michelle's physical world of the babies she had lost? Or, were they just her mind's way of dealing with some unresolved feelings of regret that she didn't even realize she had?

Chapter 20:
The Restless Spirit

The couple in this next story contacted me on social media after reading my first collection of paranormal tales. I have changed only their last names at their request. They wanted to share their experiences with a ghost whom they have co-existed with for several years. Not all spirits are evil entities; some apparently just don't have anywhere else to go.

Ryan and Kelly Armstrong, along with their teenaged daughter Ashley, moved into the three bedroom ranch style house in a quiet suburb of Houston in early 2005. The house had a fenced in back yard for their two dogs and a large garage for Ryan, who spent his spare time fixing up old cars, to tinker around in. It was a perfect fit for their family and they loved the house from the first moment they saw it.

The family got their first inkling that things might not be as perfect as they had at first seemed when their dogs began to pace and whimper every evening around bedtime. This was a behavior that the dogs had never exhibited prior to moving into the house. Around nine o'clock every night, both dogs would roam through the house, noses to the floor, madly sniffing and whining. They would pace in and out of the rooms until they reached a utility closet in the back hallway. There, they would bark frantically, tails wagging, until someone in the family would open the door. The dogs would sniff around the closet and then go about their business as if nothing had happened.

This wasn't the only time something in the house got the attention of the family's dogs. Kelly was the first to notice it. One day while everyone else in the house was out and Kelly was enjoying an afternoon on the sofa with a good book, the dogs suddenly jumped up from their daily naps and began to frantically run through the hallways, barking at the top of their lungs.

Kelly was immediately on alert. The only other time she had seen the dogs react so frantically during the day was when a prowler had been snooping around their windows. Their ferocious barking had sent him running through the back yard and out of sight. Afraid that someone might be lurking in the yard, she went from window to window peeking out to see if anyone was on the property. She didn't see a soul.

Satisfied that they were in no danger of a home invasion, Kelly shushed the dogs and went back to her reading. Just as she was settling in she heard what had sent the dogs into a barking frenzy, a cat was meowing somewhere in the house. It was loud and unmistakable. The family liked cats, but they didn't have one.

Again, the dogs began to race through the house. They would stop every now and again and listen for the meowing and then resume their mad dash to find the source of the noise. Kelly, too, was searching for the kitty.

The loud meows would seem to come from the ceiling one time and from inside the walls the next. The dogs were also flummoxed. They would dart from one end of the house to the other as the cat's call would echo from one area and then another.

The meowing eventually faded away, that is exactly how Kelly describes it. It didn't seem to her as though the cat just disappeared, it sounded like the cat had walked away into a tunnel or drum, the meowing just bounced off of the walls and then was gone.

The dogs quieted down as Kelly continued to search for the cat. She never did find it, but she has had many chances since then. At first, Ryan feared that a stray cat might have gotten trapped in the walls somehow, but he could find no place where such a breach could have occurred. The phantom cat has become a regular visitor to the house. Kelly, Ryan and Ashley have all heard it over the years, but none of them has been able to catch a glimpse of the mysterious feline.

Another bothersome thing about the Armstrong's house are the almost nightly visits from what the family now refer to as "the snorer". It all began one night about six months after they moved in to the house. Kelly was awakened from a peaceful sleep by loud snoring. She nudged her husband in an attempt to silence him.

Ryan rolled over on his side and Kelly closed her eyes, hoping to go right back to sleep. Instead, her ears were once again assaulted by the sound of someone in the room sawing logs even louder than before.

She sat up this time and nudged her husband more forcefully, she felt that if she couldn't sleep then why should he? He woke up and grumbled at his wife for waking him. She told him that he had been snoring and it was keeping her awake. He apologized and got up to use the restroom. Kelly laid back down and tried once again to fall asleep.

Her head no more than hit the pillow before the loud sounds of snoring filled the room once again. She knew that Ryan was still in the bathroom and there was no one else in the room. The dogs slept on their own beds in the living room and weren't allowed in the bedrooms at night, the door was kept closed.

She lay there in the darkness listening to the snoring. It sounded like someone was in a deep sleep. Ryan rejoined her in bed and did a double take when he saw that she was awake. He, too, could hear the snoring. The sound seemed to be coming from the bed, but they were both awake.

They lay there in stunned silence for a few minutes, listening as the snoring continued unabated. Ryan finally spoke up and called out, "Who's there?" The snoring immediately ceased. The harsh tone of his voice had apparently jarred their invisible guest from his or her deep slumber.

The night snorer has visited each family member's room more than once over the course of the family's stay in the house. Although, in the beginning, the experience was a little bit frightening for them, it had become a ritual that they no longer mind. Even guests in the house have heard the disembodied snoring. A loud "be quiet" or "wake up" usually silences the snoring for the rest of the night. Whoever the source of the snoring is, they don't seem to mean anyone any harm, they're just a noisy sleeper.

Another peculiar occurrence in the house is the random smell of food cooking which will waft throughout the house even when no one is in the kitchen and no food is being prepared. Each family member--sometimes individually, sometimes together--have smelled the enticing aroma of bacon frying or bread baking only to be disappointed upon further inspection when they find that the stove is bare and the oven is cold and empty.

At various times, other strange aromas will drift throughout the house with no noticeable source. The strong smell of a woman's perfume will suddenly fill the living room while the family is sitting around enjoying a family movie. It quickly fades with no explanation. The alarming smell of something burning is also an occasional reminder that they are not alone. The odor seems electrical in nature, but dissipates after a few moments.

The Armstrongs have cohabitated with someone from the other side for several years now. Whoever or whatever shares their home with them has never been violent or destructive, nor have they made any effort to drive the family from the house. Kelly and Ryan have come to the conclusion that the entity in their home is just as puzzled by their presence there as they are by his or hers.

Out of curiosity, Kelly began to research public records pertaining to the house in an attempt to get to the bottom of their mystery guest's origins. She checked real estate sales records to no avail. She also searched online for any mention of strange activity that may have taken place at the house, perhaps an unsolved crime or suicide.

She could find no record of anything out of the ordinary happening at her home in the decades prior to their moving in. Whoever was living in the home with them, just outside of their realm of reality, apparently had no reason for being there except that they liked the house and didn't want to leave.

Since the worst thing the entity has done in all of the years the Armstrongs have lived there is snore loudly and send the dogs on wild goose chases, not to mention cook delicious smelling invisible food, they have no plans to move. The family has made peace with the situation. Not all spirits have bad intentions. Some are just as perplexed by us as we are by them.

Chapter 21:
The Black Cow

Spirit animals are always a source of great fascination. Stories of phantom cats and dogs returning to comfort their grieving humans are fairly commonplace. Other animals, however, have been known to haunt the places they once knew. One such creature became a fixture in the community of White Sulphur Springs, West Virginia in the 1940s when my father was a boy.

The people of the small community had long exchanged stories of a mysterious black cow who roamed the countryside. Most of the locals were farmers who grew crops as well as raised livestock. No one laid claim to the mammoth cow that could be heard from early light until well into the night as it mooed and roared while making its way from one property to the other.

The townspeople who claimed to have seen the cow, or bull, said it was the size of a tractor if not larger. They said that it galloped like a horse, the thundering of its hooves echoing through the mountains on quiet days. Steam would swirl from its nostrils if it encountered you on the road. The mighty animal would stomp his foot and charge anyone unlucky enough to cross its path on one of the many back roads. As the victim closed their eyes and waited to be gored, the sound of the massive beast running towards them would fade and they would peek through half closed lids only to find that the danger had passed. The cow had disappeared without a trace.

My father was around eighteen years old when he had an eerie encounter with the legendary bovine. He was working at the time as a guard at a rock quarry. Workers would shoot the face off of the cliff and it was my father's job, among others, to keep people away while the blasting was in progress.

It was a mile's walk from work to my dad's parent's house. On this particular day it had snowed several inches and he was trudging through the heavy snow on his way home. He had what the old timers called "snow blindness". It was so bright that he could hardly see a foot in front of him as he made his way through the heavy snow.

His progress was halted when he bumped into something in the snow in front of him. As he stumbled, something let out an enraged roar. He stood frozen as a giant black form rose from the snow before him. Its eyes were blazing and it snorted only inches from his face. He could see steam rising from its fur as it began stomping one hoof in the snow. He knew he was about to be annihilated, but he was too afraid to make a sound or to move.

As he braced himself for the impact, the cow charged forward and right through him. He felt nothing but a rush of cold air as the sound of hooves crushing through the icy snow stormed past him. What followed was total silence. The cow was gone and my father was left unharmed. He said that of all the dangers he had faced in his life, first in the military and then as a police officer, nothing had ever frightened him as much as the encounter with the black cow.

People continued to see the black cow for years after my father's harrowing sighting. My great-grandfather had heard the sound of hooves thundering down the road towards their house and had run in the house and grabbed his shotgun. He was determined to end the mystery of the black cow once and for all. No one claimed to own the animal and he figured it was fair game to shoot.

He had a clear shot as the behemoth rounded the corner and ran past his front yard. He aimed his gun and fired. The cow didn't slow down or even look in his direction. My great-grandpa ran out to the road and shot again. The black figure disappeared in a cloud of dust. The man was sure that he had at least grazed the beast, but he couldn't find a trace of blood anywhere on the dirt road.

Similar stories were told for years. Men were sure that they had downed the cow only to have it disappear without a trace only to return on another day to frighten whoever was unlucky enough to cross its path.

Eventually, as most legends do, the tales of encounters with the black cow became fewer and fewer and finally came to an end. Perhaps the phantom animal moved on to other pastures or maybe it found whatever it had been roaming throughout the mountains for so many years in search of. No one will ever know, but the older residents still sit around on Sunday afternoons and tell their tales of the ominous black cow who used to haunt their mountain community.

Omens

When word got out that I was writing this book, I was bombarded with stories from people from all over who either lived in haunted houses or knew someone who knew someone who had seen a ghost. The stories were all compelling, but I tried to focus on those that stood out for one reason or another.

Omens have always fascinated me. As a child, once in a while, we would hear a loud whack on the side of our home. It literally sounded as though a giant hand had smacked the house. My mother would be a nervous wreck for days afterwards, certain that some tragedy was about to befall someone in our house. Where she comes from, those unexplained sounds are dreaded omens that mean that death is approaching.

More often than not, time would pass without incident and the omen was not for us after all. This didn't stop my mother from walking around on pins and needles each time it happened. She still reacts the same way to this day. I would like to now share some stories that people brought to me about omens that had touched them or someone close to them.

Chapter 22:
The Owl

Misty and Charles Lanthrope lived on the outskirts of Lexington, Kentucky when they were paid a visit by a most unusual guest. The couple was in their mid-fifties at the time and their children were grown and had moved on to have families of their own.

Misty and Charles raised horses on a small ranch. It was their passion and they relished everyday spent with their equines. Breeding horses took a certain amount of skill and the couple took great pride in the healthy, beautiful horses they had bred and then sold to one happy customer after another. This had provided them with a sizable nest egg and a comfortable existence.

All had gone well for the couple until the spring of 2001. One day, as Misty was walking down the driveway to go run some errands, she looked up to see a screech owl perched on the hood of her car. It was just before noon and she had never seen an owl on the property at nighttime much less during the day.

She stood for a few moments exchanging looks with the unusual bird before it took flight and disappeared into the wooded area behind their ranch. Misty thought nothing more of it and got into her car and ran her errands. The incident was all but forgotten.

A few weeks had gone by since Misty's encounter with the screech owl when one of the ranch hands hollered for her and Charlie to join him in the front stable. One of their mares, who was pregnant but not yet ready to foal, had suddenly collapsed and refused to stand up.

After all attempts to get the mare to her feet had failed, Charlie phoned their veterinarian. The veterinarian could find no visible reason for the mare to be down. Her vital signs were normal and she didn't seem to be in great distress, she just wouldn't stand up. He gave her an injection and told them that she should come around soon. He suggested that they give her a little bit of time and then try to right her. They thanked him and decided to take his advice and wait it out.

After an hour or so had gone by they tried again to get the mare to her feet, she steadfastly refused. They decided to let her go till morning. The Lanthropes went to bed feeling sure that the mare would be standing in her stall in the morning and that everything would be back to normal.

It was not to be. Early the next morning, when Charlie and his ranch hand went to the stable to check on the horse, they found her lying prone on the stable floor. She had passed away sometime during the night. Charlie phoned the veterinarian and asked him to perform a postmortem as soon as possible. He wanted to get to the bottom of what had killed the mare and her unborn foal.

There were still other mares in foal on the property, so everyone set about their day taking care of the other animals while they waited for the vet to make his determination as to what ailment had befallen the deceased mare. When Charlie entered one of the stalls further down the stable, his heart dropped. Once there, he saw another mare had gone down. She was on her side, but her head was raised. The animal was either unable or unwilling to stand.

He and his ranch hand made every effort to get the mare to her feet to no avail. She wouldn't budge. Again, like the mare on the previous day, she didn't seem to be in distress. She just refused to get to her feet.

When the veterinarian arrived, instead of having him perform the postmortem right away, they rushed him into the stall with the other mare that was down. He could find no cause for her to be off of her feet and, like Charlie and his helper, couldn't shift her no matter how he tried.

He gave the mare the same injection that he had given to the other downed horse, hoping that it would do the trick this time. He would give it a chance to work while he examined the dead mare and tried to figure out what had killed her.

Charlie and Misty paced anxiously as the doctor performed the gory procedure on the stable floor. When he was finished, he rose slowly to his feet and shook his head. Her organs all looked fine and there was no sign of colic. The unborn foal had been developing normally. He could find no obvious cause of death. A perfectly healthy mare had simply collapsed and died for no known reason. For now, he had no answers.

After the post mortem was completed, the vet and Charlie checked in on the other downed mare. She was laying all the way down now and her breathing was shallow. The doctor worked on her frantically trying to save her and her foal. It was of no use, she died writhing on the floor along with her foal.

The veterinarian performed the post mortem on the mare right then and there. Again, everything looked normal. He could see no reason why this mare had died. He collected tissue samples from both mares to send away to be analyzed. Perhaps they were suffering from some sort of virus or ailment that he couldn't detect with the naked eye. It would be weeks before they would know anything.

Things went downhill rapidly from that point on at Charlie and Misty's horse ranch. One by one, the mares would go down and not get back up. Only one of their six mares survived the ordeal. Her foal had not. In fact, not one foal was born on the ranch that season. It was an unprecedented event in their long careers as horse breeders.

When the lab results on the samples taken from the dead mares and foals finally came back, they showed no indication of anything biological or pathological that would explain the rash of deaths that swept through the ranch that year.

The events of that spring had a devastating effect on Charlie and Misty, both financially and emotionally. They eventually recovered enough to start raising horses once again, but they lived in fear of the nightmare beginning all over again. To date, it has not happened. The mares have normal pregnancies and give birth to healthy foals. Hopefully, the storm had passed.

Misty believes that the sighting of the screech owl was a warning for her to beware--dark times lay ahead. She had never seen the owl before or since and hopes it stays that way.

Chapter 23:
The White Feather

This story was related to me by Carla Mitchell of Silver Springs, Maryland. Growing up in the country, she had many encounters with animals and creatures of all shapes and sizes, but it was a feather that would stay with her as a sign that good and evil can come in many forms.

Carla grew up in an old farmhouse that had been passed down from her grandparents to her parents when she was just a child. Her grandmother had lived with her and her parents…along with her younger brother, Phillip. They raised chickens mainly for the eggs, but also had a few goats and rabbits. The family had an idyllic life for a while until her grandmother passed away in her sleep just before Christmas one year.

Carla's grandmother was nearly eighty years old and her passing wasn't completely unexpected. As the family was preparing her body for the mortician to take away, her mother noticed something odd clutched in the old woman's hand. In her grasp was a white feather. Her mother took the feather and set it aside, not giving it too much thought at the time. The mortician arrived and removed the body. Later, the room was cleaned and the old woman's belongings were divided up amongst the family.

Weeks went by and Carla's aunt came to visit from out of town. She was a city girl and Carla was captivated by her stories of life in a place where you could stay out all night if you wanted to or go to movies or dances. She was young and beautiful and seemed to live a glamorous life.

She always brought Carla gifts like fancy perfume or hair combs. She laughed easily and was always kind to her niece and nephew. Carla loved her dearly and looked forward to her visits.

Carla's aunt had only been staying with her family for a day or so when boredom finally overcame her and she told them that she needed to get out of the house for a while. She had met a young man in town and he wanted to take her out and show her around. She had eagerly accepted. She would be home early and tell them all about it. Carla watched her beautiful aunt as she waved goodbye and rushed out the door to meet her date.

Hours went by and Carla's aunt hadn't returned early as she had promised. At last, there was a knock at the door and Carla's mother answered, thinking that it would be her sister. Instead, she saw a police officer on the doorstep. He had bad news, there had been an accident and Carla's aunt and the man she had gone out with had both been killed. A friend of the family had been at the scene and recognized the young woman.

The family was devastated by having to face another loss so soon and especially this time with it being someone so young with her whole life ahead of her. The officer told Carla's mom that she would need to go claim the body and collect her sister's belongings. Carla's father worked the overnight shift at a local factory so her mother left Carla behind to watch after her little brother.

Carla's aunt's body was at the local hospital morgue. Carla's mother had the unpleasant task of positively identifying the body. The family friend had already told the authorities who the woman was, but they preferred to have a family member be the person of record as having claimed the body.

Carla's mom was led into a room and a gurney was wheeled in with a body covered by a thin blanket. The technician pulled back the cover and asked if this was her sister. "Yes," she replied. "It's her."

She took her sister's hand in her own as she was saying her final goodbyes when something fell from her sister's grasp. Carla's mother watched mesmerized as a white feather floated slowly to the floor.

She stepped back for a moment before bending down and picking up the feather. The technician was just as taken aback. "That wasn't there when I brought her in," he informed Carla's mom. They both just stood there gaping at each other for a minute before Carla's mother fled the room, feather in hand.

That night, before Carla's mom had returned from the morgue, Carla and her brother had both fallen asleep on the couch. It was very late and they couldn't stay awake until their mother got home. Carla fell into fitful sleep filled with vivid dreams, the most realistic dreams she had ever had.

In one dream, Carla was at a party and her aunt was also there. Her aunt was wearing a silver dress adorned with sequins. She swirled and spun around the dance floor as though on air. She was laughing and her eyes were bright as she danced with one beau after another. Carla was watching her, but her aunt didn't seem to notice.

At one point, Carla's aunt and her dance partner passed right by Carla as they floated across the dance floor. As they passed, something fell to the floor at Carla's feet. It was a white feather from the boa that Carla's aunt was wearing around her neck. Carla's aunt was laughing as she passed her niece and their eyes met for a second and at that moment Carla was jolted from her dream by the sound of her mother returning home from the hospital.

After Carla's mother had put Phillip to bed, she sat with Carla on the couch and showed her the feather. Carla had also seen the feather when her grandmother had passed away. She told her mother of her dream and her mom began to cry. Together, they concluded that the feather in Carla's grandmother's hand had been an omen that someone else in the family would soon follow her into the hereafter.

The dream, on the other hand, they felt was a message from their beloved sister and aunt that she was somewhere just beyond their reach, still dancing and laughing, young and beautiful for all eternity.

Chapter 24:
Demons

We've all heard that if you lead a good life, are honest, treat others as you would like to be treated, that you will spend the afterlife in paradise. For those who spend their lives causing misery to others, well, what is awaiting them in the hereafter might not be as pleasant.

My grandmother was one of three sisters. She was a good woman who raised a family during hard times, sacrificing everything for them. Her younger sister was also a woman who was devoted to her family and to her Christian faith. The elder sister, however, was a different story altogether.

I never knew my great aunt, but I have heard many stories about her. She was a difficult woman. She married young and, by all accounts, it was an unhappy union from the start. Her domineering personality left her husband in a constant state of shell shock.

Living was a day to day struggle to get by in the 1920s and 30s West Virginia. Jobs were scarce and farm life was filled with days and nights of hard labor just to make ends meet. Most families suffered through those years happy to have a roof over their heads and food on the table.

My great aunt was the exception. Her long suffering husband was the town's accountant and made a decent wage for the time. He was able to provide a comfortable life for himself and his wife. Although the couple had been married for over thirty years, they remained childless. He was a generous soul, but she was frugal and insisted that they pinch every penny. Children would just be another expense.

My mother remembers her aunt as having been a notorious germaphobe. She was constantly washing her hands and insisting that others do the same. She didn't like to be touched and recoiled at the mere mention of physical contact. She didn't welcome company and visits to her home were infrequent.

Family members who did associate with her recall being ushered outside onto the porch to talk. She didn't much like people sitting on her furniture. A cool drink on a hot summer's day was not an option. She never offered refreshments of any sort even though she kept a well-stocked pantry.

One thing my great aunt did like to do was gossip. She never missed an opportunity to talk down one of her neighbors or someone in town who she felt was beneath her. She was what people called "big feeling", meaning she thought she was better than everyone else.

My great aunt took ill suddenly and was bedridden for weeks before she passed away. Family member whom she hadn't seen in years would stop by from time to time to pay their last respects. I'm not sure with what illness she was stricken, but I've been told both cancer and blood poisoning. Whichever it was she wasted away quickly.

My mother was one of the family members who paid a visit to the dying woman to say her goodbyes. They had never been close, but they were still family. As my mother sat down next to her and took her aunt's hand the woman's eyes widened with fear. "Do you see them?" she asked my mother. "See who?" my mother asked.

"The devils," her aunt replied. She was terrified and my mother could see that she was shaking as she spoke. She went on to tell my mom that she could see devilish looking creatures climbing up the bedposts. She could also hear them whispering. They were taunting her.

When my mother asked her what they were saying...her aunt began to cry. They whispered that they were waiting to take her away. She was scared to go to sleep. She dreaded what was in store for her if she didn't wake up again.

My mother tried to calm her fears, telling her that it was just the sickness making her think she saw things that weren't there. Her aunt would have none of it. She could see them as clearly as she could see anyone else in the room. They were real and they were waiting to take her soul.

The members of my mother's family were deeply religious people, my mother included. She doesn't believe in the paranormal, but she does believe in Heaven and Hell. As much as she believes in God and angels, she also believes just as strongly in Satan and demons.

The more time my mom spent with her aunt, the more she began to see that something very real was tormenting this woman's final days. My mother wasn't with her aunt when she took her last breaths, but my grandmother was. What she related to my mother was the stuff of nightmares.

My grandmother said that her sister was so frightened in her final hours that she was almost unrecognizable. She was so weak that she couldn't raise her head off of the pillow, but her eyes were wide and her features contorted. She whispered to my grandma that the demons were now in the bed with her and that they were hitting and kicking her legs. She begged her sister to make them stop.

All my grandmother could do was to hold her sister's hand and pray for her. She died with her husband and my grandmother at her bedside. My grandmother later told my mother that the look on her sister's face when she passed was one of pure terror.

Perhaps, my great aunt was so racked with illness that she was hallucinating in her final days and the demons were only in her mind. Most of her family, however, held the belief that her years spent making other people miserable had finally caught up with her. In their words "the old Devil came for her."

An eerily similar story came to me by way of a friend of my husband's whose grandfather was also visited by what he referred to as demons on his deathbed. Otis Jakes, whom people close to him called Oats, had been a farmer all of his life. He and his wife had raised six children together before she passed away in her forties leaving him to tend to the farm and family on his own.

By all accounts, Oats had been a kind man and a good father to his children. He gave them the best life he could and they all adored him. When his children were grown and living on their own he slowed down and decided to enjoy his life.

Well into his sixties, he married a woman he had met at church. He was a loving and devoted husband and they spent many Sunday afternoons hosting family gatherings where the children and grandchildren would come to play horseshoes and eat fried chicken with all the fixings.

Oats hadn't been feeling well for a while and his wife finally talked him into paying the local doctor a visit. After an examination, some blood work, and x-rays, Oats was diagnosed with lung cancer. A life-long smoker, the news wasn't a complete surprise. He had been coughing up blood for some time. The cancer was advanced and treatment would not save him.

Rather than wallow in self-pity, Oats opted to live what life he had left to the fullest. He took his wife on a trip to the beach. They spent all the time they could with their grandkids, enjoying every minute of time they could watching the children as they played and laughed. It took their minds of off the inevitable.

In a matter of a few short months, Oats' health had deteriorated to the point where he could no longer leave the house. Soon enough, he was confined to his bed, no longer able to stand on his own.

His wife stayed by his side as his health declined. His adult children came by regularly to sit with him and keep him company. On one visit, my husband's friend David walked in and gave his grandfather a hug and then seated himself at the bedside. "Who did you bring with you?" Oats asked.

David had come alone that day. "It's just me, Grandpa," he informed him.

Oats gave David a funny look and pointed to the foot of the bed. "Who's that?" he asked.

David could see that no one else was in the room and he told his grandfather so. The old man was adamant that there was a man standing at the foot of the bed. Intrigued, David asked him to describe what he saw.

The man was small, his skin was dark and his teeth were gleaming white. He had come in the room at the same time that David had entered. David asked his grandfather if the man said anything. Oats told him that no, the man hadn't said a word, he had only stared at him and shaken his head.

David told his grandpa that it was probably the painkillers playing tricks with his mind. Oats agreed and they didn't speak any more about it on that visit. David did mention it to Oats' wife as he was leaving. She knew about the small man in the room, Oats had mentioned him before. He had also told her that there were little men who looked like devils who would come into the room and climb around on the furniture. She, too, attributed these visions to the medications Oats was taking.

As the days passed by, family members began to call each other with stories of strange things that Oats would say when they visited him. He was seeing the little demons now on a regular basis. He said that they would crawl into the bed and poke at him. He would yell for his wife to come get them off of the bed and she would run in to find him frantically flailing around at something only he could see.

No one could understand why Oats would feel besieged by demons. He was a good man who had always treated people right. Or, at least, that had been their experience with him. It wasn't until Oats' brother came in from out of town that they learned of their beloved father and grandfather's dark past.

According to his brother, Oats had been a rebellious teenager, always in trouble for one thing or another. He had been picked up more than once for breaking into local shops and had even beaten up a shop owner who had caught him in the act. Oats had served some time in jail as a young man for assault and battery.

They were surprised that Oats had been in trouble with the law, but many people act out in their youth and then settle down to become productive citizens. They assumed that Oats had been one of those people. The rest of the story was more shocking and hard for them to believe.

In his early twenties, Oats had been a suspect in a rash of attacks on women in the neighboring towns. Several of them had been hurt pretty badly and the communities had been terrorized for months by this unknown assailant. One girl who knew Oats said that she thought it was him, but it had been dark and she couldn't be certain. There was no DNA testing back then so Oats was never charged with a crime.

The attacks ended after a young woman disappeared one night after leaving her job as a nurse at the local hospital.

She was never seen again. No one knew if she was a victim of the attacker or if she had just left town. At any rate, the assaults ended and eventually the community got back to normal.

Oats' brother told the family that he had always suspected that Oats might have been involved in the attacks…he had said some things that only someone who had been at the scenes should know. At that time, Oats had been a rather menacing character and his brother hadn't pushed the matter. As Oats got older and settled down to raise a family, he had changed. He was no longer that rebellious hellion he had once been.

David and some of the other family members began to wonder if Oats conscience was starting to bother him now that his life was ending. David even got up the nerve to ask his grandfather if there was anything he wanted to get off of his chest, but his grandpa gave no reply. Whatever secrets he had, he was taking with him to the grave.

Oats continued to be terrorized by the demons in his room right up until his last moments. By that time, his wife told David that he could no longer speak, but he would point to different places in the room and tears would roll down his cheeks. She knew that whatever he had seen had frightened him to the bone. Just like my great aunt, Oats' wife said that when he died his face was frozen in a mask of terror.

Maybe it was just the painkillers clouding his mind in the end or, perhaps, past deeds aren't forgotten, or forgiven, in the afterlife.

Chapter 25:
The Doll Lady

Jeanie Smith had spent most of her adult life collecting things: costume jewelry, teddy bears, animal statues, books, and the one thing closest to her heart: dolls. Jeanie's daughter, Cara graciously shared her mother's story with me for this book. It is a tale of a bond so great that nothing could break it, not even death.

The family was originally from Portsmouth, Ohio. Jeanie and her husband, Richard, had raised their daughters in a big two-story house in the country. Once the girls were grown and on their own, the couple sold the old homestead and moved to a small community near the West Virginia border. They bought a house there which was just the right size for two people, a dog and Jeanie's collectibles, of which there were many.

Jeanie didn't get out of the house much due to her ever increasing health problems. She was suffering from congestive heart failure, among other things. She spent most of her days leafing through catalogs; ordering anything that struck her fancy. She wasn't choosy about what she purchased, but dolls were her main obsession.

One room of the house was designated as the doll's room. Jeanie had furnished it with cribs and bassinets that held many of her "babies." Others were displayed in glass cases or posed on table tops, waiting to greet whoever should come to pay them a visit. The problem was, of course, that no one ever did.

    Richard's job kept him on the road most of the time which meant that he was rarely home. Jeanie's daughters had jobs and families of their own to tend to. They stopped by on occasion and spoke often on the phone, but Jeanie led a rather lonely life except for the company of her dolls.

    Cara had become a little bit concerned about her mother's mental health when Jeanie began telling stories of how one doll or another would dance or sing or perform some other feat that Cara knew the dolls couldn't do. She humored her mother and played along, thinking that it was harmless fun and nothing to be alarmed about. As time went by, she would have a change of heart when the stories grew more and more bizarre

    Jeanie distanced herself from her family as the years passed, one into the next. Her health continued to deteriorate and calls to her daughter became less frequent as she retreated into her own world of solitude with only her dolls to keep her company. Cara began stopping by on a weekly basis to check up on her mother and make sure she was alright.

    The visits were usually brief, consisting of some small talk and maybe a cup of coffee, before the conversation would inevitably turn to what funny thing one of the dolls had said or done. They all had names, but Cara didn't know one from the next.

Jeanie would laugh as she told stories of how Missy had spun around so many times while showing off that she had gotten dizzy and collapsed into her arms. Or how Jenny had cried when she couldn't find ribbons that matched the dress that she had wanted to wear. The dolls sure did keep her busy but, she wouldn't have it any other way.

This went on each time Cara visited or spoke to her mother on the phone. Their conversations were almost always about the dolls; which were becoming more animated, at least in her mother's mind. After hearing more stories of how precocious the dolls were, Cara decided it was time to have a heart to heart talk.

As gently as she could, Cara explained to her mother that the dolls were just porcelain or plastic, they weren't real. They couldn't talk or dance and they didn't have feelings. She then braced herself for her mother's reaction.

Jeanie didn't seem bothered in the least. Yes, she told her daughter, she realized that the dolls were only dolls and nothing more. She liked to imagine them as real children just the same.

Cara was relieved. It seemed that her mother was simply reverting back to her childhood. The dolls' antics were born of loneliness and imagination. If it would make Jeanie happy in her remaining years, Cara didn't have a problem with that. She never mentioned it again.

A few months after that conversation, Jeanie's body finally gave out on her. She passed away in the hospital after suffering two heart attacks on the same day. Her family grieved and took their mother's remains back to

Portsmouth for burial. After taking a few weeks to come to terms with the fact that Jeanie was gone, they set about the task of clearing out the house.

The rooms were filled to capacity with boxes and bags of things that Jeanie had ordered over the years and never even opened. There were drawers full of jewelry that she had never worn. The dressers were covered with perfume bottles that had never been used. She had loved to buy things just to have them, whether she needed them or not.

Cara saved the doll's room for last. She knew how much they had meant to her mother and hated to get rid of them, but it had to be done. She and her sister were amazed at how meticulous their mother had been in caring for the dolls even as her own health had declined. Each doll was neatly dressed, not a hair out of place. Not a speck of dust was to be found even though the rest of the house was anything but clean.

They began boxing up as many dolls as they could. They would send them to auction. A doll collector would be thrilled to have such an extensive collection. There were too many to get to in one day so they stacked the boxes up and piled the remaining dolls in the cribs and bassinets. They would get to them on another day. The sisters shut off the lights and left the house for the night.

It was a few days later when Cara returned to continue packing up her mother's things. Her sister couldn't get the day off from work so Cara would be on her own this time. She had rented a truck to make the task of clearing out the house a bit easier. She began loading up some of the boxes she and her sister had packed up a few days prior.

After clearing most of the items out of the front room, Cara decided to take the dolls that had already been boxed up out to the truck. When she went into the doll's room and turned on the light, she was stunned by what she saw.

Most of the boxes that she and her sister had stacked up were now overturned, spilling the dolls out onto the floor. Some of the dolls that they had placed in the cribs and bassinets were still there while others were now lying on the floor.

Her first thoughts were that someone had broken into the house and ransacked the place. Strangely, no other rooms seemed to have been disturbed. She honestly couldn't tell if any dolls had been taken. There were too many to keep track of. There wasn't really anything she could do about it except to repack the dolls and try again.

Cara didn't know why, but she had an uneasy feeling that day while in the doll's room. She cut the day's work short and left early. She did manage to get a few boxes of dolls packed and loaded onto the truck. She put the remaining dolls in the cribs and bassinets once again. She hated the idea of leaving them on the floor. Her mother took good care of them and she wanted to do the same.

The next day, Cara returned with her sister and husband to finish clearing out the spare rooms. She had told them about the doll's room being in a shambles the day before, but no one seemed too alarmed by her story.

When they entered the room this time, there was no doubt in anyone's mind that something wasn't right. The dolls were once again on the floor instead of being in the cribs. They were on chairs and sitting on the chest of drawers. Cara knew that those pieces of furniture had been bare the day before; she was the one who had cleared them.

Cara was spooked and told her husband and sister so. She assured them that this was not how she had left the room. Her husband looked around for signs of a break-in, but could find none. The outside doors had been locked. The windows were all secure. No one other than Cara and her father had keys and he was living in another town.

Whatever the explanation, they decided to hurry up and get the room cleaned out and be done with it. They boxed up the remaining dolls and all of their accessories and packed them onto the truck. That was that; the dolls were out of the house and would soon be auctioned off to the highest bidder. Cara, for one, was happy that she would never have to see them again.

The house was put on the market soon after and Cara moved on with her life, deciding to put the past to rest. She gave no more thought to the strange events that had surrounded her mother's doll collection, that is, until she and her sister visited their mother's final resting place in Portsmouth.

The sisters hadn't been to the cemetery to see Jeanie's gravesite since her burial. They were waiting for her marker to be erected which had taken some weeks. When they finally made the pilgrimage there with their families, they had brought fresh flowers to place by her headstone.

They knew the general area where Jeanie was buried and as they approached her grave, they were surprised to see that someone had already placed something there. Propped up against the newly erected stone marker was a porcelain doll dressed in a velvet and lace dress. Cara couldn't be sure, but she thought she recognized it as having been one of her mother's favorites in her vast collection.

Cara's husband scoffed at the notion. He suggested that someone who had known Jeanie had left a doll as a token; it was as simple as that. Cara and her sister looked at each other. There was a way to be sure. Jeanie had always sewn her initials into all of her doll's clothing. They weren't sure why, but she had done it for as long as they could remember.

Cara bent down and picked up the doll. She lifted up its dress and searched until she found what she was looking for. There, sewn into the back of the dress in small stitching, were the initials "JS."

Cara laid the doll back down against the headstone and the family stood in silence for a while. When she returned home, she phoned her father and asked him if he had, by any chance, left a doll at Jeanie's gravesite. He denied that he had. He informed her that he hadn't been to the cemetery and had no plans to go anytime soon.

Had someone else found one of Jeanie's dolls and left it at her gravesite as a memorial to her? Perhaps, or is it just as likely that one of the dolls that she had been so close to in life had followed her to her final resting place? You be the judge.

Chapter 26:
Phantom Lights

Unexplained lights appearing out of nowhere and then disappearing just as suddenly are a surprisingly common occurrence, or so say the folks who were kind enough to share their experiences with me.

My mother, a notorious naysayer when it comes to any talk of the supernatural, related the following story to me when she found out that I was writing this book. This was the first time that she ever mentioned that she had felt uneasy at my grandmother's house. She told me that she refused to stay there by herself. She explained that there was something not quite right about that house.

I had known for years that my grandmother's old house in the hollows of Greenbrier County, West Virginia was plagued by events that could not easily be explained by conventional wisdom. The place was haunted by something and anyone who spent any time at all there could attest to that fact.

When my grandmother moved into her small rental house in the town of Alderson, everyone assumed that all of the darkness and dread that hovered over the old house in the hollow would remain there. After talking to my mother, I'm not so sure.

My mother's first inkling that something strange was going on in my grandmother's new house was the thumping she would hear in the adjacent building. The small rental unit that my grandmother occupied shared a wall with a recreation center for senior citizens. It was rarely used, save for the occasional game of bingo or holiday get together.

The kitchen door in grandma's house led into the senior center. My mother could hear people walking around in the center when there were no cars parked in the lot and there shouldn't have been anyone there. On one occasion, she summoned the nerve to go over and have a look around to see who was there. She walked through the center and just as she suspected, it was vacant.

As strange as the unexplained noises were, they weren't what spooked my mother. It was the lights that came out of the darkness only to fade away with no explanation that both worried and frightened her.

She first noticed them when she was sitting in the living room with one of my aunts and my grandmother. They were engaged in conversation when a car's headlights shone brightly through the picture window. My grandmother's house was on a dead end street by a railroad track. Cars would cross the track and then have to veer either to the left or right or else run straight into my grandmother's living room.

Everyone in the room that night assumed they had company because the lights stopped right at the front of the house and then shut off. The car hadn't turned so it must have parked, or so they thought. They waited a few moments for the sound of a car door, but there was only silence.

My mother finally stood up and opened the door to see who was waiting in the small parking area in front of the house. There was no one there. No cars were to be seen. My grandmother piped up at that moment and told my aunt and mom that she was used to this, it happened all the time.

She would be sitting in her living room, usually in the darkness because light hurt her eyes, when the room would suddenly be flooded with a bright light coming from her small front yard. At first, like my mother that night, she assumed it was a car coming across the railroad track, but she wouldn't hear a car and the light would just stop at the front of her house.

As strange as the phantom lights that shone through the window were, they weren't the ones that scared my mother the most. My father usually worked until four o'clock on Fridays, so when my parents would plan a weekend visit to my grandmother's, they wouldn't arrive at her house until around ten o'clock at night.

One night, as my parents were pulling up in front of the house, they both noticed that the senior center was lit up from the inside. Although there were no cars in the parking area, it looked as though there was some sort of festivity going on. The rooms were bright and they could see figures moving around inside so they assumed that there was a dance or party of some kind.

After getting settled in at my grandma's house, my father mentioned the shindig next door, curious about what the special occasion was. Usually the director of the center would let my grandmother know in advance of any activities they were planning as a courtesy, but he hadn't mentioned anything to her. It wasn't a big deal and the conversation soon turned to other things.

They went into the kitchen for a snack. They had been on the road for hours with nothing to eat or drink. Again, my father piped up about the party next door. He was always the inquisitive type and curiosity was killing him. He put his ear to the door, but couldn't hear a peep from the next room. Odd, it looked like quite a bash from the street.

He knocked on the door, but no one answered. He opened it just enough to peek in; the room was dark and empty. He flipped on the light and stepped into the senior center. There was no one there. The room was set up as it always was, folding chairs lining a long table which sat in the middle of the floor. There was no sign that there had been anyone there recently.

My father went back into my grandmother's house and told my mom about the vacant center. They were both bewildered and a little frightened at the same time. Was it possible that the party had ended abruptly and everyone had cleared out leaving the place seemingly untouched? It wasn't likely, but what other explanation could there be?

Again, my grandmother informed them that this was a pretty regular occurrence. She would hear what sounded like a get together next door even when she knew that no one was there. Other people had also told her that they had seen lights on in the center when the building was empty.

She took it in stride. No one ever bothered her and as long as they stayed next door, she felt that it was none of her business. One thing you can say about my grandmother was that she wasn't easily spooked. My mom, on the other hand, refused to stay in the house alone from then on and slept with her Bible under her pillow for her own peace of mind.

Chapter 27:
The Playground

This story was submitted to me from a lady by the name of Tanya Phillips. Tanya now lives in Virginia, but grew up in Wirt County, West Virginia.

Tanya's childhood home was located in a housing development that lay on the outskirts of the town of Elizabeth. The development featured mostly manufactured homes and ended on a cul-de-sac. Those familiar with the area knew that if you walked further on passed the round-a-bout in the road you would come to what residents referred to as "the park."

The park was nothing more than a small pond and what had once been a playground. The playground consisted of an old swing set, a slide and a broken down teeter-totter, but it was a place for the kids in the neighborhood to hang out. They would spend their lazy summer days playing there, twirling on the rusty swings and throwing rocks into the pond.

Rumors had circulated in the area for years that the old playground was haunted. People reported seeing the swings moving when there wasn't the slightest hint of a breeze. The sounds of children laughing and playing could be heard by locals even in the middle of the night.

Tanya had two older brothers who loved to taunt their sister with stories of the haunted playground. She wasn't sure if she believed them, but she was adventurous and never backed down from a challenge. So, when her brothers decided to stake out the playground one night when Tanya was around eleven, she begged to tag along.

Having their little sister along on their ghost hunting adventure was not what the brothers had in mind, but since Tanya threatened to tell their parents that the boys were sneaking out after dark she had left them little choice. Reluctantly, they told her that she could come along, but if she got scared and wanted to go home she was on her own. She readily agreed.

That night, after their parents had turned in for the night, the three of them snuck out of the house, armed with flashlights, to see for themselves what was haunting the playground. The plan was for them to hide behind trees and wait for the spirits to appear.

When they arrived at the park, they took to their positions and began shining their lights around hoping to catch a glimpse of something, or someone, moving in the shadows.

It was to be a long, uneventful night for the siblings. They heard frogs jumping into the pond, crickets chirped in the still of the night, leaves rustled a few times, but they didn't hear any laughing children or see anything out of the ordinary that night. That would come later.

The summer days rolled by and they all but forgot about their quest to find out if the playground was truly haunted. One evening around dusk, Tanya and her best friend were sitting at the edge of the pond, deep in conversation, when from behind them they heard the teeter totter creaking as though someone was playing on it. They turned around to look, but could see no sign of other children anywhere in the park.

Intrigued, the girls decided to explore further. They walked all around the play area, but there was no one there but the two of them. As they stood by the slide mulling over the possibility that Tanya's brothers might be pranking them, the swings began to move of their own volition. First one and then another and then all three swings were moving back and forth, unaided by anything that the girls could see.

Tanya recalls, even now, the cold chill that fell over her and her friend as they stood there watching the swings as they climbed higher and higher into the air and then back down as though someone was swinging on each one of them. The girls didn't wait around to see what would happen next, they ran to Tanya's house and never looked back.

When the girls burst through the door and excitedly told Tanya's mother and brothers what they had seen at the playground no one took them seriously. Her brothers accused her of making it up to get attention. She dared them to go look for themselves.

Tanya's brothers made a beeline to the park to check out the swings and teeter totter. Everything was still and quiet when they got there. The swings were hanging motionless. The teeter totter was setting there as usual, unused for years because of the dilapidated state it was in. They teased Tanya and her friend and called them liars.

Tanya knew what she had seen. The swings had moved on their own, of this she had no doubt. The boys didn't believe her and that made her angry. She and her friend turned around and stormed home. A little while later, her brothers returned to the house. Tanya would never forget the looks on their faces.

She said that the boys had come barreling inside, their faces as white as sheets. Her mother asked them what was wrong and they blurted out the story of what they had seen at the playground after the girls left.

Just after Tanya and her friend had walked away, her oldest brother, who at the time was fifteen, began calling out to whatever might be haunting the playground. He demanded that it show itself. He called it "chicken" and began making noises like a chicken. He and his brother laughed and turned to go home.

As they were walking away, something pushed the boy who had been making the noises. The force of the shove sent him tumbling forward onto his knees. His brother thought he had fallen and jokingly told him to get up. He tried to stand and again was shoved to the ground. Each time he got to his feet he would immediately be pushed back down to the ground.

The younger brother, who was thirteen, realized that something was wrong and tried helping his brother up. Whatever was pushing the older boy didn't touch him, but he was holding his brother by the arm and could feel the force of the shoves.

The older brother was finally able to remain standing long enough to run and both boys headed straight home. No one doubted their story. Their terrified faces convinced Tanya and her parents that something at the playground had scared the daylights out of them.

After that day, Tanya and her brothers were no longer allowed to go to the park, it was off limits. Something didn't want them there anyway, or so it seemed. Their stories were soon added to the long list of strange encounters people had experienced there.

Rumors continued to swirl around the neighborhood for years about the haunted playground. Some people said that a child had died there from a fall off of the slide. Others claimed that a child had drowned in the pond while her siblings played on the swings. None of it was ever found to be fact.

One thing was sure, something had laid claim to the playground and whatever it was the residents had had enough. The old playground equipment was torn down in the mid-1990's. A brand new playground was erected in its place.

As far as Tanya knows, the paranormal events that had plagued the park for decades finally came to an end once the last of the old playground was hauled away. Reports of strange events diminished and finally ceased altogether. Whatever had haunted the park for so many years had apparently moved on at long last.

Chapter 28:
The Crawlspace

The following story came to me, again, through social media. I talked to both the person who first contacted me and then to her brother who was the owner of the home in question. They were both straightforward people whom I had no doubt were relating the experiences just as they had occurred. It is a chilling tale indeed.

Mark Patterson (pseudonym) and his wife had been married for several years and were the parents of two children with another on the way when they began hunting for a larger home for their ever expanding family. They had looked at several houses before settling on one in a nice neighborhood in the suburbs of Cleveland, Ohio.

The home was older, but well kept. The sellers had recently painted the interior and installed new appliances. The house was huge, four stories in fact. The family would finally have the space they desired. The children would have their own bedrooms and baths. Everything was perfect--at first.

Once the movers had gone and the family was settling in to their new home, a few things occurred which struck them as a little out of the ordinary. The most disturbing was that noises from the fourth floor, which was attic space, began to wake them in the middle of the night.

They would hear thumping and banging around that would go on for hours on end. Mark thought he knew right off the bat what the source of the ruckus was: squirrels. He searched the attic, certain he would find that the furry varmints were nesting there, but he could find no signs of them.

Oddly, he noticed something that, for some reason, he hadn't seen when they had previously toured the attic. There was a small door which apparently led into a crawlspace or storage room of some sort. When he tried the doorknob it was locked. He reckoned that this must be where the squirrels were hiding out. Problem was he didn't have a key to the room.

Mark attempted to open the door by forcing it with his shoulder, but found that it was easier said than done. The door wouldn't budge. He would call a locksmith in to open the door when he had the extra money. The squirrels were noisy, but it wasn't an emergency to get them out of the house just yet.

The family went about their lives in spite of the constant banging around from the attic. The noises were at all hours now, day and night. Days would go by and they wouldn't hear a sound and then the thumping would go on all day and night. The family began to wonder what exactly the squirrels were destroying in the room. It sounded like heavy books falling onto the floor.

The noises weren't the only thing that was odd about the house. Mark and his wife both noticed that the attic door would be standing open when it should have been closed. The kids weren't allowed in the attic and the door was to be kept shut at all times. That being said, the door was constantly open even though no one in the house would admit to having been up there.

The family's youngest child, who was six years old at the time, told her parents that one day a woman opened the attic door and told her that she could come upstairs and play. The girl wasn't frightened by the woman, but she didn't go upstairs with her either. She wasn't allowed to go into the attic and she was afraid of getting in trouble.

Mark and his wife grilled their daughter for more details about the woman. The little girl said that she had long blonde hair and was dressed like any other person, in regular clothes, nothing unusual. Now, they began to wonder if someone was squatting in their crawlspace.

Maybe they had bought a house that had a stowaway in the attic.

The time had come to call in a locksmith and get that mysterious door opened and solve this mystery once and for all. The noises continued right up until the time when the locksmith arrived to open the door and let the family finally get a glimpse of what or who was hiding in the attic crawlspace.

The man they had hired to open the door had the job done in a matter of moments and the door was opened. Mark shone a flashlight into the crawlspace hoping to find bushy tailed rodents and not a woman hiding in the darkness. What he saw was even more of a surprise.

The room was empty. No squirrels and no signs that they had ever been in the small room. No books or stored items from bygone days. The room was dusty and there were cobwebs hanging from the ceiling, but there was nothing of any significance and certainly nothing that would account for all of the noises they had heard coming from the room for the past few weeks.

Determined to get to the bottom of the mystery, Mark started asking around the neighborhood to see if any of the neighbors knew anything about the history of the house. As it turned out, they all did. The house had been the subject of rumors and conjecture for years.

According to the neighbors, the house had been plagued by strange occurrences for several years. No one had died in the house, that they knew of, but a strange family had lived there during the late seventies and rumors had plagued the house ever since.

It seems that the mother was mentally unstable and social service agencies had been called in on more than one occasion to monitor the well-being of her children. No one knew for sure how many children were in the home, the numbers ranged from four to as many as ten. At any rate, she had been accused of neglecting them and, at times, of being physically abusive.

Some of the neighbors, who had actually known the family in question, insisted to Mark that the rumors were true. They said that the woman could be heard yelling at the top of her lungs at the children as they screamed and cried inside the house. One woman, whose daughter went to school with a couple of the older children, told Mark that was only the tip of the iceberg.

Apparently, a common form of punishment in the home was to lock anyone who was being particularly incorrigible in the attic crawlspace. They would remain there until their mother was satisfied that they had learned their lesson. This could be anywhere from a few hours to a few days depending on the offense.

Eventually, after having some of the children removed from the home and sent away to either foster care or to live with relatives, no one knew for sure, the woman and what was left of her family had left the area. None of the neighbors knew where she had moved to. They noticed the family packing up their belongings one day and then they were gone. No explanations or goodbyes.

Ever since then, persistent rumors had dogged the house. People who had spent any time there complained of hearing noises coming from the attic, very similar to those that Mark and his family had experienced.

Even with these new revelations, Mark and his wife had grown to love the house and had no intention of moving if there any alternatives. There had to be something they could do. After discussing their options, they decided to ask for help from an unlikely source.

Whatever dark things had taken place in the attic of the old house, and specifically in the crawlspace, the energy left behind was still present. Mark consulted a psychic medium, something he never thought he would ever do, and asked for her help in getting rid of whatever was occupying his attic.

In this modern age of having everything at one's fingertips, he had managed to locate a psychic by searching online. It was surprisingly easy to find one; there were dozens to choose from. This particular medium told Mark that she could rid his house of the residual bad energy that the attic crawlspace contained. She called it "cleansing".

It sounded like just what the family needed and they gave her the go-ahead to do whatever she needed to do to rid their house of the negative energy that was trapped there. The psychic explained to Mark and his wife that she would be using a stick of dried sage for the cleansing. They watched as she lit the sage and waited for it to smolder.

Once the sage was ready, the woman went into the crawlspace and slowly moved the sage around all of the corners. She said blessings as she did this. She then stood in the middle of the room and continued to say blessings. She explained to them later that she had to wait until the smoke moved in a certain way before she could be sure that the room was truly free from the negative energy that had been held there for so long.

The psychic blessed the rest of the house as a precaution, but assured the family that she felt no negative energy anywhere else in their home. She said a final blessing over Mark and his family and left the house. Mark didn't know if it was real or just wishful thinking, but he immediately felt a sense of calm that he hadn't experienced in weeks.

Mark reports that since the cleansing, the family has not been bothered by strange noises nor has anyone seen the woman who had attempted to coax their daughter into the attic. The door to the attic no longer opens by itself. The crawlspace seems to at last be free of whatever dark forces had been trapped within its walls. The house's turbulent past has finally been put to rest.

Chapter 29:
Angels Among Us

Most people have had experiences in which we felt that some higher power was watching over us. The following stories are examples of the very real possibility that there are guardian angels that surround us and, at times, protect and comfort us in our hours of need.

The city of Parkersburg, West Virginia used to be home to two major hospitals, one public and one private. The two eventually merged into one around 2013. When the private one finally closed its doors, stories of strange phenomena began to circulate.

I know several women who worked as nurses at the hospital, some for decades. They had all seen and heard things that puzzled them. Crying emanating from empty rooms was common, as was the sound of footsteps in vacant hallways. Sadly, hospitals are a place where many people lose their fight for life and grief and sorrow are what is left in their wake.

My friend Susan, who I have known since the early 1980's, worked as a nurse on several different wards over the years. She had many stories to tell of the unusual goings on in the old hospital, but one in particular stood out for me. It was both chilling and heartwarming at the same time.

At the time, Susan was working the second shift in the cardiac intensive care unit. Patients in that ward were usually in a life or death struggle. Some of them recovered and lived long happy lives. Some never returned home.

The patient whose story affected Susan, and myself, the most was a woman named Patricia who had suffered a stroke and had been unresponsive for days. She was receiving the best possible care, but the staff feared that she would not pull through her ordeal, and if she did, she would not be the person she had been before the stroke.

After several days in the CCU, Patricia opened her eyes for the first time. Her room became a flurry of activity as doctors and nurses poked and prodded her, trying to determine the extent of the damage caused by the stroke.

Patricia's left side was partially paralyzed. Her face drooped and her speech was slurred. Susan never forgot the look on Patricia's face when she woke up. Even with the paralysis, her face was the picture of serenity.

Weeks went by and Patricia's condition improved. She was receiving therapy for her left arm and leg and her speech was slowly returning. She was able to communicate using a pen and paper. She wrote the same words over and over. "Where is Kelly?"

Susan didn't know of anyone named Kelly who worked on the ward. Perhaps Kelly was a family member who Patricia wanted to see. When Susan told Patricia's son that his mother had been asking to see Kelly, he said that he didn't know of any friends or family by that name. Susan didn't think too much of it, Patricia had been through a catastrophic medical ordeal, confusion was to be expected.

As more time passed, Patricia's speech improved, as did her movement. She was now asking regularly for Kelly.

When she was finally able to explain who Kelly was, Susan and the other staff were stunned.

Patricia told them that on the night she arrived at the hospital, a woman had taken her by the hand and spoken softly to her. The woman told her that her name was Kelly and that she would be there to help Patricia get better. Thinking that she was a nurse, Patricia asked her what had happened to her and if she was going to die.

Kelly had squeezed Patricia's hand and whispered to her that she was not going to die. She would live to see her grandchildren grow up. She would be fine. She only needed to close her eyes and rest. Kelly assured her that she would stay by her side for as long as Patricia needed her.

Patricia had closed her eyes and drifted off to sleep. The next thing she remembered was waking up to the flurry of activity in her room. Susan knew that the story couldn't have happened the way that Patricia described it. She had been unconscious and unresponsive when she arrived at the hospital. She certainly hadn't been able to speak to anyone.

Visitors to the CCU were strictly monitored, they had to be buzzed in by someone at the nurse's station and no visitors were permitted in after eight o'clock in the evening. Patricia had been adamant that it was late at night when Kelly visited her. Susan asked her if she could describe what Kelly looked like.

Patricia remembered that Kelly had been in her late twenties to early thirties with long wavy blonde hair. She had been very pale and dressed all in white which was another reason that Patricia assumed she was a nurse. Kelly's eyes had exuded warmth and understanding. All of Patricia's fear and uncertainty had drained away as soon as Kelly had taken her by the hand.

Patricia went on to make a full recovery. She was released from the hospital and, as far as anyone knows, went on to live a normal life. Susan shared Patricia's story with some of the other nurses who in turn shared similar stories with her.

Kelly had apparently been making the rounds at the hospital for years. Several nurses and other staff members spoke of patients who had described a young nurse named Kelly who had comforted them when they had first arrived at the hospital. She had eased their anxiety with assurances that they would get better. She would see to it.

Whoever Kelly was, she helped people when they needed someone to give them hope. She encouraged them and allowed them to focus on their recovery. Whether she was a figment of their collective imaginations or a healer sent to reassure them that all would be well, she was their angel here on Earth.

This next story was related to me by a lady in Shreveport, Louisiana. The story had been passed on to her from her brother-in-law who had worked for many years as a highway patrolman. This incident was so unusual and unexplainable that he had never forgotten it.

It began with a frantic call to emergency services from a man who claimed that he had seen a woman standing in the middle of the highway on a cold, rainy night. She had appeared out of nowhere and he had nearly hit her with his car.

The man had pulled off of the roadway and searched for the woman, but was unable to find her anywhere. Terrified that perhaps he had struck her after all, he checked the side of the road and even looked over the embankment that was nearby. It was dark and he couldn't see very well, but the guard rail did appear to be damaged. There was, however, no sign of a woman anywhere.

He waited by the side of the road until the police arrived. He described to them in more detail what he had seen. He had been driving along, minding his own business, when all of a sudden a scantily clad woman had emerged from the darkness and stood in the middle of the lane he was travelling in.

The police officers were intrigued. What exactly was she wearing? The man wasn't completely sure, but it looked as though she had on only her underwear. He couldn't describe her face or anything else about her, she had appeared for an instant and then was gone.

The man assured them that he had not been drinking that night. He wasn't under the influence of any kind of medication. He offered to take whatever tests they needed to administer to prove that he was in control of his mental state.

The policemen were skeptical. The man's story was farfetched--to put it mildly. They did decide to do a sweep of the area in case he had struck someone with his vehicle. What they found would be something none of the people involved would ever forget.

When the officers shone their flashlights down over the embankment, the light came to rest on the wreckage of a car. It was well off of the road and was hidden by brush. Unless someone knew the car was down there, no one would have ever seen it.

The policeman scrambled down the embankment, slipping in the mud on their way down, to investigate the car that had obviously run off of the road and over the hill into the woods below. When they reached the car, the news wasn't good. The driver, a young woman was deceased in the driver's seat. It was what they saw in the backseat that stopped them all dead in their tracks.

In the back of the gnarled wreckage of the car was a child's car seat, and in that seat, still strapped in, was a toddler. The child's eyes were closed and they feared the worst, but when one of them reached over and touched the little one, his eyes slowly opened. It was a boy, no more than two years old, and he was alive.

Everything changed at that moment. The police officers were running on pure adrenaline as they removed the child, car seat and all, and carried him up the embankment. He was cold and shivering, but strangely quiet. He didn't cry. He just looked around calmly at all of these adults who were scrambling to get him out of the rainy night and into someplace safe.

The man who had called the police in the first place was dumbstruck by what was happening. It wasn't until later, when things had died down, that people started to piece a story together.

The policemen involved soon learned that a woman and her young son had been reported missing early that morning. They had not returned home after spending a weekend with relatives. The female victim of the auto accident was later identified as the woman who had been reported missing. Her son, who had miraculously survived virtually unharmed, was returned to his father.

Who was the woman who stood in the middle of the road and attracted the attention of the driver that rainy night? No one ever came forward and took credit for the good deed. Was she a Good Samaritan who decided to get help for the child by stripping down to her underwear and flagging down a car only to disappear into the night? Or, was the little boy's guardian angel watching over him that night making certain that someone would notice her and summon help for the child? I guess we'll never know.

My guardian angel was looking out for me one day in the early 1990s when I was still living at my mother's house. She lived on a little one way street in the middle of Parkersburg, West Virginia. Traffic on the street was, and is, horrendous because it is a short cut through town.

There is a traffic light with a four-way intersection at the end of the street. One day when I was leaving the house, I hopped in my tiny red Ford Festiva and ended up at the red light at the end of the street.

I waited patiently for the light to change. After the other traffic had stopped, my light turned green, but for some reason, I just sat there. Normally, I would have pulled out and turned left as I always did and been on my way. For whatever reason on this day, I just sat there. I didn't hear voices saying "sit still" or anything. But, I did feel something holding me back. It was as if someone had their hand on my knee preventing me from pushing on the gas pedal.

As I sat there immobile, a car came flying down the main road, running the red light in the process. This car was literally racing. I would guess they were travelling at least sixty-five to seventy miles per hour in what was supposed to be a thirty-five mile per hour zone. And, of course, they had ignored the stop light.

I sat in shock for a moment as I watched the car speed by me. Had I pulled into traffic when my light turned green I would have surely been hit by the speeding car which had raced through the red light. Whatever stopped me from moving that day saved me from serious injury and possibly worse. I have told the story many times. Nothing like it had happened to me before or since. Something saved my life that day and I owe whatever it was my unflinching gratitude.

Chapter 30:
The Little House On The Corner

Tammy Johnson, of West Chester, Pennsylvania, and her boyfriend Steven had passed by the small grey house that sat on the corner lot literally hundreds of times over the years. They both noted that the house seemed to be perpetually vacant. A "For Rent" sign would go up in the front window one week and be gone the next.

It just so happened that the apartment manager in the building they were living in at the time had recently informed them that there would be a significant rent increase in the upcoming year. It was late November 2008 and the couple was barely making ends meet as it was, a rent increase was out of the question. They would have to move and soon.

Steven was the first to bring up the little grey house that was, again, for rent. Tammy immediately vetoed the idea. There was obviously something wrong with the place. No one stayed there for very long.

Always the voice of reason, Steven argued that maybe they were just "rent skippers" who moved in, stayed for a few months racking up back rent and then fled before the landlord called in the authorities. Things like that happened all the time, he told her. It wasn't exactly a desirable neighborhood, but they could at least give the house a look.

Against her better judgment, Tammy copied down the telephone number from the "For Rent" sign and called the landlord a few days later. They set up a date and time to see the house and go over the rental details.

The couple showed up early for the showing and snooped around the yard for a little while before the landlord showed up. The yard hadn't been kept up very well. Overgrown tree branches hung low in the front yard. Bushes had grown high against the windows and what should have been flower beds was nothing more than a tangle of weeds.

The landlord arrived and ushered Tammy and Steven into the house. It was unfurnished except for the kitchen appliances. The floors were scuffed up and the walls had graffiti painted all over them. The landlord apologized and assured them that, should they decide to rent the house, he would paint the rooms for them.

The house wasn't as bad as Tammy was afraid it would be. It was small, but still larger than their apartment. The rent was considerably less than they had been paying. The money they would save could go towards buying a house eventually, they reasoned.

They were pretty much set on signing the lease when Tammy spoke up and asked the landlord flat out why no one seemed to stay in the house for very long. He just shrugged and said that he wasn't choosy about who he rented to. A lot of the people moved from state to state collecting public benefits. He explained that their benefits would run out every six months and, when they did, the people would move on to another state and start over there.

Tammy doubted his story, but supposed it was possible. At any rate, they needed an affordable place and this was probably as cheap a house as they would ever find. They signed the lease which oddly was for six month. Maybe his story was true after all.

Steven and Tammy wasted no time moving in to their new home. They did find right away that they had to keep the windows open to air the place out. It had a chemical smell that was, at times, overpowering. Strangely, neither one of them had noticed it when they saw the house the first time.

They lived in the house for weeks with no trouble whatsoever. They liked the house and, except for the smell, they were happy there. That was until one night when they were cuddled up watching a movie together and the peaceful moment was interrupted by the sound of shouting coming from the basement of the house. Tammy and Steven sat in stunned silence for a few moments listening as loud voices, a male and a female, shouted at each other from inside their house.

Tammy related later that, unlike what we've all seen in horror movies, they had no desire to investigate for themselves. They had no doubt that someone was in their basement and the people down there were embroiled in a bitter argument.

Steven called 911 while Tammy locked the basement door. They assumed that the intruders had entered the house through the small basement window. Not wanting to be in the home with the home invaders, they sat out in their car while they waited for the police to arrive.

After what seemed like an eternity, but was actually only minutes, a police car pulled up in front of their house, lights flashing. Steven got out of the car and explained to the officers that he was the person who had phoned for help. The policemen told him to stay put while they entered the home to investigate.

A few minutes later, one of the policemen came out of the house and beckoned for Steven and Tammy to join him inside. He told them that the house was clear. They could find no intruders. There was no sign of forced entry. There were no broken windows or signs of tampering with the doors or locks. They questioned the validity of the report.

Tammy and Steven said later that they could tell from that moment on that the police officers were skeptical of their story. They didn't seem too interested in taking down information or investigating further. They told the couple that they would keep in touch, but Tammy knew that she would probably never hear another word about it and she was right.

Things went back to normal in the little grey house for a while. Weeks went by with no incidents, until one day when Steven was at work and Tammy was home alone. She was in the kitchen puttering around making lunch when, again, she heard loud arguing coming from the basement.

The basement door was in the kitchen so she immediately rushed over to make certain it was locked, which it was. A man and a woman were shouting at each other. She could hear them clearly. The man was yelling at the woman to do as she was told while the woman screamed for him to get his hands off of her.

Whatever was happening in her basement was turning violent. Tammy could hear what sounded like the man striking the woman with his open hand. She could also hear things being knocked over or bumped into. In a panic, she fled the house while at the same time calling 911 on her cell phone.

When the police arrived, Tammy was pacing up and down the street, too afraid to even stand in her own yard. The police car pulled up beside her and she pointed them towards her home. They went in for a few minutes and came back out shaking their heads. They could find no one inside the house.

Tammy was crying and near hysterics this time. She argued with them. Someone was in there. She told the officers exactly what she had heard. They had to still be in there. The officers explained to her that they had searched the basement, as well as the rest of the house. There was no one there and no sign of any kind of disturbance. Again, she could sense their skepticism.

The policeman spoke with Tammy for short time, jotting down the details of what she said she had heard, and then they left, once again assuring her that they would be in touch. Afraid to go back into the house, she sat on the front stoop until Steven got home.

When Steven heard the story of what had happened at the house that afternoon, he decided that they needed to start looking for another place. Somehow, someone was able to get into their house and then sneak out without leaving a trace. It was only a matter of time before they made their way upstairs and then who knew what might happen. It wasn't a safe place to be and they couldn't stay there.

It wasn't as easy to find a new place to rent as they had hoped. They remained in the grey house while they searched for a new rental. A week or so after Tammy had heard the violent struggle in the basement, it happened again, only this time Steven was home also.

It was in the middle of the night and Steven had gotten up to use the bathroom. He made a stop in the kitchen for something to drink when he heard the sounds of a brutal struggle coming from the basement. He described it as someone being thrown around the room. A man was yelling and a woman was crying.

This time, Steven decided to find out for himself what was going on. He woke Tammy and told her to call the police. He was going to go catch whoever it was in the act. She begged him not to go downstairs, but he knew that if he waited whoever it was would be gone before the police got there.

She dialed 911 and stood by the back door while he opened the basement door and flipped on the light. All he had for protection was a hammer as he descended the stairs. He called out "Who's there?" The voices stopped immediately as soon as he spoke. He says that his legs were shaking so badly he was afraid he would fall down the stairs.

When he reached the basement, everything was quiet. Nothing seemed to be disturbed. There was no evidence that anyone had been there. He looked in every corner and conceivable hiding place, there was no one there. He yelled up to Tammy and told her to cancel the 911 call. It wouldn't be necessary.

Steven and Tammy were relieved when they found a new apartment within days of the last incident. They couldn't wait to leave the house and its mysterious intruders. As they were packing up their car with some of their belongings, a neighbor stopped them. It was the first time they had spoken to any of the neighbors since they had moved into the house.

The man asked them if they were moving out already. Steven told him yes, the house hadn't been the right one for them. Tammy could tell by the smirk on the man's face that this had not been news to him.

The man told them that no one ever stayed in the house for long. He wished the landlord would tear it down and be done with it. Tammy asked him why. The man told her that the house had, at one time, been a drug den. Methamphetamine had been manufactured there years ago. There were all kinds of criminal types who frequented the house. The landlord had made attempts to clean the place up. He had even had a crew come in to decontaminate the place after the drug manufacturers had been arrested.

Steven asked the man if any sort of violent crimes had taken place there. He wondered if perhaps someone had been harmed in the basement. The man didn't know, but he said it wouldn't have surprised him. The people had been hostile anytime he had seen them and they kept a big dog chained up in the front yard to keep people away.

Tammy and Steven never found out the details of what might have happened in the house back when it was a "meth house", but they knew that whatever violence had taken place there, somehow, it was repeating itself over and over again. She was just glad that she and Steven would no longer have to bear witness to it.

Chapter 31:
The Lost Boy

Emily Davis contacted me with the story of her brother, James, after reading my first book in this series. I featured the story of my late cousin Larry in that book and she was struck by how similar James' story was to Larry's. I agree. Here is the story of the strange haunted life of James Davis as told to me by his sister.

James Davis was born into a family which already consisted of two boys and one girl. Two more children would eventually follow. Though a large family, they were tight-knit, each member looking out for their siblings. Little James was always the child who needed the most looking after.

Right from the start, James was a frail boy. He was born prematurely and failed to thrive so his development was slower than normal. He was considered a bit "slow," but he made it through school and worked for many years as a landscaper. His life was relatively normal except for one thing: he claimed that he could see spirits.

Emily and the rest of her family had heard James speak of the entities that surrounded him from an early age. Even as a toddler, he would jabber away to an empty chair, smiling and gesturing as though there was someone there. When he learned to speak, his parents would hear him carrying on lengthy conversations with someone only he could see.

As he grew older, he would become agitated when he couldn't get anyone else to acknowledge his companions who were at the dinner table or playing with them in the yard. His family assumed that James had imaginary friends, which wasn't uncommon, and they more or less ignored his outbursts. His parents hoped he would grow out of it.

That never happened. What did change was the nature of James' relationship with his "friends". When he reached his late teens, they began to turn on him. He would show his sister scratches on his arms and legs, swearing to her that one of the people, who only he could see, had attacked him. He couldn't understand why his friends were suddenly angry with him.

The older James got, the more frequent, and more violent, the attacks became. He would fall for no apparent reason. Bruises would appear all over his body. His parents were alarmed that perhaps he was hurting himself, or even worse, that he might have some horrible disease that was causing him to bruise. They took him to the hospital for a complete medical workup.

Blood tests came back normal. James had no blood disorders that would account for the abnormal bruising. The doctors did recommend a psychiatric follow up for James. They felt that his injuries could be self-inflicted or psychosomatic in nature.

The psychiatrists who evaluated James didn't find him to be particularly self-destructive. They did diagnose him with an anxiety disorder that would require further investigation. They prescribed medication to help him sleep and they also recommended that he begin attending weekly therapy sessions. The family was relieved, he could be helped, all would be well in the end.

The weekly therapy went off without a hitch, but it didn't change anything for James. The attacks got progressively worse. Nothing changed and he told his sister that, sometimes, the entities that followed him around were even in the room while he was with his therapist. They listened to everything being said and laughed at the therapist as he was counseling James. Eventually, James stopped going to therapy altogether.

The downward spiral continued. Nighttime was the worst and James dreaded going to bed. He said that people would shake his headboard and chant words that he could not understand. He would pull the covers over his head and pray until they went away. Voices and shadows hounded him relentlessly.

James' visits from the other side began to occur more regularly as time went on. He would point out people in the grocery store who he said were "evil looking." He told his family members that the people had no real facial features and that they were around him nearly all of the time. Needless to say, no one else could see them.

Emily and the rest of the family were worried that James was losing his mind. Always fragile, he was withdrawing more and more into his own world. He no longer liked to leave the house, not even to sit on the back porch and watch the birds in the many feeders the family kept. He found no joy in life and it troubled everyone around him. He began to drink heavily, something he had never done before. Emily knew that he was using alcohol to dull his senses and make him forget the things he claimed he was seeing.

Like my cousin, James also said that the entities were calling to him at night from his bedroom window. He could hear them beckoning to him to come with them. He didn't see these particular spirits, but he heard them, night after night.

Almost identical to my Cousin Larry's story, James was found unresponsive in his bed one morning. His father was the person who made the determination that his son, his fourth born child who had been so troubled in life, had passed away in his sleep.

The cause of death was officially termed as "natural". James had fallen asleep and stayed sleeping, his heart giving out sometime during the night. His dreams of living a normal life were not to be. James Davis was only thirty-six years old.

Were the sights and sounds that tormented James for most of his life creations of his mind, or was he someone who could see and hear things that exist just beyond our reality? There's no way to know for certain. More disturbing than that is the possibility that the torment doesn't cease when life as we know it ends.

For the sake of people like James Davis and my cousin, Larry, we can only pray that they find peace at last.

Chapter 32:
The Residents

In between the towns of Parkersburg and Vienna, West Virginia one will find the regional rehabilitation hospital. For obvious reasons, I will not name the facility, but it is well known to those in the area and has been for decades.

The hospital was built on land which was, at one time, known as "the old Johnson farm." It was around this time, before the rehabilitation center was built, that three young children are said to have drowned in a nearby pond.

The identities of the children have long since been lost, but their restless spirits are said to haunt the site to this day. The children are known to play in back of the hospital well into the night. Residents have reported being kept awake by the loud laughter of children as they run and play just outside of their windows.

My mother is a caregiver for an elderly lady who spent several weeks in the rehab hospital after suffering a fall in her home. She complained to my mother that a group of noisy children kept her up nearly every night of her stay. My mother dismissed her rants, reasoning that no one would allow their young children to be out playing on the hospital grounds well after midnight. She changed her mind after learning that other people had also heard the children and that, surprisingly, their images had been caught on camera.

On another occasion, a worker was called to one of the rooms in the middle of the night by a patient who was quite beside herself. She told the worker that there were two children playing in her room. One was in the closet and the other was hiding beneath the sink.

The staff member checked the closet and the area under the sink, but there were no children hiding in either place. Just the same, she told the patient that she had removed the little interlopers so that the woman could get some sleep.

Some employees of the hospital say that they have captured images of one of the children, a young boy, on their cell phone cameras. He is said to be dressed in what can only be described as "Amish" type clothing. He wears a white tailored shirt and hat, his attire unsuited for play and seemingly from a bygone era.

All three children have been seen on the facility's surveillance cameras. Oddly, when employees have gone outside to find them, the three have vanished even though their images were caught on camera only moments beforehand. After seeing the children on the surveillance cameras, the staff concluded that the boy's playmates are two young girls. The workers who have seen them gathered this by their attire: old fashioned petticoat style dresses.

On one occasion, it was late at night and pouring rain when the cameras showed the three ghost children playing "Ring Around the Rosie" in the back garden of the hospital. As soon as the rain stopped, the children vanished.

For whatever reason, rain seems to entice the children to come out and play. I witnessed two pictures taken on a cell phone camera by an employee that showed the forms of three children in the back yard of the building. In the pictures, the white, misty images of the children can be clearly seen. The photos also reveal several white orbs floating around the children. Once again, the ghostly forms seem to be playing "Ring Around the Rosie."

Sometimes, being the new employee on the night shift at the facility comes with some unexpected challenges. On one occasion, a new girl who was manning the front desk and was blissfully unaware of the ghost children, called another employee over to inform her that there was somebody outside.

She had seen a little boy on the screen of her security monitor. Her co-worker had to give her a brief history of the children who spent many nights playing in the back yard. The three little spirits aren't destructive in any way. They don't seem to really bother anyone. They are apparently just what they seem to be, three lost children who were taken from this world too soon and remain fixed to the last place they remember.

At any rate, the employees of the rehabilitation hospital have become quite fond of them and even sit outside late at night hoping to catch of glimpse of the three little imps as they frolic in the darkness, forever young, and sadly, forever lost.

As unique as the three ghost children are, they are not the only spirits who are bound to the site of the rehabilitation center. There is also a resident ghost inside of the building whom the staff has named "George."

No one knows exactly who George was in life. He might have been a patient who passed away at the facility. He may have died on the property long before the hospital was ever built. It is even conceivable that he perished during the construction of the sprawling building. At the end of the day, it's all speculation. He may have no connection to the area whatsoever.

Whatever the circumstances of his death, he has made himself at home there where he has acquired somewhat of a reputation as a trouble maker. One worker recalls drawing blood from a patient and then setting the container on a countertop. Another employee began to joke around, prodding George to make an appearance.

"It's a full moon," the employee joked. "George is a vampire."

At that very moment, for no reason whatsoever, the lid popped off of the blood vile and fell onto the floor. The worker who had drawn the blood chastised her co-worker for goading George into acting up.

On another occasion, the same worker who had chided George into making his presence known previously was at it again. She was downstairs where the food carts were kept when she began jokingly looking for George.

"George," she called out, "where are you at?"

Just then, a clock that was affixed to a wall across the room flew off the wall and smashed onto the floor. The impact of the clock hitting the ground was so intense that the hands were knocked completely off of the facing.

On Halloween, 2015, a worker was downstairs on her way to the vending machines when she called out, "Happy Halloween, George". Seemingly in response, she heard a toilet flush in the restroom as she passed by. Thinking that another employee was in the restroom, she continued down the hallway that led to the vending machines.

After buying her snack, the employee again passed by the same restroom and, as she did, she heard a toilet flush once again. Seeing that the lights were off in the restroom, she opened the door and looked inside. The room was empty. The flushing of the toilets in that restroom is on a motion sensor, meaning that they only flush when someone stands in a certain spot in front of the commode. Since no one was in the restroom on this occasion when the toilet flushed, the employee assumed that George was at it again.

A new nurse on the night shift was introduced to George in a most memorable way. She had placed cups of water outside each resident's room to give to them later. It was the middle of the night and the water wouldn't be needed just then.

It wasn't long before she saw a hand appear from inside one of the rooms and slap the drink cup onto the floor, spilling the contents. The nurse went to the patient's room, assuming that he had spilled the water for some reason, but he was in his bed sound asleep.

As the nurse stood in the patient's doorway baffled by what she had seen, the water cup from in front of the next room was knocked to the floor and the next one and the next one. This continued until all of the water cups had been turned over and spilled onto the floor. She didn't see a soul, just the cups as they were knocked to the ground by unseen hands.

George is a constant presence at the center. He seems to get a kick out of being disruptive, although he had never harmed anyone and the nice folks who work there seem to take his behavior in stride. For whatever reasons, the rehab hospital and the ground it sits upon, are keeping George and the three children Earthbound. At least the workers at the facility accept them for what they are: lost souls who need a little bit of attention and seem to have found it with people who devote their lives to helping others, both in this world and the next.

Chapter 33:
The Homecoming

In 1969, Parkersburg, West Virginia was a nice, safe farming community where people came to raise their families in the shadows of the majestic mountains. The town would lose its innocence that summer when what began as a family squabble soon escalated into one of the worst mass murders in West Virginia history.

Reportedly, a fifteen-year old girl had begun dating her nineteen year old first cousin against her family's wishes. Her father finally put his foot down and told the girl that he would have the boy arrested and her sent to reform school if the relationship didn't cease immediately.

The girl would have none of it and allegedly conspired with her thirteen year old brother to kill their parents so she could continue seeing her cousin. On the night of June 8, while their family slept, the girl and her brother were said to have doused the family home with gasoline before throwing a lit piece of paper into the home through a broken window.

The house went up in a blazing inferno. Their mother, father and ten siblings ranging in age from six months to seventeen years, perished in the fire. Rescuers on the scene that fateful night recall hearing a woman screaming and seeing her inside the home, engulfed in flames. Unable to reach her through the flames, they watched helplessly as she burned to death. They also related that they had witnessed baby bottles literally exploding from the pressure and heat.

When all was said and done, the only family members who survived that tragic night were the brother and sister and their grandfather who had been staying in a small lean to on the property. He had miraculously escaped the fire. When rescuers arrived on the scene, they found him sitting in a chair, apparently in shock.

Initially, the fire was thought to be accidental. No one had reason to suspect otherwise. Within twenty-four hours, however, that would change. The brother, who you'll remember was only thirteen, couldn't seem to keep his sister's secret. He allegedly told a female relative that he knew how the fire had started and he would share what he knew with her if she promised not to tell on him.

The story he told was a gruesome one. He is reported to have told the woman that he and his sister had burned the family alive in retaliation for the father forbidding the girl from dating her cousin. They had even nailed the windows shut so the helpless victims would have no means of escape. The two conspirators then ran away and hid nearby, leaving their parents and brothers and sisters to burn to death.

The relative was appalled by the story and immediately shared what she knew with authorities. The girl and boy were soon questioned and both admitted their guilt. Unfortunately, they confessed to the wrong person.

The two were quickly indicted on murder charges on the strength of their confessions. Their court ordered attorneys took one look at the evidence against their clients, including the signed admissions of guilt, and knew that protocol had been breached.

It seems the siblings had confessed not to a police officer or other member of law enforcement, but to the assistant fire marshall. Being a former state trooper, he apparently thought he was in a position to secure confessions from the teenagers, but the law saw it differently.

Although the teens had technically been read their rights and had apparently refused to have an attorney present when they allegedly confessed, it was questionable that they understood what was going on. They were said to be "extremely slow" and lacking in the ability to understand the gravity of what they had done. Both were reported to have intelligence quotients of seventy.

If that weren't bad enough, the siblings had been deprived of food and sleep for more than twenty-four hours, apparently in an effort to get them to confess. It worked, but ended up tainting the case against the two.

In October 1969, a judge threw out the confessions and all evidence gleaned from them. The state was left with no case and the siblings, who had admitted burning their family alive including a baby not quite six months old, walked away scot free. No one would stand trial for the fire or the subsequent deaths.

The remains of the father, mother and ten children were buried in a mass grave in Wirt County, West Virginia. Thin metal plates with the names of each of the family members who perished on that fateful night are all that is left on this Earth to commemorate the lives of twelve people taken away in one senseless act of childish temper.

That is not, however, where the story ends. Many people believe that the restless spirits of the family, specifically the children, have never left the site of the home they had lived and died in. The building that sits on the spot where the house once stood is what makes this story all the more bizarre.

After the house burned to the ground on that balmy June night in 1969, no one had any interest in erecting another house on the site. Instead, a popular chain store was built in its place. The location is right on the main thoroughfare and a perfect place for a big retailer to set up shop.

Over forty years later, the store is still in business and doing quite well. Stories have circulated for years about the strange goings on in the store, both from customers and store employees.

Customers have recalled seeing a woman and a small child walking down an aisle only to disappear into thin air before their eyes. Shoppers have reported having their hair pulled and items "jumping" out of their carts. Others say they have seen products fall from the shelves for no reason.

Employees, especially the night crew, don't fare much better. Several workers claim that they have stocked shelves and arranged them neatly only to turn their backs and hear the items they had carefully displayed moments earlier come crashing to the floor.

The unlucky crew members who are in charge of the toy aisle seem to have the worst luck. They say that toys are constantly being moved around and removed from shelves when there is no one around. They can straighten the shelves and by the time they walk away the boxes and packages are moved around and knocked over, some landing on the floor.

Employees and customers alike report hearing a woman's voice, garbled and unintelligible, speaking to them even though there is no one around. It is said that the voice sounds as though it is coming from under water. The sounds of children's voices and laughter have also been reported, both during the day and at night, when there are no children inside the store.

Is it possible that the family, or at least some of its members, have remained tied to the place where their house used to be? Are they fated to stay bound to the grounds their home once sat upon for eternity? Is the sad fact that no one was held accountable for the heinous act that all but wiped out an entire family keeping their spirits in some sort of purgatory while they await justice?

There's no way to ever know the answers. It does seem apparent that even after four decades they can't, or won't, let go of the past and move on to whatever awaits them in the hereafter.

Chapter 34:
The Doll

The following story was a bit of a conundrum for me. It's strange, to be sure, but I'm not sure if it's paranormal in nature, truly bizarre, or perfectly innocent. It's being included for those very reasons. You can decide for yourself which category it falls under.

Mark Poole, of Columbus, Ohio was the source of this eerie tale. He was a teenager living with his mother when he had a spooky brush with the unexplained.

Mark and his mother lived on a quiet residential street in the town of Lancaster. Their back yard was separated from their neighbor's yard by an invisible fence. The fence was actually an underground electrical system with a mechanism attached to the dog's collar which would administer a mild shock if he tried to leave the perimeters of the yard. They had installed the fence so that their mixed breed dog could go in and out of the house without having to be walked on a leash.

The neighbor to the left of them was an elderly woman who lived in the home by herself. Another younger woman, whom they assumed was her daughter, came and went regularly. They didn't really know their neighbor, except to nod and say "hi" when they saw her in the yard.

One evening, Mark had let the dog out and was tinkering around on the patio when the normally quiet pet suddenly began barking fiercely. Mark stopped what he was doing and went out into the yard to shush the dog who was standing at the property line which separated Mark's home from his elderly neighbor's.

He yelled for the dog to be quiet, but the dog only grew more agitated and was running the property line in a mad effort to reach whatever was agitating him in the yard next door. Mark decided to go get the dog and bring him back inside before the neighbor complained. As he approached the dog, he saw and heard what was causing the dog's hysteria.

Lying in the grass in the neighbor's yard was a doll. It wasn't a baby doll, but a larger doll that people tend to collect rather than play with. It had long brown hair and wasn't wearing any clothing. The doll wasn't just lying there--it was talking--saying the same thing over and over again: "I'm hungry, feed me."

Mark remembers being freaked out by the doll which wouldn't stop repeating its demand, "I'm hungry, feed me." It wasn't so much what she was saying, but how she was saying it. The voice was deep and severe, not the voice one would expect to hear coming from a doll.

He grabbed the dog and ran into the house to fetch his mother. When he told her to come outside and take a look at the doll, she thought he was being ridiculous, but she followed him to the fence line to see what all the fuss was about.

The doll was still lying in the same place, and still saying the same thing over and over again: "I'm hungry, feed me."

At first, Mark's mother laughed. It wasn't every day that you saw a strange naked doll lying in the grass demanding to be fed. Mark's curiosity got the better of him and he told his mom he was going to go into the neighbor's yard and get a closer look. She balked, he had no business going onto someone else's property, but he couldn't be deterred.

When Mark approached the doll, he could see that it had soft plastic arms and a cloth body. Its eyes were wide open and it had makeup on its face. The doll was still talking away as he reached down and picked it up. He turned the doll over and over, trying to find the on/off switch…there was none that he could see. He didn't see a string or any other device that would control the doll. He couldn't even find a place for batteries. He squeezed the body and it was soft through and through. One other thing bothered him about the doll and that was how warm it was. It was a cool day, but the doll's body was as warm as toast.

Thoroughly perplexed, Mark laid the doll back down where he had found it and ran back to his own yard. He told his mother that the doll didn't have a battery compartment or any other discernable means of controlling it that he could find. Mother and son retreated back into their own home, leaving the doll to its own devices. They could still hear it talking as they walked away. "I'm hungry, feed me."

The next morning, when Mark let the dog outside, he went out also to see if the doll was still there. He looked around the yard, but could find no sign of the mysterious doll. He reckoned the neighbor must have retrieved it and he was a little bit relieved. Nothing about that thing had been normal and he hoped that it was gone for good.

A few days later, Mark's mom happened to see the elderly neighbor in the yard and she mustered up the nerve to ask her about the doll. The neighbor was bewildered. She was adamant that she didn't know anything about the doll in question. The woman claimed that she didn't have any dolls and she certainly hadn't found one in her yard. Mark's mother didn't know if the lady was telling the truth or not. Why would she lie? It was just a doll, after all.

Mark, nor his mother, ever saw or heard the doll again. They didn't know what they had encountered that day in the neighbor's yard, but Mark, for one, is convinced that it wasn't of this world. For one thing, what kind of doll repeats the same four words over and over again? And, what was the power source for the doll? Mark was, and is, a tech geek and even he could find no explanation for what was powering the strange doll. He did, however, steer clear of the neighbor's back yard from that day on.

Chapter 35:
The Resting Place

Riverview Cemetery sits in the heart of the city of Parkersburg, West Virginia. For anyone interested in visiting a graveyard that looks like a scene out of an old Hammer film, this is the place for you.

Originally, the cemetery was privately owned by a family named Cook. It was, in fact, known as the Cook Graveyard for many years before becoming a community cemetery which would be renamed Riverview. Since that time, many locals have been buried there including a few notables such as two West Virginia governors, one congressman, eight mayors and three sheriffs. They are not, however, what makes this cemetery unique.

A monument which bears the name "JACKSON" is by far the graveyard's most popular attraction. It is the statue of a woman, her head bowed in a sorrowful pose. She is leaning forward on one arm while the other rests upon the scroll before her. She is known as "The Weeping Woman."

The Weeping Woman has been the subject of local lore for years. She is said to walk the cemetery during full moons. She has been known to whisper in visitor's ears and even tug at their clothing. The thing she is most noted for is her reputation for granting wishes.

It is said that if a couple is unable to conceive a child, they need only to pay a visit to The Weeping Woman and ask for her help. Many a barren duo have claimed that after visiting the statue and leaving a token for her, usually a coin of any denomination, they miraculously become pregnant.

Wishes of all sorts are made to The Weeping Woman, but it's impossible to know how many and how often they are granted. I have shared our story in a previous book, but here is the short version for those who missed it.

In mid-2015, our family's small film production company was making preparations to begin shooting our second full-length low budget movie. As my husband and I began going over our finances for the movie, it was apparent that we had nowhere near the amount of money needed to pay for the production costs on the film.

We had visited Riverview Cemetery earlier in the year, so we were familiar with The Weeping Woman and her reputation. On our first visit, I had been awestruck by the old graveyard. It was very gothic looking with wrought iron gates and grave markers that were askew; some even broken from age and wear. The cemetery boasted headstones that dated back to the early 1800s.

Besides The Weeping Woman, there is also said to be a sea captain's ghost that haunts the cemetery on occasion. People claim to have seen him kneeling beside his own marker, clad in an overcoat and captain's hat.

We paid our respects to the captain at his final resting place and then moved on to the main attraction, The Weeping Woman. She wasn't hard to find. The beauty of the statue is undeniable. It is weather beaten and has many flaws, but something about being in its presence is very sobering.

We made no wishes that day. I stood before her and reached out and touched her hand. My eyes welled up for no particular reason. Maybe it was because she seems so sad, or maybe it was something more, who's to say?

A few months went by and we decided to have another look around the cemetery. The weather was nicer this time and we lingered in the graveyard, reading the inscriptions on the markers that were still discernable.

I felt the need, once again, to touch The Weeping Woman's hand, but that was all, no wishes were made, or so I thought.

A couple of days later, a well-known actor/wrestler passed away suddenly. My husband had met this man several times and had even appeared as an extra in a movie that the wrestler had starred in.

My husband had worked for many years chasing celebrity autographs that he would then sell on auction sites. It just so happened that he had contracted with this actor/wrestler shortly before his death to sign dozens of movie posters from the production they had both appeared in.

Usually, when celebrities die suddenly their autograph becomes highly sought after. My husband saw his opportunity and, right or wrong, he acted upon it. This is not something I've ever approved of, but my husband assures me that it's just business and since he had paid for the autographs initially, the celebrities know that they will probably be resold.

The signed posters sold very well and provided a cache for us to use to film the movie project we had been planning. We had needed the funds and now we had them. But, that wasn't the end of the story.

My husband and I were on our daily nature walk shortly after all of this transpired when he became suddenly serious…he had something he wanted to get off of his chest. He proceeded to tell me that he had, unbeknownst to me, asked The Weeping Woman for a favor on our second visit to the cemetery. He had asked her to find a way to help us finance our movie. Now, he was worried that in making that wish, he had inadvertently caused the death of the actor/wrestler. He was concerned that it was a tragic "monkey's paw" situation. You get what you ask for, but not without dire consequences.

I told him that he was being silly. The Weeping Woman wouldn't cause a man's death in order to help us fund a movie that a handful of people would ever see. Still, it was a strange coincidence. Is it possible that a wish made on a supposedly haunted statue could cause a celebrity to pass away, thereby opening the door for some unexpected income? Surely not, but all the same, I warned him not to make any more wishes on that statue. Better safe than sorry.

As a footnote to this story, the movie we had planned to film using, in part, the money from the autograph sales was plagued with problems from the start. The lead actress quit on the first day without explanation, actors got lost on their way to the set holding production up for hours, one actresses' husband fell ill and had to be hospitalized, locations fell through at the last minute and to top it off, the weather--which had been sunny leading up to the outdoor shoot--suddenly turned menacing. Production was shut down and the project scrapped. I guess the old saying holds true, be careful what you wish for, you just might get it.

We did visit The Weeping Woman a third time, but not to ask for anything, we just find the cemetery fascinating, her in particular. On this occasion, someone had placed candles around the monument. There were also coins strewn about, and, oddly, a joker from a deck of playing cards had been placed in her left hand, perhaps to highlight her reputation for playing practical jokes, who knows?

Chapter 36:
A Portal In Time

This next story has haunted me for years. I first heard this chilling tale as a teenager. I didn't know what to make of it then and still don't to this day. That being said, it stuck with me over the years and is a tale well worth sharing.

The story was told to me by a friend of my mother. She had grown up near where this event was said to have taken place in rural Tennessee in the late 1940s-early 1950s.

A farmer was working the fields one afternoon along with his team of horses and a few farm hands. There was nothing unusual about that day. It was a work day like any other until the farmer's helpers left for the day and his family came to fetch him for supper.

The farmer's teenaged son had been sent to retrieve his father, but the man was not in the field where he should have been. The horses were still there, still hitched to the plow they had been pulling all day. The farmer, on the other hand, was nowhere to be found.

The boy knew that his father would never leave the horses unattended unless something important had called him away. He called out to his father to no avail. He had simply vanished without a trace.

Worried that something terrible had happened to his dad, the boy ran home to get help with the search. He returned with his older brother and sisters, as well as the farmer's wife. They spread out and searched the entire area, calling the man's name all the while.

It was when the youngest daughter called out to her father that the man finally replied. She yelled for her mother and siblings to join her, she had found the farmer, or so she thought.

The family quickly converged on the spot where the young girl had heard her father's voice, but he wasn't there, at least they couldn't see him. They called out to him again and waited. From somewhere very far away, and yet on the spot where they were standing, they heard their father's voice.

When they called to him, he hollered back to them in response. He yelled that he was there, but he couldn't find them. His voice sounded hollow and distant as though it was coming from deep under the ground.

The man's family was baffled. They could hear him and he could hear them, but they couldn't make contact. They were sharing the same area of the field, but not in the same space in time. Not knowing what else to do, they called the local sheriff to come out and help them bring the farmer home.

When the sheriff arrived at the spot in the field where the farmer's voice had been heard, he could find nothing. He assured the family that he and his men would search for the farmer, but there was no sign of him in the field. He advised them to go home. The sheriff offered that, perhaps, the man would turn up on his own. It was not to be.

Day in and day out, the family would return to the area of the field where they believed the man had disappeared. Each day, they would call to him and he would answer. With every passing day, however, his voice would become more and more distant until one day when it ceased entirely. They never heard it again.

After the farmer's disappearance, the spot from which his voice had emanated became barren. No grass ever grew there again. The animals refused to walk near it, giving the area a wide berth when they grazed in the field.

Some people theorized that a portal of some kind had opened up in the field on the day that the farmer vanished. He had accidentally stepped through it and it had closed behind him, trapping him forever in another dimension.

Is it possible that the man had realized his mistake, too late, and stayed just on the other side of the portal trying to make contact with his family? Did he finally give up and accept his fate?

Whatever happened to the luckless farmer, whether he walked through a window in time and entered another dimension from which there was no escape or he simply wandered off for no reason, never to be seen again, the events of that day haunted the family for the remainder of their lives.

Chapter 37:
The Lighthouse Keeper

In my late teens, I did a fair bit of travelling around the East Coast of the United States. One of my stops was New Haven, Connecticut. While visiting there, I stayed at a bed and breakfast operated by a rabbi and his wife. They were lovely people, but it was the woman's father who gifted me the next story.

I stayed at this family's bed and breakfast for nearly a week and on the day before I was to move on they invited me to a get together at the beach with some of their relatives. It was a bit awkward, but they had been very nice to me and I accepted the invitation. It was on a Sunday and the year was 1984.

Everyone had gathered on the beach in New Haven for the barbeque/picnic. One person had brought a guitar and played music and sang while other people were catching up with their family members. I was out of place to be sure, but they tried their best to make me feel welcome.

My hostesses' father was particularly friendly. He had travelled to West Virginia, where I am from, many times and was anxious to talk to me about my native state. He was also interested in folklore and, since West Virginia is rich with it, I told him a few stories that I had heard over the years.

He, in turn, told me the one I am about to share with you. He had heard it from one of the investigators involved after the fact. I never forgot the tale and even used it as a basis for my screenplay/short story "Madeleine." It is chilling, to say the least.

The events took place in the mid-1970s along the coast of Massachusetts. A man had been hired to be caretaker of a lighthouse. His duties would be to man the lighthouse and provide upkeep and in return he would have free room and board on site. The location was remote and he would be isolated, there was no one else nearby and it was not a job for everyone. Human contact would be scarce for several months.

The man agreed to take the position. He was single and had no real family to speak of. He was also a bit of a loner and the thought of months of isolation didn't faze him. Little did he know, he wouldn't be alone for long.

Everything was by the book in the beginning. The man performed whatever maintenance needed to be done around the lighthouse. He walked on the beach, enjoying the ocean and all of its solitude. It was peaceful and he was content in his role as lighthouse keeper.

In his quiet moments, the man began to keep a journal of his days and nights spent at the lighthouse. At first, the entries were pretty mundane. He would keep a log of his meals. He would write about his walks on the beach and make note of the weather conditions. Nothing he wrote stood out as unusual until about a month into his tenure when the tone of his writings took a drastic turn.

The entries in the man's journal began to note some strange experiences he was having. He wrote that he had begun to notice bruises on his chest in the morning when he got out of bed. They were the size of quarters and painful to the touch.

At first, the lighthouse keeper assumed he had fallen during the night, attributing it to sleepwalking, which he had a history of. That didn't explain the sudden weakness that had come over him. He noted that he was so tired that, at times, he could barely drag his feet across the floor.

Each day, the entries in his journal became more and more desperate. The man was waking up every morning with more bruises than the day before. They were on his chest and upper arms. He feared that he had cancer or some other blood disease. He was beginning to believe that he was dying.

He also made note of the fact that the weakness that, at first, had made it difficult for him to move around, now kept him almost paralyzed for most of the day. He was no longer able to perform his duties as lighthouse keeper and knew that he would have to resign his position very soon.

The last few entries that were logged into his journal were full of hopelessness and fear. He no longer thought he had a blood disease, but he knew that he was dying. He had finally seen what was causing the bruises all over his body. Now, he knew.

He had woken up on one of the last nights of his life, only to see a dark shadow passing through the room. The shadow came closer to his cot and then knelt down over him. A shroud over its head fell away and the man could see the face of a woman, but he knew that it wasn't really a woman…it was an unknown being attempting to take on the appearance of something familiar to him.

Whatever this entity was, it began sucking on the lighthouse keeper's chest. He lay there unable to move, unable to fight. He wrote that he could feel his life being drained from him by this shadow creature.

Weeks went by and, with no word from the lighthouse keeper, his employers sent someone out to check on his well-being. What they discovered at the lighthouse would haunt them from then on. They found the man, lying on his bed in an advanced state of decomposition. Investigators were called in to determine his cause of death. Since there were no signs of a break-in or foul play of any kind, his death was eventually attributed to natural causes. It was assumed that he had died in his sleep.

The lighthouse keeper's journal was taken into evidence in the investigation into his death. It was bizarre and those who read it interpreted it in different ways. Some of the authorities thought that he had, perhaps, lost his mind from the solitude and had imagined that something was sucking his life away. Maybe it was a metaphor for the loneliness he was feeling.

There were a few, including the investigator who shared this story with my hostesses' father, who took the journal literally. He believed that something had taken the lighthouse keeper's life--something dark and sinister with no connection to this world. Unfortunately for the investigator, believing in something and proving it are two different things. The mysterious death of the lighthouse keeper remains classified as natural to this day.

Chapter 38:
The Neighbor Who Wasn't There

Everyone grows up in a neighborhood that boasts at least one creepy house that no one wants to go near. I was no exception. This particular house was actually two streets over from where we lived, but my friends and I walked past it every day for years. It was so run down and decrepit, it had to be haunted, or at least that was what everyone said.

There is a laundry list of things that made us think that this house was spooked. For one thing, no one ever saw anyone come and go from the place. The trash would be at the curb every week for pick-up, but no one saw who put it there. Although weeds grew out in tendrils across the walkway and around the house, the grass was always brown and dried up and nobody ever mowed it. There were no cars parked on the property, so whoever did live there walked wherever they needed to go, and yet no one ever saw them.

All that being said, it seemed that there was someone inside the house. A light would burn in the front window every night and be off in the day time. My friends and I roamed the neighborhood every day and, as nosy as we were, we never saw a soul stirring about the place. We did see something nearly every night and that was a sudden rush of bats that would escape out of a broken window on the third floor at dusk. It became a nightly routine for us to stand across the street and watch as, at first, one or two bats and then dozens would flood from the upstairs of the old house. That was as exciting as it got until one fall when there was suddenly a burst of activity at the house.

One of the people who lived next door to the house was the first to send word around that he had seen someone milling around. He couldn't tell if the person had been a man or a woman since they had been covered from head to toe in dark clothing. He was certain, however, that they had come from inside of the mystery house. The person in black had walked around to the back of the house as the nosy neighbor kept watch. They then returned to the front yard and re-entered the house through the front door. It doesn't sound like much, but when no one has been seen in a house for years and they suddenly appear it's a pretty big deal in a small town.

More and more people reported seeing the person, always shrouded in dark apparel from head to toe, coming and going in the next few weeks. The person did the same thing every time they were spotted. He or she walked to the back of the house and then returned to the front and disappeared inside once again. A few neighbors even ventured out of their homes and tried to strike up a conversation with the mystery person, but he or she just retreated inside without acknowledging them. Most people just watched from the safety of their own homes, peering through the curtains at the eccentric neighbor.

Just before Halloween, moving trucks appeared at the house. Now, we would finally get a good look at the mysterious inhabitant of the house who had eluded us for so many years. It was not to be. Someone was moving in, not out.

The new neighbors turned out to be a couple who were planning to renovate the house and then sell it for profit. They were young and nice, but we were all curious about what had happened to the previous owner. This is where the story takes a strange turn.

As it turns out, the previous owner had died years earlier leaving behind no heirs. The property had been deeded to the state to be sold at auction at a later date. No one had lived in the house for years. It had been vacant for at least six years prior to the young couple moving in. So, all of those years that we had speculated on who lived there, the house had sat empty.

Who had been the person turning the lights on and off? Point of fact, how were there lights anyway with no electricity? Who had taken the trash can out to the curb and then retrieved it, sight unseen? And, again, if no one lived in the house, there wouldn't have been trash pick-up there. Who was the person clad in black who had been seen coming and going from the house in the weeks before the new owners moved in?

As nosy as everyone was in our little neighborhood, no one could ever answer those questions. Maybe a vagrant had been squatting there, but how would they have known that the house was being sold? And, no one ever saw them leave the house, just walk from the front yard to the back.

Even after the house was renovated and the couple moved out, people speculated on the mysteries surrounding the place. According to one of the neighbors, the couple who had fixed the place up reported hearing footsteps and doors closing on their own during their stay at the house. They hadn't known about the neighbors' sightings of the strange figure dressed in black until they were moving out. Only then did they relate that they too had seen the figure, in the form of a shadow, from the day they moved in until the day they moved out. They hadn't wanted to believe it was anything supernatural so they just kept working on the house and ignored the otherworldly presence that was sharing the house with them. Fortunately, they weren't easily spooked. As for the rest of us, we always thought that place was haunted and as it turns out, we just might have been right.

Chapter: 39
Lucky

I sat on this story for several months to be sure it wasn't just imagination or wishful thinking. Enough has happened that I feel comfortable now in including this story. It involves a close friend and client, or more specifically, her dog.

Stories about animal spirits are always endearing to me and this is no exception. When I'm not writing, I work as a professional cleaner/home organizer. One of my dearest clients has, or had, three dogs one of whom is at the heart of this story.

In the late spring of 2015, my client texted me with the bad news that one of her dogs had passed away. He was quite old and had been in a bad way for several months prior to his passing. I had worked for her for many years and, in turn, had known her dog since he was a pup. It was sad news, but he had been very ill and was now in a better place.

This client also had two other dogs, but they were much quieter and more docile than the one who had died. One was a female and the other one male. They weren't barkers, at least not around me, and they never had been.

Lucky, the one who had passed, had always barked when I came to work at the house. I had a key and would let myself in, he would let out a shrill howl and then follow that with little growls and yips until I walked into the house and he realized that he knew me. Only then would he wag his tail and greet me. Once in a while the other two would come to the door to see who was there, but they didn't bark, they just stood there quietly waiting to meet whoever had come to visit. Sometimes, they didn't even get up off of the couch to investigate, but Lucky always did, without fail.

It was several weeks after Lucky died that I began to realize that he might not be gone in spirit. I had been to the house a few times since his passing and nothing had been out of the ordinary. No dogs barked at me when I put my key in the door and entered, that was Lucky's job and he was no longer around. The other two couldn't care less.

On about my third trip there after he died, I put my key in the lock and was immediately greeted by Lucky's familiar howl, followed by his low growl and little yaps. There was no way I was hearing what I was hearing, so I opened the door expecting to find one of the other dogs taking over for Lucky. They were there alright, but in their usual spots--one on the loveseat and the other in the floor in front of the couch. They weren't making a sound.

Not totally convinced that one of the other dogs wasn't playing a prank on me, I went about my job cleaning the house. Several times that day I caught sight of a shadow out of the corner of my eye as it passed through the hallway. I knew it wasn't the girl dog, she was white. It could have been the other dog, but when I checked on him, he was in his usual spot on the loveseat. That was his comfy place and he very seldom left that area when I was at the house.

Another strange thing I began noticing was that one of the bedroom doors, which was kept closed but could be pushed open, was always open now. Lucky was the only dog I had ever seen push his way into that room. The other dogs had never shown any interest in it. Now, I found myself closing that door more than once when I was in the house even though I knew that the other dogs were in the living room.

On some of my trips to the house, there was nothing unusual to speak of. I would hear no barking nor any sign of Lucky's presence. On other occasions, events would occur which would cement in my mind that Lucky truly was still paying occasional visits to his old stomping ground.

One Tuesday, as I let myself into the house, I was again greeted by Lucky's howl and low growls. As I came into the house, the other dogs were not in the entry way, they were in their usual spots in the living room.

The three dogs had always taken certain positions to plant themselves in while I cleaned. The female would lie in front of the couch, the younger male would lay on the loveseat, and Lucky would curl up on the one big cozy chair. My client always kept a pillow on the chair, which Lucky would knock onto the floor. It became my routine to pick the pillow up off of the floor and set it aside lest he knock it off again.

On this day, when I went into the living room, the pillow that should have been on the chair was on the floor in front of the chair. Since Lucky no longer laid claim to the chair, I placed the pillow back where it belonged and then went about my business.

When I came back into the room a bit later, the pillow was once again lying on the floor. The other two dogs were still in the spots they had been when I had left the room earlier. Puzzled, I placed the pillow back on the chair and continued working. I had no more that turned my back before I heard the soft thud behind me. I looked to find the pillow back on the floor in front of the chair once again. Defeated, I placed it on the couch where it remained for the rest of my work day.

On another visit, I was in the living room with the two remaining dogs when I heard a dog walking around on the linoleum floor in the kitchen. The familiar 'clickety-click' of toenails on the hard surface was a sound I knew well. Of course, when I checked the kitchen, there was nothing there; no dog or any other creature to be found.

Little things have happened every time I have been to that job since Lucky died that remind me that he is still around. He had an awful habit of lifting his leg on a bag of dog food that my client keeps on the kitchen floor, propped up against a wall. He was the only dog who did his business there, who knows why, but it was the one thing I didn't miss about him. Every now and then when I'm cleaning the kitchen I will move the bag and there it is…a pee puddle just like the old days. Having a dog's spirit remain in a house is a wonderful thing, but it isn't always peaches and cream.

Chapter 40:
The Missing

Morgantown, West Virginia in Monongalia County is home to West Virginia University, or as it is better known, WVU. Today, the university is renowned for its college football team, but back in the winter of 1970, it made headlines for its role in a tragic case of kidnapping and murder.

Karen Ferrell and Mared Malarik, both nineteen years old, were dorm mates and students at WVU. Morgantown was and is a small college town where crime had never been an issue. The girls made plans to hitchhike from their Evansdale dorm to Morgantown to see a movie. It was January 18 and it was bone chillingly cold.

The girls found a ride to the movie with no problem. Afterwards, they went back out into the sub-zero temperatures and attempted to find a lift back to their dormitory. Witnesses later said that they saw the girls get into a car with a man in his forties. That was the last the girls were seen alive by anyone, except for their killer.

Search parties combed the area from which the girls went missing for months afterwards with no sign of the missing duo. Months would go by, winter passing into springtime, before police would get a break in the case.

In March, a thirteen year old boy found a purse along US119. The purse was identified as having belonged to Mared Malarik.

In early April, a young boy found a driver's license in a remote area south of Morgantown. It was weathered, but the identification could still be made out. The license bore the name of Karen Ferrell.

State Police and National Guardsmen descended on the area in a renewed effort to find the girls. Ten miles from where the driver's license had been discovered, Mared Malarik's glasses were found lying at the side of a dirt road. The searchers were getting closer and they knew it.

Also, in the same area, the search team found a prescription medicine bottle bearing the name Karen Ferrell along with her purse and a makeup compact. A few miles south of Morgantown, near the site of the old abandoned Weirton Mine off of County Road 76, the bodies of Karen Ferrell and Mared Malarik were finally recovered. The girls had been decapitated…their heads nowhere to be found.

Six years went by before someone was arrested in connection with the kidnapping and murders of the two young coeds. He was thirty-six year old Eugene Paul Clawson. He had confessed to the crimes and seemed to know details that only the killer would know. There are still people to this day who claim that he was innocent of the crime for which he was sentenced to life in prison. Officially, the case is closed.

The ravine where the girls' bodies were found is located near a popular local recreation area known as Cheat Lake. People from all over West Virginia flock there year round for its beautiful scenery and fishing. It added insult to injury that such a heinous act had been perpetrated near a place that is known for its beauty and serenity.

Rumors have persisted for years that the girls can be seen running through the woods of Cheat Lake. Many a passing motorist has claimed to have seen their headless bodies frantically searching the brush for their missing heads. There have even been several automobile accidents on State Route 857N that have been attributed to motorists being distracted by visions of the girls.

My father used to fish on Cheat Lake several times a year. He and his fishing buddies would set up a camper in the area and fish during the day, then sit around the camper drinking and talking well into the night. He knew well the story of the murdered coeds since he happened to be a West Virginia State Trooper.

My father couldn't swear that he had encountered the ghosts of Mared and Karen in the woods, but he did say that they would hear movement outside the camper and then find nothing when they went out to investigate.

He also said that he would catch glimpses of someone moving around in the woods when he was fishing, but no one would ever materialize.

When I sent out feelers for this story, one man's encounter with the girls grabbed my attention. His name is Charles Kimes and he claims to have had brushes with the spirits of the murdered girls on not one, but two occasions.

Charles fishes for walleye and bass on Cheat Lake regularly, or at least he used to. On one such outing, he was driving his pickup truck to the Lake when he saw a woman, fully clothed, dashing through the woods. It was early in the morning and she seemed out of place running through the woods. His first instinct was that she needed help, so he pulled over and got out to offer assistance.

As he got closer to her, he could see that what he had thought was a woman was only a body with no head. He also noted that the body didn't seem quite real, it was very vague, more like the outline of a body than an actual physical form.

Not being familiar with the story of Karen and Mared, Charles got back into his truck and barreled home, no longer in the notion of fishing. When he told people of his encounter in the woods, they filled him in about the two girls and the presumption that they were forever haunting the woods in a desperate attempt to find their missing heads.

Months went by before Charles mustered the nerve to return to Cheat Lake. When he did return, he brought his brother with him. The men drove to the same area of the woods where Charles had seen the headless ghost months earlier. He didn't really want to see it again, but he was curious and this time, he had a witness.

There was no woman in the woods this time. Charles admits he was a little bit disappointed. He and his brother moved on to their usual fishing spot and spent an uneventful day visiting and reeling in their respective catches.

As they were leaving the Lake, Charles' brother suddenly grabbed him by the arm. "Do you see what I see?" he whispered. Charles did see it. In the distance, the men could just make out the forms of two females moving through the woods. One seemed to be frantically searching for something in the leaves while the other seemed in a daze. They weren't close enough to be sure, but since they could see no features, it didn't look to them like the bodies had heads.

Charles and his brother left Cheat Lake in a hurry that evening. That was over three years ago and he has not been back since.

This is a tragic tale in so many ways. The horrible murders of the two innocent young women with so much to live for who only wanted to see a movie on a cold winter's day is heartbreaking enough. The fact that they can't seem to rest until their heads are found just adds to the senselessness of this awful crime.

I hesitated to write this story, not wanting to disrespect Karen and Mared in any way. The story has been widely reported for decades, so I'm not breaking any new ground here. I included it because of the many sightings of their restless spirits. Maybe one day, some hunter or camper will discover their missing heads and the girls can finally rest in peace.

Chapter 41:
After School

One of my dearest friends has worked for many years as a school custodian. She started out working temporary positions before being hired on full-time at a local elementary school. She works the after school shift when the students have all gone home for the day, well, most of them anyway.

Even though my friend has worked at the school for years, she didn't share her knowledge of the strange goings on right away. She says that she noticed some strange things about the building soon after being hired, but kept them to herself unaware that she wasn't the only one who had encountered the mischievous spirits.

Some evenings when she would be cleaning in one room she would hear doors closing in rooms down the hall even though there was no one else on the floor at the time. On more than one occasion, she was spooked by the sound of children's laughter and the sound of feet running up and down the hallways. After hours at this particular schoolhouse was anything but peaceful.

One night, as she was using the polishing machine on the hallway floors, she looked up to see a little boy, no more than six years old, standing in front of one of the classroom doors. Thinking that he had somehow gotten left behind after classes had dismissed for the day, she turned off the noisy machine and called out to him.

She says that the boy giggled and then ran into the classroom closest to him--right through an unopened door. Not believing her eyes, she decided to investigate further. She checked the classroom door. Sure enough, it had been shut tight. She opened the door and went into the room, but the lights were out and there was no sign of the boy or anyone else.

Curious, she later asked some of the other people who worked at the school if they had any strange encounters with children in the building after hours. As it turned out, several teachers and custodians alike had either heard rumors of children playing in the hallways at all hours or they had seen them first-hand.

Although the sightings were reported in different areas of the schoolhouse, a young boy seemed to be the apparition most often seen. He had been spotted in the cafeteria, running up and down the hallways, in the restrooms, in classrooms and in the stairwells.

The possibility, as remote as it may seem, that a child has somehow been living in the school undetected is easily put to rest. These sightings have taken place over many years and the boy is always said to be around six or seven years old. A child surviving in the building on his own for years would surely age. And that wouldn't account for his apparent ability to walk through doors without opening them first.

Some of the school employees have done some detective work to try to determine who the little ghost boy might have been in life. Although, they couldn't come up with anything concrete, there had been stories circulating for years that a child had died after a fall in one of the stairwells sometime in the 1960s.

I asked my friend how the boy had been dressed when she saw him, were his clothes outdated? She couldn't be sure. She hadn't realized when she saw him that it would be significant until he disappeared so suddenly. By then, it was too late. She hadn't paid attention to his clothing.

Over the years, she has heard the boy much more often than she has seen him. The sound of running in the hallways is the most common occurrence in her experience. Disembodied laughter is also quite common. She says that it seems to bounce off of the walls at times. On more than one occasion, she had been frightened enough to move on to another part of the school until the activity died down.

Oddly, some of the other workers have reported hearing what sounds like more than one child playing in the hallways when there is no one to be seen. Could this be left over energy from decades of the halls being filled with children? Is the young boy's spirit doomed to forever roam the hallways of the schoolhouse after falling victim to a tragic accident on the grounds?

It's been said that when a person dies, they need for someone who is still living to show them the way home lest they be trapped in the area where they died for eternity. One hopes this is not the case and that maybe, someday, the boy will find his way back home.

Chapter 42:
A Soldier's Honor

This story is one that I have shared before in my book "Tales Too Strange To Be Fiction." It was included in that book for its bizarre nature. Since not everyone has read it, it's being offered now because it recounts the tale of soldier's ghost who was asking nothing more than to be heard.

My father-in-law, Larry Parmiter, Sr. was a career Navy man. He travelled the world and served America proudly in more than one war. He eventually worked his way up through the ranks to become a CW04.

On one of his many layovers at port, this time in Mexico, Larry Sr. became the unwitting conduit in the saga of a young sailor, named J.J., who needed to clear his name.

J.J. had been assigned the Friday night watch from four o'clock until eight o'clock. At the end of his shift, Larry Sr. had asked J.J. if he would be up for the extra duties of folding laundry and sheets for the ship's barber.

The air conditioning wasn't working and it was upwards of one hundred degrees on board the ship that night. In spite of the heat, J.J. agreed to perform the additional chores.

Monday morning at four o'clock, the ship's crew gathered for roll call. J.J. was uncharacteristically absent. His commanding officers didn't think too much of it. They thought maybe he had gone into Mexico over the weekend and had drunk a bit too much and was sleeping it off. They decided to let him be for the moment.

At seven o'clock muster, J.J. again missed roll call, so Larry Sr. sent someone to J.J.'s room to check on him. The man found J.J. asleep on his bunk, his face purple. He looked as though he had sustained a brutal beating. The crewman phoned Larry Sr. and told him he'd better come take a look for himself.

Larry Sr. knew immediately upon seeing J.J. that he hadn't been beaten, he was mottled from decomposition. The sailor had died sometime over the weekend.

When the men attempted to lift J.J. off of his bunk, his beard stayed glued to his pillow and his stomach burst open from the buildup of gases in his system. J.J. had been deceased for some time.

It was later determined that J.J. had died of a heart attack. The sailor had suffered from heart ailments in the past, but his death at the age of forty still came as a shock to his fellow Navy men.

A routine inventory of his belongings while the ship was still docked, revealed a gun that no one had been made aware of. The serial number was traced back to the San Diego County Sheriff's Department.

There was no reason that J.J. should have been in possession of the firearm and everyone's first thought was that he had stolen the pistol and stowed it away in his belongings. The ship left port and was once again at sea when Larry Sr. had one last communication with the young sailor whose honesty was now in question.

Larry Sr. was sleeping in his bunk when J.J. came to him in a dream. The sailor told him something over and over again. He was emphatic: "I did not steal that gun." When Larry Sr. woke up, he decided to investigate further into how J.J. had come into possession of the pistol.

As it turned out, the San Diego County Sheriff's Department had awarded J.J. the pistol in gratitude for his service. He had never mentioned the gun to any of his ship mates, for whatever reason.

J.J. hadn't been a thief at all. He had been an upstanding citizen who had been given an honor that not many ever receive. Thanks to one final declaration to his commanding officer, he could now rest knowing that his good name would remain untarnished.

Chapter 43:
Theater Macabre

Growing up in Parkersburg, West Virginia, one of my favorite places to go for entertainment was the old Burwell

Theater. It had been a staple in the town for as long as anyone could remember. My high school was just a couple of blocks from the movie house, so it became a favorite stomping ground for me and my friends.

The theater boasted an old fashioned marquee which would display the name of the movie that was playing at any given time. Besides that, the other thing that set the Burwell apart from any of the other theaters in town was the fact that the seats rocked which made watching a movie there the next best thing to being in your own living room. It was a great place to spend a Saturday night.

One of my high school classmates worked in the ticket booth at the Burwell in our senior year. She regaled us with stories of the spooky goings on at the old movie house. Whether she was just trying to impress a bunch of gullible teenagers or she really was working at a haunted theater, we didn't know for sure. Whichever it was, we enjoyed the stories, but they didn't deter us from spending time at the Burwell whenever we got the chance.

She had only worked at the theater for a short time before she started hearing stories from other employees about some strange events that had taken place there.

According to her, the ushers would check the theater between showings to make sure that no one was trying to stay behind and avoid paying for the upcoming show. One of the ushers had shared with her that on one occasion, he had begun his walk down the aisle and could clearly see someone seated in the front row. He could only make out the back of the person's head, but he could tell that it was a man.

When the usher approached the patron, whom he assumed had not purchased a ticket, the man had vanished. The usher had not taken his eyes off of the man. He was there and then he was gone. Thoroughly flummoxed, the usher high tailed it out of the main theater to the relative safety of the front lobby.

My classmate, who worked the ticket booth, also claimed that sometimes when she and some of the other employees were gathered in the lobby talking between movies, they would hear the movie begin playing in the auditorium. Someone would run up to see who was operating the projector, since the projectionist was either not there or in the lobby with the other workers.

The projection room would be empty, but the projector would be running. They would make jokes about the phantom projectionist from then on, even though the actual projectionist that day didn't find it very funny. He told them that he had noticed things being moved around in the projection room, even though he was sure he had been the last one in there. Reels would turn up where they shouldn't have been. Equipment would be turned on when it should have been off; little things that he had dismissed until the incident with the movie starting by itself.

Another thing that some of the employees noticed was that at night, as they were closing up, they would hear noises upstairs even though they were all cleaning the lobby or the auditorium. When they would go up to investigate, they would find all of the lights on, but no signs of anyone.

The one event that frightened my school chum the most and eventually led to her quitting the job was what happened one evening when she was sent to clean the restroom. When she walked in and switched on the light, she said that a man wearing a long dark coat was standing against the wall, smoking a cigarette. She apologized and fled the restroom.

Since the theater was closed at the time and there shouldn't have been anyone in the building except for employees, she asked a male co-worker to go into the restroom and tell the man to leave. When the co-worker went to investigate, there was no one in the restroom. And, even though my friend was sure that the man had been smoking, there was no smell of smoke in the air.

My friend only worked at the theater for a few months before moving on to less eventful employment elsewhere. She did tell anyone who would listen that she thought that the place was haunted. For whatever reason, theaters tend to be a place where spirits like to settle. Maybe it is the fact that so many people come and go in the lifetime of an old movie house. Perhaps they are drawn to the fantasy of the world of film just like the rest of us.

The Burwell was torn down in 1990, which is why I feel comfortable using the actual name. Businesses that are still in operation don't always want the reputation of being haunted. It's just not good for business.

It is interesting to note that after the theater was demolished, a well-known chain store was erected in its place. Even though there are many other branches of this store in the general area that do quite well, the one that took the spot of the old Burwell went out of business. The building stands vacant now and has for years.

Chapter 44:
The Oval Mirror

In the world of antiques, oval shaped picture frames and mirrors are said to be more valuable than their square or rectangular counterparts, or so I'm told. One woman's account of the bizarre events that plagued her after she purchased an old oval mirror at an estate sale might make you think twice before buying that valuable antique you've had your eye on. You can never be sure what the mirror has witnessed, and held onto, for all of those years.

Kay Chichester, of Richmond, Virginia, is a great lover of all things antique. Now in her fifties, she has been a collector since she was in her late teens. It isn't unusual for her to spend entire weekends travelling hundreds of miles in search of unique items from bygone eras.

One treasure she will never forget was something she happened upon at an estate sale close to her home in Richmond. The sale had been advertised in a local paper and Kay had been waiting eagerly for the doors to open on that Saturday morning in April, 2005.

Kay says that she knew she had lucked into the sale of a lifetime when she pulled up in front of the house. Everything about the place said 'antique' and she was excited to get inside and start sorting through the treasures.

The house was filled to capacity with a lifetime's worth of goods. Kay overheard the man who was hosting the sale telling shoppers that the house belonged to his mother who had recently passed away. He had no room for all of the things she had left behind so he was selling just about everything.

The late homeowner had been a collector of fine art, hand-blown glass, old china and so many of the things that Kay coveted, she couldn't believe her luck. She began digging through boxes and it wasn't long before she had armfuls of bric-a-brac to add to her collections.

As Kay made her way from one room to another, she was overwhelmed at the number of antiques the woman, whose house this had been, had collected. The volume of items was staggering. Kay wanted so many things, but knew she had to be selective since her home was already brimming over with finds from previous sales.

It was in the old woman's bedroom that Kay spied the one antique in the house she knew that she had to have. It was an oval mirror that was hanging over the head of the bed. The glass was foggy, but Kay could still make out her reflection. The detail work on the frame was breathtaking. What appeared to be cherubs had been meticulously carved into the framework by hand. If she could have nothing else, she wanted that mirror.

Unfortunately, Kay was unable to find a price tag on the mirror so she went searching for the man who was in charge of the sale. She had her fingers crossed that the mirror was still for sale and not already spoken for by another shopper.

Kay found the man, still in the front room, talking with other perspective buyers. She asked him about the mirror and he told her he would have to see it. He followed her into what had been his mother's bedroom and Kay showed him the mirror that she was interested in purchasing.

The man was puzzled as to why the mirror wasn't priced. It was indeed for sale. Apparently, someone had neglected to put a sticker on it. Kay nearly fainted when the man told her he would take ten dollars for it. She wasn't an expert on antique mirrors, but she knew that this one was worth many times that amount. She paid him without hesitation.

The man helped Kay carry the mirror and her other newfound treasures to her car. She thanked him and was on her way. She couldn't wait to get home and find a place for her latest, and probably most valuable, antique.

Once home, Kay lightly dusted the mirror and found a place to hang it in the hallway. It was heavy and she was careful to find a solid place on the wall to hang it so it wouldn't fall. She stood in front of her latest treasure, admiring the intricate detailing. This mirror had been quite a find and she was delighted with her purchase.

The mirror became a great source of pride for Kay and she showed it off to everyone who visited her home. They all agreed with her that it was beautiful, except for her daughter who told Kay that she didn't like it at all. Something about the mirror didn't feel right to her. She told her mother that when she looked into the mirror, she felt as though someone else was looking back at her.

Kay thought that her daughter was being silly. She had looked into the mirror many times and had never felt the least bit uneasy. That is, until one day when she was running late for work and she happened to stop in front of the old mirror for one last primp before she walked out the door.

As Kay put her face close to the glass and fussed with her hair, her face in the reflection became distorted. The mirror was always hazy, but normally you could still see your face in it. On this occasion, her reflection looked like something you would see in a funhouse mirror. Her eyes were elongated and her mouth drawn downward.

Kay was startled by the face that was looking back at her from the mirror. It was her face, but not really her face at all. She was so alarmed by the bizarre reflection, that she went into the bathroom and looked at her reflection in that mirror to see if her mind was playing tricks on her. The face staring back at her from the bathroom mirror was normal, except for the fact that she was ghostly pale.

Shaken, Kay darted past the hallway mirror, avoiding her own reflection, as she hurried out of the house for work. Kay told some of her co-workers about the odd incident with the mirror, but she didn't think they understood how frightening it had been. She decided that maybe she had overreacted. It was only a mirror and she had been in a hurry. Her imagination was getting the better of her. That had to be the answer, at least that's what she told herself.

Even though Kay talked herself into believing that the strange experience with the mirror had just been an overreaction on her part, she found herself avoiding looking at her reflection when she passed through the hallway.

On the rare occasions when she would take a quick glance at her image in the old mirror, it was always the same. Her face would be drawn out and unrecognizable. This wouldn't have bothered Kay so much if it had not been for the fact that when she had first seen her reflection in the mirror at the estate sale, and many times after that at her own home, her face had appeared normal. No elongated features. No contortions. Just her face looking the way it was supposed to look. Something had changed, but she didn't know what, or why.

Kay didn't want to get rid of the mirror, she still loved the way it was made and hated to part with it. But, what was the point of having a mirror that you were afraid to look at? She needed to get someone's opinion who would understand her apprehension. She decided to talk to her daughter about the strange images that were reflected in the antique mirror.

Kay's daughter listened intently to her mother's account of how the mirror, which had been perfectly normal in the beginning, now only reflected Kay's face as a distorted, twisted, version of her actual face.

As it turned out, Kay wasn't the only one who had noticed this oddity. Her daughter told her that, upon seeing the mirror for the first time, she had noticed the same thing. She had tried to tell Kay at the time, but knew how silly it sounded so instead she had just told her mother that the mirror made her feel uneasy.

In reality, when Kay's daughter had looked at her reflection in the mirror, the face that looked back at her was not her own. Instead, the image that was reflected was a bizarre caricature of her face. She was so disturbed by the sight of her own face that day that she had wept for the duration of the drive back to her own home two hours away.

Kay asked her daughter what she thought should be done with the mirror. Her daughter's opinion was that the mirror was cursed. For some people, but not everyone, the mirror reflected some turmoil or ugliness that couldn't be seen in other mirrors…or by the naked eye. It wasn't right and it wasn't the way things were supposed to be. To her way of thinking, the mirror was evil. Instead of looking at your own reflection, you were looking at what the mirror wanted you to see or what it perceived your face to be.

Kay's daughter suggested that her mother take the mirror to an incinerator and burn it. She felt that it was only a matter of time before whatever was haunting the mirror somehow seeped out into the world around it. If that happened, she felt that there would be no getting rid of whatever dark force was trapped inside of this antique.

The thought of destroying such a beautiful antique was out of the question for Kay. She felt that her daughter was being overly dramatic. At the same time, she also believed that the mirror might be possessed. She reasoned that if a house or person could be possessed, then why not a mirror? She would hold off on burning the mirror until she talked to someone who might be able to fix the problem. She would contact her pastor and ask for his advice.

When Kay explained the situation she was having with her antique mirror to her pastor, he was surprisingly sympathetic. He told Kay that his mother and grandmother had both collected antiques all of their lives. He knew a thing or two about relics himself and he shared a bit of wisdom with Kay.

According to the pastor, mirrors (and cameras) were antiques to be avoided. He said that since they capture images, whether it was a permanent image or a temporary one, they retain a memory of that image forever. He explained to her that many cultures shun these objects for that very reason, believing that, eventually, souls can become trapped inside of them. This is the reason, he explained, that some people cover mirrors when someone dies so that their departing soul can't take refuge there.

All of this was news to Kay. Now, she began to fear that perhaps the old woman whose house she had purchased the mirror at was somehow trapped inside of the glass, unable to move on to the next world. She shared this theory with her pastor. He assured her that her fears were probably unfounded, but if it would ease her mind, he would perform a blessing on the mirror and attempt to rid it of any dark energy. Kay readily agreed.

It was several days before the pastor was able to pay a visit to Kay's home to perform the blessing. He later told Kay that as he had walked through her front door that day, a cold chill had stopped him in his tracks. He hadn't mentioned it at the time, knowing that she was already on edge, but he had felt the presence of something otherworldly and it had not been welcoming.

Kay showed the pastor into the hallway and pointed out the antique mirror on the wall which had now become a burden to her. The pastor stood in front of the mirror and began reciting a prayer of blessing and goodwill. He noticed, as did Kay, that his reflection in the mirror was quite shocking. His features were twisted and his mouth seemed to be frozen in a snarl. What was being reflected in the mirror was not his face and he knew it. Shaken, he continued reciting the prayer.

The pastor had performed countless blessings in his years in the pulpit. He had blessed homes, families, even pets, but no prayer of good spirit was changing whatever had cursed this mirror. His reflection remained a contorted travesty of his true face and the feeling of foreboding was more than he could bear. He was out of his league and he knew it.

Kay's pastor apologized profusely as he told her that he would not be able to help her. His advice to her was to destroy the mirror. It was infected with something malevolent and she needed to get it out of her house immediately. He stressed to her that time was of the essence. The mirror had to go and the sooner the better.

Kay knew that her daughter and her pastor were right. The mirror had to be destroyed before it brought something into her home that she wouldn't be able to get rid of, if it hadn't done so already. She called her daughter who said that she would arrange to have it incinerated.

The day after the pastor's visit to Kay's home, her daughter retrieved the mirror and took it away for disposal. Although, she had refused to admit it before, Kay felt an almost instant sense of relief the minute the mirror was out of the house. It was as if a dark cloud had lifted and light was once again allowed in.

Kay still frequents antique malls and estate sales and she still brings home all sorts of ancient items--except for mirrors and cameras. She decided to heed the warning from her pastor. One bedeviled object in a lifetime was enough for her. She had learned her lesson the hard way.

Chapter 45:
The Thrift Store Santa

When I put out feelers asking people to share any unusual experiences they may have had involving objects that were Christmas related, the number of responses was a bit overwhelming.

Although most of the stories were intriguing, none caught my attention like the one you are about to read. It would begin and end with a trip to a local second-hand store. The events that took place in between would shake a family to its core and leave them wondering just what sort of entity they had brought into their home.

Steve Sellers, his wife and their two children spent many a Saturday afternoon frequenting the various thrift stores, flea markets and antique malls in and around Columbus, Ohio. On one particular weekend in 2001, they happened upon a second-hand store that they had missed on their previous outings.

As the family pulled up in front of the store, the first thing they noticed was a Santa that was on display in the window. It was November and the store was already lit up with Christmas lights and decorations. The Santa was propped up against a sled with fake snow at its feet. The kids' faces immediately lit up at the sight of Jolly Ol' Saint Nick winking at them from the other side of the glass.

Once inside the store, Steve and his wife tried to look around at the various wares, but the children kept pulling them towards the window. They were only interested in the Santa. Steve relented and they decided to take a closer look at the Christmas display.

Upon closer inspection, they could tell that the Santa had seen better days. The figure was about five-feet tall with rosy cheeks and one eye that was closed in a permanent wink. The face was plastic, but the body was soft. The clothing was a bit ratty and worn. Santa's hat stood straight up and the white puffy ball that should have been on the tip had been torn and was barely hanging on by a thread. The thing that disturbed Steve about the Santa was that it was missing two important appendages--its hands. There were just empty sleeves where the hands should have been.

Nevertheless, Steve's children begged him to buy the Santa. One look at the price tag, which dangled from one sleeve, told Steve and his wife that it was time to move on. The figure was way too expensive for their budget. Over their children's loud protests, Steve told them that they would have to look for something else.

As they were leaving the store, a man approached them. He introduced himself as the shop's owner. He was an older gentleman who grinned as he spoke. He had overheard the conversation at the window and he was willing to make them a deal for the Santa. He explained that it was for the kids, his way of sharing the holiday spirit. He knocked several dollars off of the price tag just for them.

Even with the price adjustment, it was still too steep for Steve. What he didn't tell anyone at the time was that he didn't really want the Santa. He thought it was kind of creepy and the sight of it made him feel anything but festive. Little did he know at the time just how accurate his gut feeling would turn out to be.

The store owner was very flexible on the price and kept lowering it until Steve couldn't refuse. He ended up getting the Santa for a fraction of the original price. His children were overjoyed as he loaded the musty smelling old Santa into the back of the car. This would be a Christmas to be remembered, though not for the reasons one would think.

Although Christmas was still over a month away, the family went ahead and set the Santa up in front of their living room picture window, just as the store had done, so that anyone passing by would see it. Santa was holding up one handless arm as if he were greeting passersby.

Things took a turn for the strange on the very next day after Steve had purchased the Santa. Even though they had stood the figure in front of the window when they brought it home…when they woke up the next morning it was standing in the corner of the dining room beside the china hutch.

After establishing that neither he nor his wife had moved the figure, Steve questioned his children. He knew it was unlikely that they had moved the Santa…it was bigger than either of them, but they were the only other people in the house. They both denied having touched the Santa. No one in the family would own up to having relocated the Santa, so Steve moved it back to the spot in front of the window and let the incident go. He supposed that someone was trying to be funny and felt that there had been no harm done.

Later that very same day, Steve and his wife were sitting in the family room watching television while the kids' played in their bedrooms. Steve could hear the children laughing and jumping around, probably on their beds which they weren't allowed to do.

Steve's wife was on her way upstairs to tell the children to stay off of the beds when she noticed something strange in the front room. The picture window was bare. The

Santa was gone...again. She went back into the family room and asked Steve if he had moved the Santa. He assured her that he had not bothered the figure since placing it back in front of the window earlier that day.

Steve and his wife went upstairs to confront the children. Someone was being mischievous and enough was enough. As Steve and his wife reached the top of the stairs, the Santa was standing on the landing, a wink on its face and an arm held up in greeting.

This was too much. Steve didn't think for one minute that the children could have dragged the figure up the stairs and propped it up on the landing, but what other explanation could there be? He confronted the children once again. They denied having moved the Santa. Though not completely convinced that they were guilty, he punished them anyway. Life isn't always fair and he was tired of the shenanigans.

Steve lugged the Santa back down the stairs and, once again, set it in front of the window. That night, Steve's wife woke him up to tell him that she thought she heard something downstairs. She wasn't sure, but it sounded like the front door had opened and then closed.

Steve hadn't heard anything, but he armed himself with the heavy flashlight that he kept on his nightstand and crept downstairs to investigate. He switched on the lights at the foot of the stairs. The front door was closed and locked. There were no signs of a break-in.

The rest of the downstairs was undisturbed as well. Steve checked every room and even the garage. No one was lurking in the shadows. All was well except that as Steve passed back through the front room he noticed that the Santa, who was supposed to be facing the street, was now facing into the house.

Steve knew that he had place the Santa facing the right way when he had put it back in front of the window earlier. He was also pretty sure that he would have noticed if the figure was turned the wrong way when he had turned off the lights and locked up at bedtime. At any rate, he turned the Santa back around, facing the street, and went back to bed.

The following day, when Steve went outside to retrieve the morning newspaper from the sidewalk in front of their house, he noticed that something was missing from the front window. The Santa was gone once again.

Steve hurried back into the house and searched throughout the room for the wayward Saint Nick. He found what he was looking for in the kitchen. The Santa was standing, on its own, in the doorway that led from the kitchen into the laundry room.

Bewildered, and a bit unsettled, Steve stood for a few moments staring at the Christmas decoration that wouldn't stay put. It was early and the kids were still in bed. His wife was sleeping as well and, at any rate, it didn't matter. Steve knew in his gut that they hadn't moved the Santa on this occasion or any of the other times.

The same feeling of apprehension washed over him that he had experienced the first time he had encountered the Santa at the thrift store. Steve had thought the Santa creepy right from the start and now he just wanted it out of the house. For the time being, he put it back in front of the picture window for the umpteenth time since they had brought it home.

Once the whole family was out of bed and downstairs having breakfast, Steve told them that he was going to throw the Santa out. He told them it was because it smelled bad and he thought it might have parasites.

He didn't want to tell them the real reason he wanted to get rid of it—that he thought it was possessed. Whatever its story was, Steve didn't want whatever had attached itself to the Santa to, in turn, latch onto his family. The Santa would go...case closed.

To Steve's surprise, no one argued to keep the Santa. Nothing but accusations and arguing among the family had taken place since they had brought their thrift store treasure home. Steve's wife did have one suggestion. She thought that it would be a better idea to take the Santa back to the second-hand store where they had purchased it. That way, someone would get use out of it since it had, at one time, been a rather pricey item. Steve reluctantly agreed.

He neglected to tell his wife that he had been a little bit worried about throwing the Santa away. He had seen enough scary movies to know that, sometimes, haunted objects find their way back to the person who threw them out. Steve was already aware of this particular Santa's penchant for travelling so he didn't want to take any chances.

So, after breakfast, Steve loaded the Santa into the car and headed back to the thrift store to return it. He went alone this time, not wanting to take the chance that one of the kids would change their mind and cause a scene. The Santa was history and that was final.

When Steve arrived at the thrift store, he took the Santa out of the back of the car and carried it into the store. The shop owner recognized Steve, and the Santa, right off the bat and grinned when he saw them come through the door.

Steve told the man that he wanted to return the Santa. He also informed him that it was a donation…he didn't want his money back. The man's grin spread even wider as Steve spoke.

"Spooked you did he?" the man asked.

Steve feigned ignorance and asked the shopkeeper why he would ask that. The man didn't say too much, but he did tell Steve that he had had difficulty keeping the Santa in one spot. He said that he would position the Santa in the window one day only to have him turn up in another part of the store the next day. No one worked at the shop except for the owner so there was no explanation for the Santa's displacement.

The old man went on to tell Steve that it hadn't bothered him one bit. He had dealt in antiques and second-hand goods his whole life. He explained to Steve that this wasn't the first time he had encountered an object that moved about on its own.

He had seen items move right before his eyes with no explanation. He had heard bells ring when there was no one holding them. Cuckoo clocks would go off even though their pulleys were broken and the mechanisms were destroyed. He told Steve that he could tell him stories that would give him nightmares.

Steve thanked the man, but told him that he had heard enough. He did have one last question for the shopkeeper. He asked the old man why he had stayed in the business for so many years surrounded by objects that were possibly haunted. He wondered if the old man ever got scared being around so many questionable antiques.

The old man's ever-present grin widened as he shrugged his shoulders and laughed. "I don't bother them and they don't bother me," was his simple response. With that, he took the Santa from Steve and positioned it in front of the window in the same pose it had been in a few days earlier when Steve and his family had first seen it.

Steve wished the shopkeeper a Merry Christmas as he departed the store, for the second and last time. He liked the owner well enough, but he decided to steer clear of second-hand items for a while.

As he got into his car, Steve couldn't help but see the Santa winking at him from the store's front window. 'Merry Christmas to you, too', Steve thought as he backed out of the spot and left the Santa behind. This was one holiday memory best forgotten.

Chapter 46:
The Wampus Cat

The Wampus Cat is, according to folklore, a harbinger of death. It is said that if someone hears the ominous cry of this woodland creature, a death will soon follow. By most accounts, a person very close to whoever hears the mournful sound will die and be buried within three days. The legend of the Wampus Cat began in Tennessee, but my relatives in West Virginia are very familiar with this creature of folklore. They were my source for this story.

As a child, I had never heard of a Wampus Cat. That is, until I was ten years old and my uncle passed away. He wasn't really my uncle. Dan was my father's cousin, but we always called him Uncle Dan. He and my father were more like brothers than cousins and it seemed only fitting.

Dan had always lived a hard life. He liked to drink a bit too much. He also smoked like a chimney. All in all, it didn't come as a complete surprise when he died from a sudden heart attack when he was only in his forties.

I remember my family joining the other mourners at a relative's house after the funeral. I sat there silently listening as the adults shared stories about their lost loved one. My Uncle Dan's brother, Virgil, told everyone that he had known someone was going to die, he just hadn't known who until the call came informing him that his brother was gone. He knew, he said, because he had heard a Wampus Cat crying in the woods a couple of nights earlier.

Virgil said that he had been sitting in his living room, watching television, when he heard what sounded like a woman's cries echoing through the woods that lay behind his house. He was familiar with the legend of the Wampus Cat, but had never paid it much attention. He had assumed, like everyone else, that it was simply make believe.

All the same, he was on pins and needles, wondering if death was stalking someone close to him. It was the very next day that he got word that Dan was dead.

I watched silently as the adults in the room all nodded their heads in understanding. After a few moments of silence, Virgil's wife chimed in with her story. She had also heard a Wampus Cat in the woods behind their house. She had kept the story to herself for several years for fear that no one would believe her. Now that Virgil had told his story, she felt safe in sharing hers.

Virgil's wife nervously told the room full of mourners that she had been awakened one night years earlier by the sound of a woman's shrill crying that cut through the quiet of the night and jolted her out of bed. Virgil was away on a hunting trip at the time and she was in the house alone.

She had looked out the windows, but hadn't seen anything unusual in the woods that surrounded the house. She could still, however, hear the woeful cries as they split through the night. Terrified, she sat up the rest of the night with the lights on, too fearful to go back to bed.

Virgil's wife said that she knew that the cries were a warning…something terrible was going to happen to someone close to her. Since Virgil was in the mountains hunting, she was sure that the cries were for him. To her great relief, he returned home the next evening, safe and sound. She didn't tell him about the Wampus Cat or how it had scared her so.

Sadly, word came to her the following morning that her mother, who had not been ill a day in her life, had died in her sleep. Virgil's wife didn't say if anyone ever found out the reason her mother had passed away suddenly, but it was obvious that she was still shaken by the whole incident. Again, the adults in the room all nodded and agreed with her. The Wampus Cat had been sent to warn her that death was coming for someone, and soon. With her mother's passing, the death foretold had come to pass.

I asked my mother later, when we were alone, what a Wampus Cat was. She shushed me and told me that it was nothing. Forget about it. It wasn't real. I always wondered if she really believed that or if she just didn't want me to be frightened. At any rate, it was obvious to me, even as a child, that the people in the room that night believed that the Wampus Cat was real and that if you heard her cries, death would follow close behind

Chapter 47:
A Face In The Crowd

Growing up in a small town in West Virginia, I formed some lasting bonds with several of the kids in our neighborhood. Aside from my best friend in the world, Roberta, the person I was closest to was a boy who lived on the next street over from ours. His name was Vincent Gilbert.

I knew of Vince for several years before actually meeting him. His reputation preceded him, to put it mildly. Vince buddied around with a boy who was considered to be the neighborhood bully. He was not a nice kid and the rest of us avoided him like the plague. Since Vince hung around with him, I assumed he was a creep also and likewise avoided him.

That is, until one day when a friend and I rode our bikes to a nearby store and left them unattended in the parking lot. When we came back out, our bikes had been vandalized. As we looked around for the culprits, we saw Vince and the notorious bully standing at the side of the building laughing at us.

Being an average eleven year old girl, I ran home and tattled to my big sister. I told her that my bicycle had been damaged and that I knew who the guilty party was. I didn't know where the bully lived, but I did know where Vince lived. I pointed his house out to my very protective sister and she grabbed an aluminum baseball bat and headed for his front door.

Unaware of the trouble he was in, Vince answered the door and found a very angry nineteen year old standing on the doorstep, baseball bat in hand, little sister cowering behind her. The look on his face went from the usual smirk to jaw-dropping fear when she laid into him, verbally, for smashing my bike.

After my sister let Vince know, in no uncertain terms, that if he ever came near me or any of my possessions again, she would be back and that the bat wouldn't be for show next time, he nodded his head and slowly retreated into the safety of his home.

That seemed to be that. Problem solved. Vince and his bully friend gave me and my friends a wide berth and all was well, at least for a little while. I'm not sure how much time past before I had my next encounter with Vince, but it was under much different circumstances.

My friend, Roberta, and I were roaming the neighborhood one day, as we were prone to do, when we were approached by a frantic Vince. His dog had gotten loose and he couldn't find him anywhere. He was desperate to locate the big Golden Retriever who never strayed far from his master's side. Even though we didn't particularly like Vince, we agreed to help him look for his lost dog.

After wandering up and down the streets calling the dog's name, we finally found him rooting around in a neighbor's garden. Vince was relieved to have his dog back and we were happy that we could help. The whole experience that day is memorable because, for the first time ever, I saw the human side of this boy who had been someone to avoid up until then. From that day on, Vince was a different person to me.

Vince started stopping by my house from time to time to go ride bikes together or walk to the local park, which was really just a swing set and slide. He was actually quite shy and nothing like the evil boy I had him pegged as. The more time we spent hanging out, the more I grew to like the quiet boy with the brown tousled hair and crooked front teeth.

Vince and I remained good friends until we were around sixteen. It was then that Vince told me that he and his family were moving to South Carolina. It was amazing how things had changed between us over the years. There had been a time, not so long ago, that I would have rejoiced at the news that this menace was moving away.

That was, of course, before I got to know him and realized that he was a sweet person who had just been hanging around with a bad influence. Now, I was upset and sad to see my friend go, but it was what it was.

A few weeks later, we said our goodbyes and that was that. We promised to keep in touch, but I didn't hear from him after he moved and assumed that he had forgotten all about me. As it happens, he would pay me a visit that I didn't expect and could never explain.

When I was seventeen years old and in my senior year of high school, I worked part-time at a fast food restaurant to save up money for a graduation trip to England. I usually worked the dinner rush when the place was packed with hungry diners.

On one particularly busy evening, I was manning the cash register when I noticed a guy standing off to the side near the exit door. He was looking right at me and when he caught my eye, he smiled. I recognized that crooked smile in a heartbeat. It was Vince. He was back from South Carolina.

I couldn't wait to finish up with my line of customers so that I could go talk to Vince, but by the time the crowd had died down, he was gone. I assumed that he had grown tired of waiting around and had left. I checked the parking lot to see if maybe he was out there smoking a cigarette, something he had done even as a kid, but he was nowhere to be found.

Disappointed that I hadn't been able to reconnect with my friend, I went back inside and finished my shift. I had no way of getting in touch with Vince. This was long before cell phones or the internet. I still lived in the same house I had grown up in, so if he wanted to find me, he knew where to look.

Vince didn't show up at my mom's house that night or the next morning, as I had hoped. I did, however, have another encounter with him. My friends and I were at our local mall, which was the only fun place for teenagers to hang out at in those days, when I saw a tall boy with tousled hair walking towards us. He smiled when he realized that I had seen him. It was Vince. He hadn't changed much at all and I knew him instantly. I couldn't wait to spend some time catching up with him and hearing all about his new life down south.

The mall was busy that day, as it is every Saturday. Somehow, I got jostled around by all of the people and lost sight of Vince for a moment. Even though he had been walking right towards me only seconds earlier, he was gone. I had lost him.

My friends and I looked all over the mall for him, but Vince had disappeared into the crowd and we never did find him. That would prove to be the last time I would see him. I had missed my opportunity to spend some time with my old friend. I was very disappointed, but there was nothing I could do except to hope he would turn up again sometime. It was not to be.

At school the following week, one of my friends who hadn't been with us at the mall that day, asked me if I had heard about Vince Gilbert. Thinking she was going to tell me that he was back in town, I told her that I had seen him a couple of times, but hadn't been able to talk to him.

She looked at me like I was out of my mind. No, she meant had I heard what had happened to Vince. Now, I was the one who was puzzled. What was she on about? She proceeded to tell me that, over the weekend, Vince had taken his father's paddle boat, and his pistol, out onto a lake near their home in South Carolina and had shot himself. He was gone, a suicide at the age of seventeen.

I was speechless. I told her that it couldn't be. I had seen Vince in West Virginia, in our little town, on Friday and Saturday. That couldn't be, she explained, her parents were good friends of Vince's family and she knew that the story was true. He had killed himself on Friday. No one seemed to know why. She didn't know who I had seen, but it couldn't have been Vince.

   Well, I knew better. I had seen his face as clear as a bell on both occasions. I knew Vincent Gilbert when I saw him, and I had seen him on Friday and Saturday. There was no doubt in my mind.

   Did Vince take the time before moving on to whatever destiny awaited him in the next life to let me know that he was okay? Was that why he was gone both times before I could reach him?

   Those are questions that cannot be answered. All I know is that I saw him, my enemy turned friend, after he had left his earthly body and before he had departed for parts unknown. I wish that there had been a chance to tell him that he wasn't at all what most people thought. He wasn't a trouble maker or a menace, but a vulnerable kid with a sweet soul and a crooked smile who never forgot a friend.

Chapter 48:
Gretchen

This, all too close to home, story involves a framed portrait that my husband bought at an antique store. It was during a period in which we were collecting oddities for a store we were planning to open. We were on the lookout for any items that we found bizarre or creepy and boy did we hit the mark with this one.

When he brought the portrait home, I immediately hit the roof. It was just awful and I didn't want it in the house…not even temporarily. The picture was very old and its subject was—let's just say--unusual looking.

The portrait was of a woman, I think, with her hair parted in the middle and slicked down. The lips were pursed and the eyes were as angry as two hornets. The frame was square with an oval inlay surrounding the actual picture. It was obviously old and probably valuable. That being said, I hated it.

I have encountered people in my life who gave off bad vibes, but nothing like the waves of bad karma that emanated from this antique. Just having this relic in the house was casting a pall over everything around it, but my husband loved it and insisted we keep it for our oddities store. After all, he reasoned, this had been someone's mother, grandmother, sister, daughter or wife. In other words, she had meant something to someone at one time and we needed to show her some respect.

Thoroughly ashamed of my initial revulsion at the sight of the portrait, I relented and agreed to keep the picture of the androgynous person from the past until we could display it in our, as yet unopened, shop. We decided to name her 'Gretchen'. We were pretty sure the person in the picture was a woman and, for whatever reason, Gretchen suited her.

   Almost immediately, our lives began a downward spiral. My husband was, at that time, the most sought after karaoke host/DJ in our area. He worked nearly every single night and was always in demand. Within a month of bringing Gretchen into our home, all of that changed.

   First one, and then another, and then all of my husband's karaoke jobs fell to the wayside. Either the places he worked at went out of business, or the owners decided to try someone new, or the establishments nixed the idea of karaoke altogether. Whatever the excuses, the jobs were history, each and every one of them.

   My aunt, who was in good health and still going to work every day, fell in her driveway and later died in the hospital. We inherited her wonderful dog that also died unexpectedly a few months later.

   My mother-in-law, who was only in her mid-sixties at the time and had recently moved into a new home, began to behave erratically and was later diagnosed with dementia. Her mental health began to rapidly decline and life as she had known it came to an abrupt end. She could no longer live on her own and lost the new home she had been so proud of.

   Bad luck seemed to be heaped upon us as well as many of the people close to us. A good friend of my husband's died from a sudden heart attack at the age of thirty-six. My younger brother suffered two strokes, which left him needing months of physical therapy in order to regain his ability to walk.

All of these things happened within months of each other. It seemed that every time we picked up the phone, it was more bad news. On top of all of that, since my husband had lost his jobs, we couldn't afford to open the oddities store. All of our planning and saving and collecting artifacts for our much anticipated venture into owning our own shop had been for nothing…it wasn't going to happen.

As if we needed more bad luck, the furnace in our home—which was less than a year old-- went on the blink and had to be repaired. Our hot water heater also blew and had to be replaced. My van, in the span of a few weeks, managed to get not one, or two, but three flat tires. Might I add that it wasn't the same tire over and over again; it was three different tires that went flat for no good reason.

The stress of everything: the sudden deaths and illnesses, losing our dream of opening a store and our household items going haywire, caused so much turmoil in our marriage that we nearly divorced. Our young daughter was also feeling the negativity and commented on the fact that she just wanted our lives to go back the way they had been before everything started to fall apart. In other words, before Gretchen came into our lives.

It may sound silly, and it could all be coincidence, but a dark cloud entered our home with Gretchen's arrival. I couldn't stand the sight of her any longer so I put her portrait in our basement facing the wall, I had had enough of those angry eyes to last me a lifetime.

Fortunately, things were about to get better. My husband knows a lot of people who deal in antiques and collectibles and he had told a few of them about Gretchen and our theory that she was cursed and, in turn, was passing that curse on to us.

One of his acquaintances couldn't get enough of the Gretchen story and he offered to take her off our hands. Needless to say, we couldn't hand her over fast enough. He didn't care that we thought she was bad luck. It was love at first sight for him.

It is worth noting that, almost immediately after giving Gretchen away, our luck improved. My husband began working again, this time at his leisure. We didn't open our oddities shop, but we do now have a used DVD store that does quite well. The upheaval in our home finally settled down and the clouds lifted. Things were back to normal for us and for that we were truly thankful.

Chapter 49:
The Spirit Magnet

My cousin, Donna Jennings, is someone who is very familiar with the paranormal. She, and her brother Larry, seemed to always be just a bit closer to the other side than most people ever are or care to be. The following four stories all revolve around Donna and her uncanny ability to attract those who have passed on from this life in spite of her efforts to the contrary.

Donna has known since she was a child that she was different. She feels things more deeply than most people, and although she has no explanation for it, she has been touched by the spirit world on countless occasions in her life.

One of the first incidents occurred when Donna was staying at our grandma's house in the hollows of West Virginia. I have written about the house in previous volumes in this series. The old house was haunted. Anyone who ever set foot inside the place will tell you that. Donna knew better than most just how frightening the old house could be.

When she was in her early teens, Donna was spending the night at the house in the hollow when she came down with a fever. She was very ill and decided to sleep in the living room so she wouldn't disturb our grandma and our Aunt Imogene, who was also staying over.

Sometime during the night, Donna kicked her covers off. She was burning up with fever and the blankets were only making things worse. No sooner had the covers been tossed to the side before someone pulled them back over Donna. Since our grandma and aunt were the only other people in the house that night, Donna assumed it was one of them.

Not to be outdone, Donna defiantly threw the covers onto the floor. She was roasting hot and couldn't bear the added heat the blankets provided. Again, someone covered her back up before she could protest. It was pitch black in the room so she couldn't see who was meddling with her blankets. Whoever it was, they continued to make sure she was tucked in all through the night, whether she liked it or not.

In the morning, Donna's fever had broken and she was feeling better. At the breakfast table, she confronted grandma and Imogene, telling them that they had just about burned her up by keeping those covers over her all night.

Grandma and Imogene were both puzzled. They protested that they had been in their beds all night. Neither one of them had even gotten up to check on Donna at all. Whoever's unseen hands had pulled the blankets over Donna time and time again during that feverish night, they hadn't belonged to any living person in the house.

When Donna was older and married to her first husband, Danny, they moved, along with their baby daughter to Florida. There, they rented a small apartment until they could afford to buy a house. It consisted of a kitchen, one bedroom, a bathroom and a small living room. It was cramped quarters, but the young family made do as best they could.

Donna remembers being visited by something that terrorized her one night while Danny and the baby were sleeping soundly in the bedroom. Donna had fallen asleep on the couch while watching television. The room was set up so that a coffee table separated the couch from the TV. She was jolted awake sometime during the night by loud buzzing as the station she had been watching signed off for the night.

As Donna stood up to turn off the television, two arms reached for her from the other side of the coffee table. She tried running one way and then the other, but the arms grabbed for her no matter which way she attempted to run. She could see no actual body, just the arms with two long hands on each end. The hands were opening and closing madly as they grabbed for her.

In sheer panic, Donna lunged past the arms and made it to the bedroom door. As she opened the door and shot into the bedroom, she felt one of the hands make contact with her arm. She was screaming when she finally pulled free and made it into the bedroom with her husband and baby. She closed the door behind her and locked it.

Strangely, Danny and the baby were still sound asleep. Donna was sure that she had been screaming the whole time the arms had been after her, but her family had slept through the entire incident.

Still in a panic, Donna grabbed the baby out of her crib and put her in the bed with Danny. Donna then got into the bed as well and huddled close to her family. She stayed awake the rest of the night, her eyes glued to the bedroom door, terrified that whatever was on the other side would find its way into the room with them.

In the morning, Donna told Danny what had happened. Danny's first thought was that they had probably been burglarized. He told Donna to stay locked in the bedroom while he explored the rest of the apartment.

While Danny checked the apartment for intruders, Donna had to go to the bathroom. When she went into the room and looked at her reflection in the mirror, she could see that she had three long scratches on her arm. Whatever had grabbed at her in the living room had left its mark.

When Danny came back into the bedroom, he said that he could find no signs of a break-in. There was no one but them in the apartment and the front door was locked. Whatever Donna had encountered in the living room the night before hadn't come in through the door and it hadn't left that way either. Donna wasn't surprised. She felt sure that whatever it was that had attacked her didn't need a door to travel by. Not the kind we are accustomed to anyway.

Another story involving Donna occurred many years later. Donna and Danny had long since divorced and Donna was now remarried. She and her second husband also have a daughter together. Donna also has several grandchildren. This story involves one of them, her grandson Colton.

When Colton was around three or four years old, Donna had taken him to visit her in-laws. It was quite a drive from Donna's house to her in-laws, but Colton didn't seem to mind. There was one thing about the drive that Donna didn't care for. One house in particular that they had to pass by gave her a bad feeling and she dreaded the sight of it.

There was nothing special about the house that gave Donna such a feeling of gloom. It was a large, white, well-kept home that one might see on any street in the southern United States. That being said, the house couldn't have been creepier to Donna.

As they passed by the house on this occasion, Donna could hear Colton immediately begin talking to someone. He said 'hi' and then launched into some chatter that she couldn't make out. Curious, Donna asked him who he was talking to.

"My friends," was his innocent reply.

"Oh, yeah," Donna played along. "What are they saying?" she asked.

"They want me to take you to the barn," was his answer.

"Why do they want me to go to the barn?' she asked.

Colton shrugged his shoulders.

She wanted to know more, but didn't want to frighten Colton.

"Where do your friends live?" she asked.

"Back there," Colton replied, gesturing back towards the white house.

Donna thought for a moment, she didn't remember ever seeing a barn at the white house.

Donna didn't press Colton any further. She let the matter drop, but she still wondered if they had, perhaps, picked up a passenger at the white house; a passenger that only Colton could see.

After a while, she heard Colton tell his friends "goodbye" and that was it. He didn't speak of them again.

The whole incident bothered Donna so much that she made a point of slowing down and taking a closer look at the house on their trip home. Sure enough, set back behind the white house, was an old barn. You wouldn't notice it from the road unless you were looking for it. Donna doubted that it would have been something that Colton would have ever seen.

Later on, Donna did a little investigating into the old white house. It turned out that it was for sale and had been for some time. People who bought the place usually sold out soon afterwards. The house had changed hands numerous times in only a few years. A local realtor told her, in confidence, that they had even tried renting out the house in lieu of selling it, but renters never stayed either.

The last Donna heard, the house had been sold once again. She never did find out who Colton had been talking to, or why they wanted him to take her to the barn, but she did know that the house never lost its ability to make her blood run cold. Whoever the new owners were, she wished them luck. She felt sure that they were going to need it.

Although there are many more stories involving my amazing cousin, I will end, for now, with this one. Donna had always been very close to everyone on my mother's side of the family except for our Uncle Bernard. It wasn't that she didn't like him, she had just never bonded with him in the same way that she had with the rest of the aunts and uncles.

Uncle Bernard was a bit aloof and I have to admit, I wasn't close to him either. He was just a little on the standoffish side and hard to get close to. Whereas the other members of the family would laugh and kid around with each other, Bernard would keep his distance, content to smoke his cigarette and not be bothered. Each to their own, as the saying goes.

I was very young when Uncle Bernard passed away. He was in his early forties when he was struck down by a massive stroke. All of the family members gathered at my grandmother's house after his funeral to pay their last respects.

Bernard and my grandmother, Bernard's mother, were extremely close. He was her first born son and he held a special place in her heart. She never quite got over losing him so young. She mourned him until her own passing more than twenty years later.

Until the day she died, my grandmother kept a photograph of Bernard in his military uniform on her nightstand beside her bed. Donna spent more time with our grandmother than the rest of the cousins and they too were extremely close.

Donna didn't, however, ever warm up to Uncle Bernard even after his death. She didn't like the photograph and avoided looking at it. She could feel Uncle Bernard's eyes glaring a hole through her from behind the picture's glass. It gave her the creeps and always had.

When my grandmother passed away, the family once again gathered at her house, only this time it was to go through old family heirlooms and decide who would take home the various mementos my grandmother had collected in her lifetime.

As they were clearing out my grandmother's bedroom, one of my aunts asked Donna if she would like to take the photograph of Uncle Bernard, which had been so dear to our grandmother. Donna told my aunt point blank that she didn't want the photograph. She had never liked it and had no use for it. Let someone else take it was her final thought on the subject.

After everything was boxed up and everyone had said their final goodbyes, the family all departed my grandmother's house in Alderson for the last time. Donna took the mementos she had chosen to remember our grandmother by and headed back home to North Carolina. Once there, she stored the boxes in her garage until she was ready to unpack them. There was no hurry, she needed some time to rest and mourn grandma in peace.

Donna has a large bookcase in her living room that takes up one whole wall. This is where she displays not only books, but family photos and various items of home decor. One day, a few weeks after returning from our grandmother's house, Donna was dusting the bookcase when she made a startling discovery.

On the top shelf, among the photographs of her children and other close family members, was the photograph of Uncle Bernard in his military uniform. Donna was flabbergasted. She had made a point not to take that picture. She had packed the boxes herself and she knew, without a doubt, that she had not brought that photograph to her house. Besides that, she still hadn't unpacked the boxes. They were sealed and sitting in her garage, untouched.

She removed the photograph from the shelf, Uncle Bernard's eyes glaring at her disapprovingly, and put it in storage. She didn't throw it away out of respect for our grandmother who loved Bernard so, but she didn't want to ever see it again and certainly not displayed in her living room.

Donna never could explain how the picture had found its way into her house. She had been the only one who had packed the boxes she brought home and none of them had been opened once they were put in her garage. Was Uncle Bernard trying to make amends from beyond the grave?

Or, was he taking one last opportunity to remind her that he wasn't going to be as easy to be rid of as she thought? Maybe someone was playing a trick on her, but who? I guess only she, and Uncle Bernard, know for sure.

Chapter 50:
The Discovery

My father, Bill, was a West Virginia State Trooper for over twenty years. In that time, he dealt with everything from traffic stops to murder investigations. He has a plethora of stories, some of which I have shared in previous books.

One case he was involved in stood out for him and for me. It involved a woman who went missing without a trace, or at least that's what the person responsible for her disappearance thought, until over a year later when a discovery on a hunting trip would shine new light on the cold case. What makes the story unique is that one of the members of that hunting party had a connection to the case and a long-held desire to solve it.

In the early 1970s, my father was one of the members of law enforcement who was called in to investigate the disappearance of a woman. She had been involved in an acrimonious relationship with her estranged husband when she suddenly came up missing. Her family reported that she had been fearful of her soon-to-be ex-husband and they suspected that he may have harmed her, or worse.

Days turned into weeks and then into months as the investigation dragged on. The missing woman's husband claimed to have no knowledge of his estranged wife's whereabouts. Contrary to the reports given by the woman's family, he told investigators that they had been working things out and that he had no reason to harm his wife. He claimed to be as worried about her as anyone else. He volunteered to help in any way possible.

The people investigating the woman's disappearance, including my father, felt that the man had probably killed his wife, but they couldn't prove it. They didn't have a body or any evidence that could be used against the husband. All they could do was keep him on their radar and hope that, eventually, he would slip up.

A year went by with no sign of the missing woman. Her family hoped, in vain, that she would turn up somewhere. They had always held onto the small possibility that she had run away from her abusive husband and had started a new life someplace else. After so many months with no word from her, they had finally given up hope. She was gone and she wasn't coming back.

The woman's husband, on the other hand, had gotten on with his life. Even though he had assured investigators at the time of his wife's disappearance that he would help them in any way he could, he had stopped cooperating when it became clear to him that the police suspected him of killing her. His concern for her well-being came to a screeching halt when he realized that his every move was being scrutinized, especially the fact that he wasted no time finding other women to keep him company. He was moving on, his missing wife seemingly forgotten.

He was wrong. At least one investigator, my father, had never stopped thinking about the young woman whose life, he was sure, had been cut tragically short. She had left behind children who would never know what became of their mother. As a young father himself, my father had a hard time facing the possibility that the case might never be resolved.

My father makes no claims to any psychic abilities, or even a belief in the supernatural. He does, however, think that the woman tried to reach him from somewhere beyond our reality. He thinks this because, even though he never knew her in life, she appeared to him in his dreams.

It only happened a few times, but in these dreams, the woman would tell my father that it was okay. Just wait. It would be alright in the end. He didn't know what she meant, but he hoped it meant that the case would be solved, someday, somehow.

He could never have guessed then just how the case would eventually be solved or the role that he would play in that resolution. That is until one early autumn morning when a party of hunters that included my father, cousin and a family friend, stumbled upon something in the woods that would blow the cold case wide open.

As they were making their way through the piles of leaves and sticks and thick brush in the heavily wooded area in Elkins, West Virginia, my father's friend saw something lying on the ground that brought the hunt to an unexpected stop and made the hunters local celebrities for a time. There, half covered in fallen leaves, they had found a human skull.

My father had been an outdoorsman his entire life. He had been on countless hunting trips all over North America and had never, ever, seen anything like what he saw that day. As gingerly as they could under the circumstances, they retrieved the skull and retreated to their truck. They weren't sure what they had, perhaps a lone hunter or woodsman had perished in the forest years earlier and had never been found, maybe animals had carried the skull there from someplace else, or maybe, just maybe, a victim of foul play would have their day in court at long last.

After taking the skull to his police barracks and then having it sent to the coroner's office in Charleston, my father waited to hear any news of who the skull might belong to. It was determined that the skull had been that of a woman between thirty and forty years old. The skull had also given them a gift that every investigator dreams of. In a sheer stroke of luck, most of the teeth were still intact. This meant that if they could match the teeth that remained in the skull with the dental records of known missing persons, they might be able to identify who the skull belonged to.

Since they knew the gender of the skull's owner and approximate age, investigators began scouring their missing person's reports for anyone who might fit the general description. The investigation blanketed the state, since, if the woman whose skull they had found had been a crime victim, she could have been transported to the woods from another location.

Eventually, the investigation was narrowed down to a handful of women who had been missing for some time and who fit into the age bracket of the skull. Of course, investigators realized that the skull could belong to someone who had never been reported missing, but they were hoping that luck would be on their side and they weren't disappointed.

After comparing dental records from the missing women to the teeth that were found in the skull, investigators found their match. The skull was proven to belong to the same woman whose disappearance had haunted my father.

She hadn't run away with another man, or started a new life far away from her loved ones. She had been taken by violence and the police involved in investigating her disappearance in the first place felt sure they knew who was responsible. They decided to pay her husband a visit, and this time, they had some leverage.

Investigators found the husband right where they had left him over a year earlier. He was still moving from one woman to the next and drinking himself into a stupor on most days. When they confronted him with their newfound evidence, the skull belonging to his wife, the positive identification, and the revelation that she had been murdered, he broke down and confessed to having killed her in an alcohol induced rage.

Unfortunately, the man was deemed to be mentally unfit to stand trial. His mental health had always been in question and the years of guilt-induced alcohol consumption had deteriorated what was left of his mind to the point that he was nearly incoherent most of the time. He was committed to a state mental health facility until such a time that he would be considered suitable for trial. It never happened. He died in the state's care a few years later, never having truly answered for the crime against his wife.

The great coincidence of this story is that my father, one of the original investigators in the case of the missing woman, would be a member of the small hunting party who happened, by sheer chance, to find the skull in the woods. There are countless wooded areas and forests in the state of West Virginia that hunters lay claim to every year. There are also countless places where someone could dispose of a body after a misdeed.

What were the odds that this particular killer would hide his victim's remains in an area that one of the original investigators hunted in? What are the greater odds that, after a year of exposure to the animals and elements, my father's small hunting party would find the skull in the woods and that enough teeth would be left in the skull that it could be positively identified? None of it seems possible, but it happened. The story was even featured in a detective magazine that was popular at the time.

Whoever this woman had been in life, she had stayed as close to this world as possible to make sure that she hadn't been forgotten and that her case would eventually be solved, perhaps even having a hand in the final outcome. How else could one explain all of the amazing coincidences that took place in order to bring her case to a close and identify her killer once and for all?

Chapter 51:
A Local Haunt

The Mid-Ohio Valley boasts a variety of family owned and operated businesses. One of those local establishments is the subject of the next story. The owners of this once thriving business did not want their name used in case they ever decide to re-open, so I will call them the "Smith" family. They are a large family consisting of the parents as well as four grown children.

The Smith's first opened their family style restaurant in the mid-1980s. They specialized in home cooked meals such as meatloaf sandwiches and chicken-fried steak. Business was good and the whole family pitched in waiting tables and working in the kitchen. An added bonus was that the restaurant was located right next door to the parent's residence. It became a home away from home for the entire family.

The restaurant had been open for nearly a year before anyone noticed anything strange about the place. It began when one of the Smith's daughters arrived to open the restaurant early one morning and discovered that the dining room furniture had been rearranged.

Not only had some of the tables been moved from their usual spaces, but the chairs had been arranged on top of the tables instead of on the floor where they should have been. The daughter's first thought was that someone was playing a practical joke on her. Nothing else in the restaurant seemed to be disturbed and the door had been locked when she got there. The restaurant had an alarm system so a break-in was unlikely.

She and her siblings often goofed around with each other and she figured this was their idea of a joke. She put the dining room back together before the customers arrived, not giving the incident too much thought.

When other family members showed up for work, she did mention to one of her brothers that the little prank they pulled had caused her to run late that morning. He swore up and down that he didn't know what she was talking about. When she confronted the rest of the family, they also denied any involvement.

Little did she or the other members know at the time, but the furniture being moved around would turn into a regular occurrence. As it would turn out, that would be the least of their worries.

Soon after the first incident of the dining room being rearranged, the appliances started going bad one by one. First the ovens, which had been purchased new only a year earlier, started malfunctioning. They would blaze hot and burn food or remain cold no matter how long they were on. Food would never come out right. The stove tops would do the same thing. Repairmen were called in and the stoves would work fine for them only to malfunction again as soon as they left.

The refrigeration system also broke down. The Smith's would get in a load of fresh fruits and vegetables and put them away in the cooler only to come in the next day and find everything moldy and unusable. Again, when repairmen checked the system, it worked without a glitch.

Bread also became an impossible item to have on hand. Packages of buns and rolls would mold in a day's time. Meat, their most expensive food product, would be fresh one day and rancid the next.

The stress was taking a toll on the entire family. Business was quickly going downhill. Customers would be turned away because the food supplies on any given day would be spoiled before the first meal was served. The Smiths were losing money on a daily basis. Something was sabotaging their restaurant, but what?

The family also began to worry that they were not alone in the restaurant when they were there after hours. They all report hearing doors slamming and a strange humming sound when there was no one else around.

The final nail in the coffin came when Mr. Smith and one of his sons arrived one morning and found that the glass partition which separated the kitchen area from the dining room had been smashed. Large shards of glass littered the floor. Mr. Smith found it hard to believe that anyone could have broken the divider which was made of a heavy duty, supposedly unbreakable, glass without setting off the alarm or having anyone hear anything. The family lived, literally, a stone's throw away.

The Smith family made the painful decision to shut down the restaurant they had worked so hard to build. Between the lost food products and the property damage, they couldn't afford to run the business any longer. And, since things seemed to be escalating, they didn't want to find out what was in store for them next. They closed the business and moved on to other things.

The family never did find out who, or what, was so determined to run them out of business. They had never had any problems at their home. Whatever it was, it focused solely on the restaurant.

Not wanting to completely give up on their dream, the Smiths have kept the building which once housed their family restaurant in hopes of someday reopening. Their hope is that, given time, whatever destructive force drove them out of business will move on and leave them in peace.

Occasionally, they spend some time in the building that used to be the family business. Sometimes, the visits are to reminisce about the good times they once had there. More often, they are an attempt to determine if the entity that took so much from them is finally gone.

The eldest daughter, who was the source for this story, says that the general consensus among the family members is that the building is not safe. There is a feeling of dread that they can't get past. Perhaps, it is the memories of the strange occurrences and destruction that took place there that still haunts the family, or maybe it is something else, something unexplainable that refuses to share its space with them.

For now, the place that had, at one time, been the site of one family's dream restaurant sits boarded up and empty. Well, perhaps not quite empty. Only time will tell.

Chapter 52:
The Soul Collector

This story is one that is either sheer coincidence, or one of the eeriest tales I've ever heard. It involves a strange bond between a mother and her sons, a bond that, apparently, knew no bounds.

Jeffrey Adler is a forty-three year old man with the mind of a child. His mother had been at an advanced age when she became pregnant with him and the delivery had not been an easy one. She had labored for fourteen torturous hours before the baby was finally delivered. Jeffrey had been deprived of oxygen for a brief period which caused some damage to his brain.

Several medical professionals advised Jeffrey's mother, who was already raising a ten-year old son when Jeffrey was born, to place her brain damaged child in a facility for the mentally infirm, but she steadfastly refused. Her mind had been made up right from the start. She would raise her son and give him as normal a life as possible, no matter what anyone said.

To her great credit, she did a wonderful job raising Jeffrey. She didn't allow his special needs to be an excuse for failure and neither did he. He has some noticeable difficulty with speech, but his mind is sharp and his conversation on point. She taught him well.

By the time Jeffrey was eighteen, he had graduated from a public high school and was already learning a trade. He loved building things and hired on as a laborer at a local construction company. He learned quickly and has made a decent living for himself and his mother for many years.

Jeffrey never left his childhood home. He stayed with his mother, who still helped him with everyday things like cooking and laundry, things that Jeffrey never quite caught on to. She also made sure the bills were paid and that Jeffrey's future would be secure if anything ever happened to her. She wasn't getting any younger and everyone knew, including Jeffrey, that she wouldn't be around forever. Still, when the blow came it was devastating for everyone involved.

Jeffrey's mother had only been feeling ill for a brief time when she visited her doctor. The diagnosis was grim…bone cancer which had spread throughout her body. She had very little time left.

When his mother explained to Jeffrey that she would be leaving soon and that he would have to learn to take care of himself, he more or less understood. He knew that she was sick and accepted, grudgingly, that she would be going to heaven soon.

Jeffrey's brother, who lived in another state and had a family of his own, had put in a request for time off from his job so that he could spend time with his mother before she passed. He was still waiting for an approval from his superiors when word came to him that his mother had died. Now, he had to change the request to one for another sort of leave--bereavement.

Jeffrey had been at his mother's bedside when she passed. They had been holding hands, and even though she hadn't been able to communicate in those final days, he had talked to her for hours on end. He felt that she could still hear him, even if she couldn't respond. He had told her to hang on and wait for his brother, Roger, to arrive so that he could say goodbye. The disease was too advanced and she just didn't have the strength. When the time came, she had to let go.

At least, that's what everyone thought at the time. Almost immediately, Jeffrey began to change. Even though he looked the same and talked the same, he was different. He knew it and so did the friends and neighbors who had gathered around to help him make the arrangements for his mother's burial. They knew that Jeffrey wasn't able to deal with so many details so they all decided to pitch in.

As it turned out, it hadn't been necessary. Jeffrey had taken care of everything without anyone's help. By the time Roger arrived, all of the arrangements had been made.

Some of the mourners took Roger aside to tell him that Jeffrey had begun to behave strangely just after his mother had passed. They had noticed that he had started making references to things that had been said between this person or that person and his mother even though he hadn't been present when the conversations had taken place.

Jeffrey had also taken over all of the household chores, which--try as she might--his mother had never been able to trust him to do. He seemed unable to comprehend the knobs on the appliances or to understand exactly how they operated. All of a sudden, he was an expert at things he hadn't been able to do only days before.

They also noted that he began using phrases that his mother had often used, but that were foreign to him. She prefaced almost everything with the exclamation "By God" no matter what the subject. No one had ever heard Jeffrey use that particular exclamation until after his mother had passed. Now, it flew out of his mouth in every other sentence.

As days passed, Roger took notice of all of the changes in Jeffrey's personality. Roger hadn't lived with his brother for years, but spoke regularly with him on the telephone. Jeffrey had always been soft-spoken. He wasn't one to be brash or loud, ever. He also had a very long fuse and seldom lost his temper.

Their mother, on the other hand, had been a strong woman who had raised two sons by herself, one of whom came with a whole set of challenges she had to face. She didn't suffer fools lightly and she wouldn't hesitate to speak her mind. She was loud and commanded attention everywhere she went.

Now, Jeffrey was behaving just like his mother. Where he had been quiet and reserved, he would now demand to be the center of attention. He would strike up conversations with complete strangers, something his mother did all of the time when she was living, but Jeffrey had always been too self-conscious to attempt.

Roger began to suspect that Jeffrey was trying to take on their mother's personality, perhaps because they had been so close and he missed her. Maybe this was his way of grieving. Whatever it was, it was beginning to bother some of the people around them.

One neighbor, who had been extremely close to Jeffrey's mother, stopped coming around because Jeffrey made her feel so uncomfortable. She told Roger that his brother talked to her about things only she and their mother should have known. They had shared secrets for years and the neighbor was a bit put out that Jeffrey's mother had broken their confidence by sharing what was supposed to be private with Jeffrey.

When Roger asked Jeffrey how he knew so many things about the neighbor, Jeffrey couldn't answer. He told Roger that he didn't know how he knew the things he knew; he just did. He wanted to get all of the new things that were filling his head out, but he didn't know how. Jeffrey told Roger that he was afraid. Something had changed the minute their mother had died.

Jeffrey told Roger that he thought that their mother's soul had entered his body when she died. Roger explained to his brother that such a thing was not possible, but Jeffrey insisted. He said that he had felt something strange as their mother took her last breath. All of a sudden, his mind had been flooded with all sorts of images and thoughts that he didn't understand. He cried when he related the story to his brother. He assured his brother that he didn't know why he was talking and acting like their mother. He wasn't doing it on purpose.

Roger thought a lot about what Jeffrey had told him. He knew it wasn't possible for a living person to house a dead person's soul. What he hadn't told his brother was that, in the last conversation Roger had had with their mother, she had said something that didn't made sense to him at the time.

His mother had told Roger that she knew she would be dead very soon. She also told him that she felt sure he wouldn't make it home in time to say goodbye to her. She wanted to see him one last time, but it wasn't to be. She told Roger that if she could figure out a way, she would hold on until she could spend some time with him, like the old days when they were still a family.

Roger wasn't exactly sure what she meant. He had every intention of making it home in time to say his final goodbyes. He didn't know then that her time was indeed going to be short. She died the following day.

As crazy as it sounded, Roger began to wonder if, somehow, his mother had taken up residence in Jeffrey's body so that she could see Roger one last time. He knew it was a ridiculous notion. He had been home now for days and Jeffrey was still acting strangely. If their mother had just wanted to see Roger one last time, she could have done that by now. Even so, everything about Jeffrey now reminded Roger more of his mother than his brother.

Their mother always had a nervous habit of clearing her throat when she talked. She did it without being aware of it herself, but everyone else noticed it. Now, Jeffrey was doing the same thing. One other odd habit she had was laughing after she had said something that wasn't remotely funny. It was a nervous tic that she didn't seem to do on purpose; it just happened. Jeffrey had never done either one of those things until now.

Roger decided to test his theory. He had to be heading back to his own home soon and he wanted to try something. He sat down with Jeffrey and held his brother's hands. He looked deep into Jeffrey's eyes and spoke to their mother.

He told her that he was sorry that he hadn't been with her when she passed. He told her that he loved her and that he was glad they had been able to spend the last few days together. But, he told her, he had to go home and so did she.

Roger told his mother that it wasn't fair for her to stay any longer. Jeffrey had his own life to live and she would be taking that away if she remained. He asked her to move on to whatever was waiting for her in the next life. He asked her to let Jeffrey be Jeffrey.

And, just like that, Jeffrey began to cry and all of the tension he had been holding onto for days vanished. He hugged his brother and they talked, for the first time since Roger had been in town, as two brothers who had lost their mother. Jeffrey was, once again, the person he had been before their mother passed.

Jeffrey went back to being the mild-mannered, hard worker who everyone knew and loved. The brashness was gone, as were the strange mannerisms and tics that had put everyone off. Things went back to normal.

Roger went back to his home and family, though he and his brother speak on the telephone regularly. Jeffrey still works and lives on his own, except for weekly visits from a helper who makes sure that the house is kept up and the bills are paid.

Did Jeffrey's mother's soul really enter her son's body so that she could make up for lost time with Roger? Surely, such a thing can't be possible. Even so, how else does one explain the many changes in Jeffrey? Did he take on his mother's personality and mannerisms out of grief? Had the whole thing just been a series of coincidences? Or, is it possible that a mother's determination to see her son one last time can transcend everything, including death?

Chapter 53:
Black As Night

This account is one that came my way recently and has not been featured in any of my previous books. Christy Potts, of Pittsburgh Pennsylvania, is the source of this chilling tale.

Having spent many a summer vacation with my family at my grandmother's spooky old house in the hollows of West Virginia, I relate to this story all too well. Christy's experiences are remarkably similar to mine except for the fact that she and her family actually saw the person, or what had at one time been a person, who was terrorizing them.

Christy's grandparents lived on a farm in rural Pennsylvania. Whereas my grandmother's home had been small and a bit rundown and antiquated, this property was sprawling and modern--at least for that time period. It consisted of the main family home as well as a large barn and a garage that housed the farm equipment.

The first time Christy can recall noticing something strange at her grandparent's house was one day when she and her little brother were playing in the yard next to the barn. The family kept a few cows which roamed during the day and spent their nights in the barn. This occurrence was in the afternoon when the cows were grazing.

As she and her brother were running in the yard and playing whatever game they had come up with that day, they were suddenly aware that something was in the barn. They could hear the stall doors being opened and closed, one after the other. Thinking that it was their grandpa cleaning out the stalls, they went back to playing.

Again, their play was interrupted by the sound of someone in the barn, but this time whoever was in there was wreaking havoc. They could hear what sounded like the slop buckets being hurled against the walls. Curious, they opened the barn door to take a peek inside.

Sure enough, the buckets were haphazardly lying on the floor, as well as the tools that their grandpa usually kept hung on the walls. They looked around for their grandpa, who they called "Pap," but he wasn't there. No one was.

Christy and her brother ran out to the field, where their Pap was working and told him that someone had been in the barn. He told them to never mind, he'd see to it later. Christy didn't understand her grandpa's dismissive attitude, but as long as she and her brother didn't get the blame, she didn't care. She and her brother went back to playing and the incident was not spoken of again.

That same night, while the family was eating supper, they could hear the cows carrying on loudly in the barn. They sounded panicked and Pap and Christy's father ran out to check on them. When they came back inside and returned to the table, they didn't say a word about what they had seen. When Christy's grandma asked if everything was alright, Pap just nodded and continued eating. The subject was not discussed any further.

Later on, during that same visit, Christy remembers being in the yard again only this time she was alone. She was digging with some of her grandparent's gardening tools when something stopped her cold. She suddenly sensed that someone was standing very close to her. She could feel their eyes upon her and, whoever it was, they were seething with anger.

Christy says that she was too frightened for a moment to look up. The rage from whoever was standing beside her was palpable. When she did get the courage to raise her eyes, there was no one there. She knew, without a doubt, that someone had been standing there. You know when someone is beside you, and this person had given her such a bad feeling, there was no mistaking it.

When she told her mother what had happened in the yard, her mom didn't seem surprised. She just told Christy that if it ever happened again, she would be alright, just come into the house. It was kind of a relief for her that her mother didn't tell her she was imagining things, but strange that she accepted it without question.

On another visit to the house, Christy was picking flowers in the field for her mom and grandma when she, again, felt the malevolent presence that she had encountered that day in the yard months earlier. She decided to do as her mother had told her and get inside the house.

Whoever was in the field with her was angry, she could feel their eyes boring into her. She started out walking toward the main house before feeling the sudden urge to run. The thing that was so furious with her was walking very close behind her. She felt that if she stopped, whatever it was would crash right into her. But she didn't stop, she kept running as fast as her legs could take her.

As soon as she reached the front porch, the thing, so filled with rage, that had been following her was gone. The horrible feeling that had surrounded Christy lifted and it was as though a storm had passed.

She ran into the house, crying, and told her mother and grandmother about the thing that had chased her from the field all the way into the house. They were quiet for a moment and then Christy's grandmother suggested that she go wash her face and calm down. She told the girl that she had gotten too much sun. Christy did as she was told, but she knew better, it hadn't been the heat that had frightened her. There had been someone in the field with her that day. She just wasn't able to see who it was.

A couple of days later, Christy was outside helping her Pap with his chores when he sent her inside to fetch him something to drink. As she was approaching the house, she saw someone standing in the shadows at the corner of the garage.

The person was wearing men's work clothes, but had long hair. As Christy grew closer to where the person was standing, the solitary figure stepped out of the shadows. It was a woman with messy hair and filthy clothes. Christy had never seen the woman before, but the terrible waves of anger that emanated from her were very familiar. Christy had felt them before, first in the yard and then again in the field.

The woman's face was normal except for her eyes, which Christy says were as black as coal. She could see nothing in them except for hollow darkness. The woman began walking towards Christy, one arm outstretched.

Christy ran screaming into the house. Her grandmother immediately came to her aid, asking her what in the world was the matter. When Christy told her about the woman by the garage, her grandmother finally broke down and told her granddaughter what she knew about the angry presence Christy had been seeing around the farm.

It turned out that Christy wasn't the only one who had encountered the spiteful spirit over the years. Farmhands and family alike had seen her, usually around the barn or in the fields, for decades.

Anyone who did have the misfortune of seeing the woman or feeling her presence, reported basically the same thing. They would be overcome with a feeling of dread as though a dark cloud was hanging over them. Sometimes they would actually see the source of their horror. It was a woman, usually dressed in men's clothing. If she was in the barn, she would be destroying equipment or slamming the stall doors. If in the yard, she would usually just stand and stare at whoever happened to be nearby.

If anyone dared to look back at her, she would begin walking towards them, usually with one or both arms outstretched. No one had ever stayed around to see what would happen if she actually made contact. The overwhelming feeling of doom that surrounded her made them run before she reached them. Whoever she was, her rage was intense. She exuded it from every part of her being.

The other thing that everyone who reported having seen the woman agreed upon was that her eyes were otherworldly. They were as black as night, just two deep hollow places where eyes should have been, but weren't. Even so, there was no doubt that she could see. Christy attests to the fact that the woman looked right at her before walking towards her that day by the barn.

Christy's grandmother went on to tell her that Christy's own mother had seen the woman many times while growing up on the farm. The woman never aged or changed in any discernable way. Months would go by and sometimes even years with no one seeing her, and then she would reappear and stay around for a time before vanishing once again.

The visitations were such an unpredictable occurrence that Christy's grandparents just tried to ignore the woman, only acknowledging her existence when a terrified farm worker or visitor would unwittingly encounter her, usually in the fields.

She was unhappy and obviously destructive; they had seen the results of her fury in the barn on many occasions. That being said, in the many years that she had haunted the place, she hadn't harmed any of the people or animals on the farm.

The one thing that made the whole thing bearable was that the woman was never known to enter the main house. No one had ever reported seeing her inside the residence in the many years she had haunted the property. As long as she stayed outside, they would tolerate her.

The fact that she seemed to take most of her anger out on the barn and its contents made Christy's grandparents suspect that something had happened there long before they bought the place. They attempted to research the history of the land to determine if perhaps someone had been killed in a riding accident or other farm tragedy, but they had no luck.

Christy accepted the story her grandmother told her that day. She continued to feel the woman's presence on the farm for years afterwards, though she never actually saw her again. Her grandmother passed away a few years ago, but her Pap continues to reside at the family farm.

Someday, the farm and its angry resident spirit will be passed down to her mother and then to Christy and her brother. When I asked her what she would do if that happened she hesitated before answering. "We'll see," was all she could say. "We'll see."

Chapter 54:
The Midnight Caller

Mary Parsons had always thought of herself as a level-headed woman. She had worked for nearly twelve years as an executive assistant to a very well-to-do accountant in a suburb of Richmond, Virginia. She had been raising her son as a single parent since her divorce in early 1993. Nothing in her life up to that point could have prepared her for the unusual events that would befall her beginning in late 1996 and continuing for over a year and a half. During that time, her sanity would be questioned and her faith in everything she held dear would be tested. She couldn't know it then, but it would all begin innocently enough with a late night phone call.

It was around Thanksgiving, 1996 that Mary's nightmare began. She was sitting in her living room reading a book that had been an early Christmas gift from her mother. It was nearing midnight and her eyes were getting tired, so she decided to turn in for the night. Just as she was getting up from the sofa, the telephone rang.

Mary's heart sank instantly. No one ever called at this late hour unless they were the bearers of bad news. Hesitantly, she picked up the receiver and said "Hello?" There was no response from the other end of the line, except for static. There was obviously a bad connection so she repeated "Hello?" Once again, she received no answer from the late night caller.

Assuming that it was either a wrong number or a prank call, Mary hung up the phone. She glanced at the clock that sat on her living room mantle and noted that it was exactly midnight. Not giving the mysterious phone call another thought, she turned off the lights and went to bed. For reasons unknown to her at the time, Mary tossed and turned all night, unable to sleep for more than an hour or two at a time.

The following morning, Mary was up before nine to make preparations for the busy day ahead of her. Her ex-husband would be arriving to pick up their son for a few days' stay at his home for the holidays. Mary was then planning to spend the afternoon Christmas shopping with her sister. That evening, she was having dinner with a man she had been dating for several weeks. She had a full day and many things to do.

As Mary was preparing breakfast for her son, there was a knock at her front door. Packages that she had ordered from various catalogs had been arriving at the house on a regular basis, so Mary assumed that this was another early morning delivery.

When she opened the door expecting to see the familiar delivery man sporting his brown uniform, she instead found herself looking into the tearful face of her sister, Kay. Knowing immediately that something was terribly wrong, Mary blurted out the first thing that came to her mind, "I don't want to know". She can't explain why she said those words, she just knew that bad news was coming and she wasn't ready to hear it.

Kay was so distraught that she was barely coherent as she broke the news to Mary that their mother had died sometime during the night. Mary didn't believe her. It couldn't be true. Kay explained that she had just come from their mother's home. There was no mistake. This was real. Their emotions were all over the place from shock to grief and even a pang of guilt.

Their mother was a headstrong woman who had insisted on living in her own home, unassisted, even though she was well into her eighties. However, to ease her daughters' minds, she had worked out a system with a neighbor who lived across the street. She would open her living room curtains every morning at seven o'clock. If the curtains were still closed after seven, something was wrong and the neighbor had been told to call either Mary or Kay immediately so they could go check on their mom. Their fear was that she would fall during the night and this was a way that she could remain independent, but still have some safeguards.

Kay explained to Mary, that on this morning, the neighbor had reported that the curtains had not opened at the usual time. Worried, he had phoned Kay who lived only minutes from their mother's home. When she arrived at the house, she knocked on the door, but her mother didn't answer. Kay then let herself in.

Kay can still recall the eerie silence in the house...it was deafening. As she walked slowly through the hallway, calling out to her mother, she knew that something was very wrong. When she reached the doorway of her mother's bedroom, her worst fears were confirmed. Her mother was still lying in her bed, her head and one arm hanging off to the side just slightly. It was an unnatural position and Kay knew that her mother was gone.

Rushing to her mother's bedside, Kay frantically looked for any signs of life. Her mother was cold to the touch, a cold like no other that Kay had ever felt before. The woman who had seen both of her daughters through so many hard times had died alone.

After phoning for an ambulance, Kay waited there, holding her mother's hand, until help arrived. Emergency workers, and then a coroner, took turns asking questions and examining the body. They surmised that she had died from a heart attack or perhaps a stroke in her sleep. Nothing was disturbed in the house. It didn't appear that she had left her bed once she had lain down for the night. The coroner estimated that she had been dead anywhere from eight to twelve hours. Everything was pretty straightforward. An elderly woman had died in her sleep. They saw it all of the time.

After what seemed like an eternity to Kay, they took her mother's body away. It now fell on her to tell her sister what had happened. Mary was even closer to their mother than Kay had been and she knew that the news would be devastating. It was with a heavy heart that she made the drive to her little sister's house. She knew that their lives would never be the same from that morning on. She couldn't know at the time how right she would be.

Instead of spending the day shopping, as they had planned, the sister's instead made funeral arrangements. They called relatives far and wide and told them of the tragedy that had befallen the family.

Mary's son was too young to fully understand why his mother and aunt were so sad. Mary had explained to him that his grandma had gone to Heaven. Not wanting to expose him to any more grief than necessary, she put on a fake smile and helped him pack for his visit with his father.

After her son had been picked up, Mary and Kay spent the rest of the afternoon talking about old times. It was during this conversation that Mary suddenly remembered the phone call she had received the night before. Now, she wondered if perhaps her mother had tried to call her daughter for help, but hadn't been able to speak. Maybe, she had been the mysterious midnight caller.

The sisters decided to drive over to their mother's house to see if they could piece together what might have happened during that fateful night. Again, the eerie silence in the house made Kay, and this time Mary, uneasy. They searched the house looking for any sign that something was amiss.

Their mother's only telephone was located on the wall in the kitchen. It was still on its cradle. They doubted that their mother could have made a call from that phone, especially if she was having a heart attack, and then put it back in its proper place before making her way into the bedroom and climbing under the covers. It didn't add up. They felt sure that she had not been the source of the hang-up call the previous night. It wouldn't be easy, but there was nothing to do except to chalk the call up to a wrong number, bury their mother and move on with their lives.

Mary made it through the holidays with support from her remaining family and friends, as well as her new beau. It had been hard, but she had come to terms with the loss of her mother. Mary vowed that 1997 would be a year of change for her and all for the better. She would focus on her career, raising her son and perhaps even remarrying if the opportunity were to arise.

Three months into the new year, Mary was roused from a deep sleep by the sound of her bedside telephone ringing. Half asleep, she answered, mumbling something close to "Hello?" Only the sound of static greeted her from the other end of the line. Now, fully awake, Mary sat upright in bed. She grasped the phone tightly and, again, said "Hello?" Just as had been the case months earlier, no one spoke. The static continued to crackle on the line before the call abruptly ended.

Immediately, Mary was gripped by a feeling of dread. Gathering her senses, she dialed *69 in hopes that she could find out who had placed the call. The number was anonymous. Unable to go back to sleep, Mary tossed and turned the rest of the night. She did notice one thing before she lay back down after hanging up the telephone...the digital alarm clock that sat on her nightstand informed her that it was now 12:06. This meant that the time of the anonymous call had been right around midnight just as it had been three months prior.

Mary was on pins and needles the following day, sure that bad news was on the way. This time, there was no early morning knock on the door, and that eased her mind slightly. She got her son off to school and went to work for the day, still apprehensive, but hoping that she was just overreacting. Nothing out of the ordinary happened. They both made it home safely at the end of the day. Mary breathed a sigh of relief as they sat down at the dinner table that evening. The storm had passed.

As she and her son were going over the events of their respective days, the phone rang. Since they were in the middle of their meal, Mary let the answering machine pick up. Whatever it was, it could wait until they had finished eating.

Later on, while her son was in his room doing his homework, Mary remembered the call. She played the message on the machine. It was from her ex-husband. He sounded solemn and a bit down as he asked her to please give him a call as soon as possible. Figuring that he was cancelling his weekend visit with their son, something he had done frequently in the past when business took him away unexpectedly, Mary dialed his number.

When her ex answered the phone, Mary could tell immediately that something was wrong. His voice broke as he spoke. He told her that he had been feeling under the weather for a while and had finally seen his doctor. He went on the tell Mary that he had been diagnosed with lymphoma, a cancer of the lymphatic system.

Mary didn't know what to say. Her ex-husband had always been healthy. He stayed in shape, ate right, didn't smoke and only drank on special occasions. She was stunned at the news that he was now battling cancer.

Composing herself, Mary tried to reassure her ex that he would be fine. He wasn't so sure. The cancer was stage three. He would have to immediately begin treatment. He told her that he would be fighting for his life. He also told her that he didn't want their son to know. He wanted life to go on as if nothing was wrong for as long as possible.

They spoke for a while longer, making a few changes in their visitation schedules, before her ex asked to speak to their son. Mary took the phone into the boy's room and then left him alone so he could talk to his dad.

Mary couldn't help but make the connection between the bizarre phone call she had received and the news that her son's father had just been diagnosed with this devastating disease. She told herself that she was being ridiculous, but it certainly had been a strange coincidence.

Again, Mary let the memory of the midnight caller fade into the past as she dealt with the immediate stresses of her life. She was working full-time, raising her son alone while her ex-husband underwent cancer treatments, trying to maintain a relationship with her new beau; all the while still grieving the loss of her mother. These were not good times and Mary's nerves were constantly on edge.

Nearly a month to the day of the last midnight call, Mary was again sound asleep when the silence of the night was interrupted by the telephone's loud ring. Wide awake at once, Mary hesitated before answering. She knew from experience that there wouldn't be anyone on the line, but she forced herself to pick up the receiver anyway.

Just as she had feared, the only sound on the other end of the telephone line was static. It seemed even louder than before as it assaulted her ear. Her mind was at a breaking point as she yelled into the phone "Who is this?" time and time again. There was no reply. The static continued for a few moments and then, just as it had on the two prior occasions, the line went dead.

Mary's mind was racing. Who would it be this time? Her son, or maybe her sister? She didn't know, but she was sure that bad news was on the way. Mary didn't know who was placing these calls or where they were coming from, but she did know one thing for sure, they were a warning to her that something terrible was either happening at that moment or about to happen. There was nothing left for her to do but wait for the inevitable.

Sure enough, the next morning when Mary went into work, she was met by chaos and panic. The accountant she had worked for, and respected, for so many years had been charged with embezzling funds from dozens of clients over the years. Investigators from the state were going through all of his files and seizing computers when Mary walked into the office.

Even though she had been his right arm for years, Mary had no inkling that this man, a respected member of the community, had been doing anything illegal. Her surprise and disappointment soon turned to worry when she was informed that she, too, was under suspicion.

After being questioned on numerous occasions by investigators, Mary was finally cleared of any wrongdoing. Although that was a huge relief and a burden lifted off her already fragile shoulders, there was still one glaring problem: she was now out of a job. The accountant would be facing a trial and, most likely, jail time. His days as a businessman were over and he had taken her down with him.

The economic times were tough and finding a new job that paid as well as her old one was not easy. Mary sent resumes to as many places as she could think of, but she had very little success. When she was fortunate enough to be granted an interview, she would ultimately be passed over for the job. She feared that the misdeeds of her previous boss had tarnished her reputation in the eyes of potential employers.

With bills piling up and no income coming in, Mary ended up taking a job as a clerk in a local department store. The job paid only a fraction of what she had been earning, but it was better than nothing and it might be enough to keep her head above water until something better came along.

Several months went by as Mary tried to sort out her life. She had moved up to head cashier in a very short amount of time and was hired on full-time at her new job. She actually enjoyed the work and decided to stick with it for the time being. Her ex-husband had responded well to his treatments and, although he was tired most of the time, he seemed to be making a recovery. Mary was still dating the same man and they had become nearly inseparable. Things seemed to be improving for Mary and she allowed herself to relax and stop worrying about the bad luck that seemed to be plaguing her.

And then it happened, it had been several months since any bad news had come her way when Mary was awakened, once again, by a call at precisely midnight. This time her boyfriend, who was now her fiancé, was in bed beside her when the call came in. Mary roused him from his sleep and asked him to answer the phone.

When Mary's fiancé picked up the receiver and said 'hello', he looked puzzled and handed the phone to Mary. She could hear, even before putting the receiver to her ear, the loud buzzing sound coming from the other end of the line. Static was still blaring as Mary hung up the phone.

She hadn't mentioned anything to her fiancé, or anyone else, about the strange calls until now. Her fiancé listened quietly as Mary told him the story of the mysterious calls that always seemed to precede bad news. Just wait and see, she warned him, tomorrow something awful will happen. To Mary's surprise, he didn't ask any questions or scoff at the notion. He just shrugged and turned off the light. Mary thought his response was odd, but she didn't say anything. Instead, she lay in the dark staring at the ceiling. Bad news was coming, she was sure of it.

Mary, her son and her fiancé had planned a trip to a local park the next day. They were going to have a picnic and let the boy play on the swings while they enjoyed the warmth of summer. Everything went off without a hitch, in spite of the phone call. That is until they were driving home that evening. It was still light out as they made their way through traffic. There had been an accident on the four-lane that led to their home and cars were backed up in every direction.

After everything had been sorted out and the policemen on the scene began directing traffic, Mary's fiancé drove past the gnarled up cars that had been involved in the accident. Ambulances had already taken the people who had been in the cars to the hospital, but the vehicles remained in the street. Mary wasn't sure, but one of the cars looked very much like her ex-husband's. It couldn't be, he had returned to work not long before and was away on business. She had spoken to him a few days prior and he wasn't due home until the following week. All the same, she would call him when she got home to make sure everything was alright.

Once the family got settled in for the evening, Mary placed the call to her ex-husband. He carried his phone with him at all times, but he didn't answer. She didn't want to make too much of it, he was a busy man and probably was having a business dinner. She would try him again later.

It was later that night when Mary received a phone call from her former father-in-law. His voice was barely audible as he broke the news to Mary. His son, Mary's ex-husband and the father of her child, had been killed in a car accident earlier that day. He had, apparently, been on his way to Mary's house to pay a surprise visit to his son. Mary was devastated. She can't remember what she said or how the conversation ended. She was numb.

A million things ran through Mary's mind. In the years since their divorce, he had never--not once--ever just dropped by to see their son. It was completely out of character for him. She also couldn't get over the fact that he had battled cancer, and was winning, only to lose his life in a traffic accident. Worst of all, she would now have to break the news to her son that he would never see his father again.

Before telling her son, Mary told her fiancé what had happened. He looked somber, but said nothing for a few moments. Finally, he spoke. He told Mary that his family had come from Armenia when he was just a child. He had been brought up to believe that everything was predestined. Nothing happens in this life that has not already been planned someplace else. He didn't expect her to understand, but he thought that the phone calls were coming from that place.

Mary knew it was crazy, but she found herself believing that what her fiancé was telling her could be possible. How else could she explain the phone calls, with no one on the other end, always coming the night before a tragedy? But, she wondered, why was this happening now? And, why was she the victim of these foreboding calls?

She asked these questions aloud to her fiancé. He couldn't say for sure. He did tell her that he believed that loved ones who had passed on were capable of contacting those who were still living. He also felt that they were aware of things that were going happen in the future and could warn those they left behind, although they usually didn't. Not everyone who crosses over to the other side wants to meddle in the lives of the living, but some do. The calls weren't causing bad luck, he reasoned, the events that followed would have happened anyway.

Mary's fiancé explained to her that this was not a bad thing. He told her that he was raised to believe that people who had passed on to the afterlife could then see everything that had ever happened and everything that would ever happen. Someone was staying one step ahead of Mary's future, but was only choosing to warn of the bad, not the good.

They sat together long into the night and went over all of the people in Mary's life who had passed away. They narrowed it down to an aunt on her father's side who had died a few months before the first midnight call. She and Mary had never been very close, but they had a cordial relationship. The only reason Mary suspected her to be the source of the calls was the fact that she was, for lack of a better term, a busy body.

Mary could see her aunt going out of her way to interject herself into situations that she really should stay out of. Maybe she thought that she was helping Mary, but that was not the case. No one wants to get bad news, but it happens to everyone. Having tragic events be preceded by static-filled phone calls at midnight didn't help the situation.

Mary realized that she had experienced more tragedies in her life than most. Her father had died in an accident at work when she was a child. An infant brother had died in his crib and she never did find out what happened to him. Mary had lost many friends over the years to disease, accidents and suicide. Horrible events mar everyone's lives. The phone calls were the only thing that set Mary apart from most.

Her fiancé suggested that she have a priest bless her house, including her telephones, and that she also have him speak to her aunt. If it wasn't the aunt making the calls, it wouldn't hurt anything. If it was her, then she might be convinced that she was doing more harm than good and move on to other activities in the hereafter.

Mary hadn't attended church in years so her fiancé arranged for a local priest to come to Mary's house and say the blessing. The priest had been informed of the calls and of the suspected source. Whether he believed them or not, the priest said a prayer for Mary, her son and her fiancé. He then blessed the house. The holy man also spoke to whoever was contacting Mary from beyond. He implored them to cease interfering in the lives of the living and to leave the family in peace.

Months passed without incident. Mary and her fiancé married, her son gave the bride away. All of the deaths and loss that had dragged Mary to the depths of despair had not broken her. Even though her young son grieved for his father and feels his loss to this day, he accepted Mary's new husband into his life and they have a loving relationship that any father and son would envy. He has grown into a fine man and has recently made Mary and her husband grandparents.

Even though Mary's life has highs and lows like everyone else's, the darker events are no longer preceded by late night telephone calls from places unknown. She lives her life day to day, taking the good and the bad as it comes…just as it is meant to be. That is, when those from the other side keep fate's secrets to themselves.

Chapter 55:
The Long Goodbye

My relationship with my father was always a tricky one. On the one hand, we were family and we loved each other. On the other, we were two very different people who butted heads more often than not. Growing up in that environment was not necessarily good for either one of us, but we eventually got past it.

Once I was an adult, a married woman with a family of my own, my father and I came to an understanding. The past was the past. We both would do things differently, in regards to our relationship, if we could. We let bygones be bygones and lived our lives in the present instead of the past.

My father was a great cheerleader for my writing career. He read my books and loved each and every one of them. He even contributed a few stories that I went on to include in earlier volumes of this series, among others. Every time I talked with him, which was about every month or so, he would ask when my next book was coming out. He was a fan.

In early September, 2016, my sister called me to let me know that our dad had fallen in the home he shared with his second wife—our parents had divorced over twenty years earlier. He was being taken by ambulance to a nearby hospital. It was nothing major, he was just being taken in for observation since he was eighty-six years old and had banged up his face pretty badly.

Thinking that my father would be in and out of the hospital in a day or so, I waited until the following day to pay him a visit. I hadn't seen him in person for nearly three months and I was shocked by his appearance.

My father had always been thin but he was, literally, skin and bones. His face was black and blue. He was happy to see me and he seemed coherent. We spoke for a while. They were running a lot of tests and x-rays on him. He was annoyed and just wanted to go home. His wife was nowhere to be found, so I wasn't sure why he was still in the hospital when he just wanted to leave.

Every day, I would hear that he was going to be released and then everything would change. They wouldn't let him return home because he was now suffering from pneumonia. He was getting weaker by the minute and, worse still, he didn't even know me half the time when I would visit.

As I watched my dad deteriorate in the hospital, I couldn't help but to reflect on the last few months leading up to the fall. My father had been a career law enforcement officer. He loved being a trooper and then a corporal in the West Virginia State Police. He told me often that he had seen things I would not believe in his years serving the people as a policeman. He asked me on many occasions to come out to his house and sit down with him so that he could tell me his life story. My father wanted his daughter, the writer, to pen his biography.

For reasons I will never fully understand, I balked. It is to my great shame, and everlasting regret, that I didn't take him up on his offer. I made excuse after excuse as to why there just weren't enough hours in the day to make the trip to his home and record his stories.

Part of me thinks that by writing down my dad's life, that would mean that it was at an end. We were finally in such a good place as father and daughter that I didn't want it to be over...not yet. Also, I always thought that there would be time. Even though he was in his late-eighties, my father was still relatively healthy. He wasn't suffering from any terminal illnesses. I would write his memoirs some other day--or week--or month, but not now.

And then, just like that, he went into the hospital for routine treatment after falling in his bedroom and never came home--at least not in life. I received the call from my sister during the second week of our father's hospital stay. He had died six days before his eighty-seventh birthday.

I can't begin to describe the aching pain that immediately settled in the pit of my stomach. It was as though grief, sadness, regret, loss and shame all united and decided to wage an assault on my gut. The pain was terrible and it would not go away. I didn't feel like eating or talking or doing anything. I just wanted to be left alone.

This went on for nearly a week. I cried until I couldn't cry anymore, but it didn't help. The pain never subsided for even a second. I could barely stand, the ache was so acute. Finally, I asked for help from the one person I knew could send me some relief from my terrible ache: my dad.

I had always heard that our loved ones who have passed on can, sometimes, return to us in dreams. This is when our minds are most at ease and open to anything and everything. So, before falling asleep, about eight days after my father died, I asked him to come to me. I needed to see him one more time and talk to him. I was ready to hear any story he wanted to share. I would take anything. Just, please, talk to me. These were my words to my father. I hoped that, wherever he was, he could hear me.

When I woke up the next morning, nothing had changed. The pain in my stomach was as bad as ever. It just felt like the worst kind of emptiness you can imagine. The dream theory hadn't worked for me. I wondered what I was supposed to do now.

That night, I was sitting on the couch watching a movie with my husband when I began to doze off. It was somewhere between being awake and asleep that I saw my father for the first time since his death. He was standing in our driveway beside a red truck. He had a huge smile on his face and was looking right at me and my family. What made the vision so real to me was his attire. He was wearing a fishing vest, a fisherman's hat with hooks in it and he was holding a fishing pole.

No one on God's green earth loved fishing as much as my dad. It was his passion for as long as I can remember. And, there he was, happy as could be, decked out next to his truck getting ready to go fishing.

I opened my eyes and just sat there on the couch, trying to remember every detail of what I'd just seen. It was beautiful and seeing him smiling was the greatest feeling in the world. Unfortunately, he hadn't spoken to me. The familiar ache was still there. Nothing about that had changed. Maybe the vision had just been wishful thinking, who knows?

That same night, I asked my dad again to visit me in my sleep. I needed to know that he was alright and that he held no hard feelings toward me. It might seem selfish, but I just wanted him to know that I loved him and I needed his love in return.

I woke up the next morning feeling wonderful. I can't describe the euphoria I felt upon opening my eyes and facing the new day. The pain was completely gone. But, much more than that, I felt as though I was walking on air.

I knew, without a shadow of a doubt, that I had spent the night talking to my father.

What was spoken between us in my dream state, I'll never know. I recall seeing my dad's face. I know he was there, but that's all. Whatever he said to me, it made everything alright. Honestly, I feel only a warm sense of love and bonhomie when I think of my father now. Not a smidgen of regret. He took it all away. Believe it or don't…my father gave me the wonderful gift of total forgiveness and undying love as only a father could do.

I wasn't the only one grieving the loss of our father. My sister and brother were both coping in their own ways. My brother, who was the closest of all of us to our dad, is not one to share his feelings so he kept to himself and I respect that.

My sister went about her days making funeral arrangements along with my father's widow. She kept busy so that she wouldn't have to deal with grief head-on. She knew that, sooner or later, she would give in, but the time wasn't now.

A little over a month after our father's death, my sister bought a new flat-screen television for her bedroom. The old set had not been moved in years and it was so bulky she had to rock it back and forth in order to slide it off of the chest of drawers on which it sat. It was what she found underneath the bulky set that sent her reeling.

There, among the dust bunnies and other bits of refuse that had gathered under and around the spot where the television had been, she saw three coins. Unlike everything else in the vicinity, they were shiny and looked like they had just been placed there. When she picked them up and examined them, she noticed immediately that they weren't just any coins…these were special in more ways than one.

The three shiny quarters were bicentennial. This might not be significant to most people, but it had a deeper meaning for our family. My father had been collecting bicentennial quarters since they first started becoming popular forty years prior. Many a day was spent with our family sitting around counting my dad's collection of bicentennial quarters. We would arrange them and stack them up for him. He even had special commemorative cases to keep his cache safe. They were only quarters, but he loved them. He was overjoyed anytime a new one would come his way.

My sister knew that my dad had not been in that room for years. There was no way he had placed those coins there when he was alive. It couldn't have happened. My sister didn't collect them. Only our father had been enamored of the collectible quarters and we all knew it.

She took this as a sign from our dad that everything was good. He was doing fine and still up to his old tricks. He knew that she would know what the coins represented, a father who couldn't depart for places unknown without first leaving behind something for her to remember him by, three of his cherished bicentennial quarters, one for each of the children he had loved in this life and would continue to love in the next.

Chapter 56:
A Dancer's Final Act

Susan Spencer remembers her sister, Sara, as the hub around which her family revolved. Sara was the middle child of three, but she was the youngest girl and everyone adored her. With a smile that lit up a room and a fiery determination that could not be denied, this girl was special and everyone knew it.

Sara had wanted to be a dancer ever since anyone who knew her can remember. They laugh and say that she could dance before she could walk. At the age of five, her parents enrolled her in her first professional dance classes. Their daughter never looked back. She was a dancer and always would be.

By the time that she was in her mid-teens, Sara was such a prodigy that she was the featured dancer in nearly all of the dance school's performances. She lit up the stage whenever she showcased her talent. People couldn't take their eyes off of this obviously gifted performer. Sara was telling her family that she would pursue a career in the performing arts. Someday, they would see her name in lights.

After graduating from high school, Sara decided to make the move from her family's home in West Chester, Pennsylvania to the metropolis of New York City. That is where her star would truly shine. She was young and beautiful besides being one of the best dancers anyone had ever seen. She knew that once talent scouts and agents saw her, she would be famous in no time.

Sara's family tried to talk her out of the move. They agreed that she had a unique talent, but urged her to stay close to home for a while. She could study dance in college, get a degree and then try her luck in the big city.

Sara wouldn't hear of it. She was career oriented and didn't want to spend time in school when she could be honing her craft on stage. No amount of pleading from her parents could sway her. They worried about their naïve young daughter. She had led a relatively sheltered life and had no idea how dangerous the world could be for someone so trusting.

In the end, there was nothing they could do other than to see her off on her new adventure. They made sure that she was taken care of financially, at least until she found a job. So, with that, they reluctantly let their daughter find her way in the world. She assured them that she would be alright.

Susan remembers seeing her sister drive away that day, her hand waving out the car window as she disappeared around a corner. She couldn't have been happier for her baby sister. Even so, for reasons she can't explain, Susan walked back into the house with her parents and burst into tears. She knew, in her gut, that she would never see Sara again.

Sara soon began reporting back to her sister that paying jobs for dancers were not easy to come by. She was going to as many auditions as she could, but she had only received a handful of callbacks. Sara was still hopeful that her career as a dancer would happen. It was just going to take more time than she had hoped.

Sara also had a secret. She confided in Susan that she had taken a job in an upscale after hours club as a stage dancer. She danced topless, but none of the patrons had any physical contact with her. She was embarrassed, but she had bills to pay and the money was excellent. She would quit once she started getting paid for her theater work.

Sara made Susan promise that she wouldn't tell their parents. She hadn't wanted them to worry about her. Susan agreed. The idea of her little sister dancing topless in front of a roomful of strange men did worry her, to say the least. She asked Sara if there was security and her sister assured her that there was. She told Susan that she needn't worry. She could take care of herself. Unfortunately, Susan believed her.

Susan spoke to her sister every few days over the following months and nothing out of the ordinary seemed to be happening in her life. She had landed a few off, off, off Broadway shows and she was busy rehearsing while at the same time holding down her lucrative job at the gentleman's club. Even though Sara acted like everything was fine, Susan could tell that something wasn't right. When she mentioned her suspicions to her sister, Sara finally told her what was troubling her.

A man who was a regular at the club had been harassing Sara over the past few weeks. He asked her out on several occasions, but she had declined. Something about him was creepy and, besides, she had already made up her mind to never date any of the patrons of the strip club.

Susan didn't think that this sounded like a big deal and she told her sister so. Sara agreed, except that she said that his persistence was beginning to frighten her. She was afraid to walk out to her car alone after her show. On more than one occasion, he had been waiting in the parking lot for her. He knew which car was hers and would be leaning against it when she exited the building. As soon as he saw that she was being escorted out, he would get into his vehicle and speed away, tires squealing.

Again, Susan cautioned her baby sister to be careful. She also told her to call the police if this guy didn't stop bothering her. Sara assured her that she would. That was the last phone call that the sisters would share. A short time later, Sara would be a missing person and Susan would be left wondering if her sister had identified a suspect during that last call.

A week went by and then two without a word from Sara. No one in the family had heard from her. They had all been calling her for days, but she never picked up her phone. Worry was beginning to consume each one of them.

Only Susan knew about Sara's job as a topless dancer. She was also the only one in the family who was aware that her sister was being harassed by one of the patrons. Without telling her parents, Susan drove to New York to check on Sara. She was hoping that all was well and that her sister's busy schedule had simply made her lose track of time.

Upon arriving in the city, Susan went straight to her sister's apartment, but no one answered her persistent knocks on the door. She then made a trip to the club where her sister said that she had been working as a dancer. They weren't open yet, so Susan sat in her car and waited for someone to show up so she could get some information about Sara's whereabouts.

As she sat there, she spotted something that made her blood immediately turn to ice. Sara's car was parked in a lot adjacent to the club. She ran over to the vehicle to make sure that her eyes weren't deceiving her. They weren't. The car was Sara's. She knew by the tell-tale troll doll that her sister had attached to the rearview mirror. Susan knew now that something wasn't right, there were numerous parking tickets on the windshield. Sara would never have left her car unattended for that long.

After what seemed like an eternity, Susan saw a man unlocking the door of the gentleman's club. She approached him and introduced herself. She told him that she was Sara's sister and that she hadn't been able to reach her for days. The man said that he couldn't help her. Sara hadn't shown up to work her last three shifts. He assumed that she had quit.

Susan pointed out to him that Sara's car was still there. She asked him when Sara had last worked. He thought it had been on Tuesday night. It was now Monday. Almost a week had gone by since anyone had seen Sara. She mentioned to him that a frequent guest at the club had been more or less stalking her sister and wondered if he had any idea who the man was. He said that he couldn't help her. Men were constantly hitting on the dancers. It was impossible to keep track of who was bothering who.

After leaving the club, Susan went to the nearest police precinct and filed a missing person's report. She told the officer who was taking the information that she knew about the person who had been doggedly pursuing her sister prior to her disappearance, which wasn't much. Sara had told her that he was in his thirties and that he worked in the financial district. Susan thought that his name was Mark or Mike, but wasn't sure. Not much to go on, but at least it was something.

The officer told her that people went missing in the city all of the time. They usually turned up safe and sound in a few days. He would look into it. That was it. Susan had been expecting the police to immediately investigate this as foul play, but they didn't seem overly concerned. Dejected, she drove back to Pennsylvania to break the news to her parents. Sara was lost somewhere in New York City and she didn't know what to do about it.

The family continued to call Sara's phone day after day, several times a day. She never answered. Eventually, the phone service was shut off. Her apartment was also lost over time. They had driven up as a family and collected Sara's belongings. They kept in contact with the manager at the club where Sara had worked in case she showed up there, but she never did.

They also made regular calls to the officer in charge of Sara's case hoping for some sort of breakthrough. He had talked to the other dancers in the club about Sara and the mysterious patron who had frightened her so. Some of them were aware of the situation. They didn't know the man personally, but Sara had told them that he wouldn't take no for an answer. Sara's car had been impounded, but a thorough search of its interior had produced nothing helpful to the investigation. No one seemed to know anything more than they had from the beginning of the family's nightmare. Sara was gone without a trace and no one seemed to be able to tell them what had happened to her. And then, from the most unlikely source, came their answer.

The call that would bring closure, in a way, to the family came several months after they realized that Sara was missing. The officer who had been working the case phoned Susan to tell her that a man had confessed to the abduction, sexually assault and murder of Sara. Susan was floored. Her worst nightmare had become a reality. Sara was dead. She had been murdered. She could hardly process the information the officer was providing. Even though she had feared that this would be the outcome, that didn't make it any easier to hear. The officer than asked her if she could come to New York. There was much more to the story than he could share over the phone.

Susan agreed to meet him at the precinct the following day. She would call off work and make the trip alone. She didn't want her parents to be exposed to the gory details of what had happened to their child. It was going to be hard enough for them to accept that she was gone forever without knowing every last detail.

When Susan arrived at the police station the next day, she was ushered into a room where the officer she had been communicating with and another man were already waiting. They asked her to have a seat. It was then that the officer in charge, the one who had taken the initial report, told her a story that she would never forget. It was the story of her sister's final act.

Three days prior, a man had walked into the precinct and informed anyone who would listen that he had killed a girl several months earlier. He looked like he hadn't slept in weeks. His eyes were wild as he begged for someone to put handcuffs on him. They had never seen anyone so eager to be placed under arrest.

Even though the man hadn't asked for a lawyer, they called one for him. He didn't care. He wanted to talk. As soon as he said that the girl he had killed had been a dancer at a strip club, the officer in charge of Sara's missing persons case took over the interview. The officer related to Susan that the man could, literally, not get the words out fast enough. The story he told was unbelievable, but he swore it to be the truth.

The man began with what they already knew. He had been a customer at the club where Sara danced. Although he had frequented the establishment on and off for months before she began dancing there, once he saw Sara on stage, the man was mesmerized. He couldn't take his eyes off of this girl who was so different from the other dancers. She moved with beauty and grace and he knew that she was special. He wanted to get to know her better and waited around after her show to talk to her.

The man soon learned that it was not easy to get close to the performers. They were sequestered away from the patrons most of the time. He decided to wait for her outside and speak to her as she was leaving.

He soon found out that Sara was not interested in getting to know him in the same way that he wanted to get to know her. He said that she acted a bit scared when he approached her, but that was to be expected. She was polite, but not receptive to his invitation to go out for a drink. She had hurriedly gotten into her car and sped away. The man said that he was a little angry at the snub, but that was all.

Not one to give up easily, the man attempted on several other occasions to talk with Sara after her show had ended. Each time, he would wait by her car and each time, she would be escorted out by one of the security men who worked the door. Feeling more and more frustrated, the man stayed away from the club for a few days in the hopes that Sara would let her guard down. His patience paid off in spades.

After lying low for a brief time, the man began hanging around the parking lot behind the building every night. He wasn't sure if Sara's schedule had changed and he didn't want to run the risk of missing out on seeing her. His luck was in and he found her on his first try. Everything lined up in his favor on that fateful night. Sara, who usually parked in the club's lot had parked across the street and, for the first time since he had been watching her, she walked to her car alone.

There were very few people on the street that night which was unusual…the area was usually bustling as people left for the night. He had moved his car as close as he could to where Sara was parked and as she walked toward her vehicle; the man had jumped out and grabbed her arm.

Leading her forcefully away from her car and closer to his, the man had told her that he had a gun and that if she screamed he would use it. He hadn't really had any weapon at all, but Sara--young and naïve--had believed him. Incredibly, she walked with him to his car and offered little resistance as he forced her into the passenger seat. Keep in mind that this was his version of the events of that night, Sara is not here to give her side of the story.

The man stressed to the police that he had no intention of harming Sara. He had only wanted to talk to her. He believed that if she got to know him, she would like him as much as he liked her. He wasn't expecting her to fight, but as soon as he pulled away from the club and began driving through the city, Sara's self-preservation kicked in. She began to scream and even tried to jump out of the car. Not knowing what else to do, the man punched Sara several times in the head and face. She slumped over in the seat and was quiet. Panicked, the man parked behind a group of darkened buildings where there didn't seem to be anyone around.

Sara was moaning so he knew that she was alive at that point. Things were not working out as he had planned. She would go to the police if he released her, he knew that. Her face was bleeding and one of her eyes was swelling up. He couldn't chance what she would do if he let her go. He made up his mind that he would strangle her and leave her body in one of the many dumpsters that lined the buildings all around them. No one would ever find her. This had not been the way he had wanted things to end, but there seemed to be no other way out for him. What was best for Sara never even entered his mind.

Although he claimed that he had no intention of harming Sara that night, the man sexually assaulted the young girl before following through with his plan to strangle her. When the deed was done, he dragged her body to the nearest dumpster and left her there amongst the trash. He then drove home and showered and tried to convince himself that what he had done was an accident. He would have to forget about it and move on with his life.

That same night, the man said that he had experienced the worst nightmare of his life. Sara was there, in his dream, and she was furious. She screamed at him that he had taken everything from her. He had ruined everything she had worked for. Her face had contorted into a white mask and her hands had elongated and grabbed at him, scratching his face and ripping chunks of flesh out of his throat. He woke up drenched in perspiration, his own hands over his neck. His heart was racing. Never had a dream been so real. He remembered every last detail down to the tears that had run down Sara's face as she railed at him.

Assuming that it was just his conscience working on him, the man tried to forget the nightmare as well as the events that preceded it. He went to work as usual and tried to act like everything was fine. No one around him would ever know what he had done, he was sure of it.

The nightmare that had seemed so real would not be an isolated one. He began having them regularly. They were almost identical, night after night. Sara would come to him, crying and angry. Why had he taken everything from her? What right did he have to end what was hers? The nightmares always ended with her hands tearing at his throat. He would wake up terrified each and every time.

Weeks went by and the nightly visits from Sara continued. The man began to think that these weren't dreams at all. He believed that his victim was tormenting him from beyond the grave. Sleep was becoming unbearable. He found himself nodding off during the day and staying up all night in an attempt to avoid the confrontation he knew was waiting for him once he closed his eyes for the night.

Two things, besides the nightmares, had sent the man to the brink of insanity. The first one occurred on his way home from work one night. It was early in the evening, but already dark outside. Traffic was thick as he made his way home and he found himself sitting in gridlock. Suddenly, out of nowhere, Sara was standing in the street in front of his car. She had slapped her hands down on the hood and glared at him through the windshield.

Unable to move, the man put his head down on the steering wheel and stayed that way until the honking of car horns behind him forced him to look up. Sara was gone. There was nothing in the street in front of him except for other cars moving slowly through the city.

A few more weeks went by and the nightmares continued. On top of that, the final straw took place one night when the man had stumbled into the bathroom, half-awake only to find a woman lying in his bath tub. The lights were off, but the room was always illuminated by street lamps. He could clearly see her form and he knew immediately who it was. Sara was there, in his apartment and she was even angrier than she appeared in his nightmares.

While the man stood in his bathroom, frozen to the spot, Sara leapt up from her position in the bath tub and grabbed him around the neck. Her eyes bore into his. She didn't say a word, but her intention was clear: she wanted to do to him what he had done to her. He wanted to beg her for forgiveness, but her grip on his neck was so tight that he couldn't make a sound. He felt himself losing consciousness. The last thing he remembered was falling slowly to the bathroom floor. When he woke up, it was morning and Sara was gone. He had had enough. He needed to make things right. That was the day that he walked into the police precinct and confessed to Sara's murder.

The cops didn't know what to make of the story at first. Initially, they thought he was a nut, but after checking into details of the story, they weren't so sure. The buildings he described were there as were the dumpsters. Sara's car had been found where he said he last saw it when he abducted her. Worse yet, when his car was examined, blood later determined to be Sara's was found on the passenger side door. This, along with his confession, was enough to send him to prison for a very long time. That is, if he wasn't deemed mentally unfit for trial.

It was determined that, although the man had clearly suffered some mental trauma, he was not insane by any clinical definition. His confession would stand.

It is up for debate, as it was then by the investigators who worked Sara's case, what exactly led to his confession. Was it simply that his guilty conscience wouldn't allow him to forget what he had done? Could it be that he was tormenting himself, using Sara's vengeful spirit to punish himself for his unspeakable crimes?

Those things are certainly possible. Sara's sister Susan, as well as the rest of the family she left behind, believe that their shining star…the spark that had burned so brightly in her brief life…had used that determination that had always driven her to excel one last time. She had reached her killer from the other side and forced him to atone for what he had done. She took from him, in a way, what he had taken from her: life. Hers was gone and his would never be the same. She had seen to that as only Sara could.

Chapter 57:
And Then There Was One

Feuds between neighbors are nothing new. Usually, they end with one party giving the other the cold shoulder for the remainder of the time they are forced to live on the same street. Every once in a while, however, one neighbor is so vindictive and unforgiving that their anger can never be appeased. This is the story of one such family. They were, well and truly, the neighbors from Hell.

Greg Roush had grown up in what was, for him, an idyllic environment. His family, which consisted of his parents and four brothers, lived far up in the mountains of West Virginia. This is actually how I came by this unique story. Greg had attended school with one of my cousins who ended up putting him in touch with me. It is indeed a small world.

At any rate, Greg spent his childhood playing outside winter, summer and all seasons in between. He and his brothers did all of the things that country boys do. They swam in the streams that ran down the mountain. They hunted and fished. They caught frogs and snakes and any other creature they happened upon. They enjoyed every moment of their young lives. That is, until a new neighbor moved into one of the other homes in their slice of paradise. It was June of 1977. The date is burned into Greg's memory. He was fourteen years old and life as he knew it would be changed from that day on.

There were only six of seven houses in the whole area and they were all separated by a good bit of land. Everyone had always gotten along up till then. They exchanged tomatoes and other produce from their respective gardens. If one neighbor saw that another needed help mending a fence or repairing a roof, they would lend a hand without being asked.

The new neighbors made an impression almost immediately upon their arrival. Greg and his family were in the middle of eating supper when the sound of someone pounding on the front door interrupted their meal. Greg's father excused himself from the table and went to answer the knock.

The rest of the family couldn't hear exactly what was being said, but they did know that whoever was on their porch was not happy. After a few minutes, Greg's father returned to the table. Greg could see that his hands were shaking.

When one of the boys asked who was at the door, Greg's father told him that it was the fellow who had moved into the house that sat closest to theirs. The man said that someone had been rummaging around in his yard, some of his tools were missing off the back porch and he, more or less, accused Greg and his brothers of being the thieves.

Greg's father had assured the irate neighbor that his boys would never steal anything, much less tools from the house next door. The man had laid into Greg's father and warned him that he'd better never catch the boys on his property. If he did, they would be sorry they had ever been born.

The way the man had spoken that day, not just the horrible things he said, but the way he had said them, had angered Greg's father and also frightened him. This man was clearly unstable. Greg's father warned his sons to never, under any circumstances, go near the neighbor's house. They agreed and the matter was settled. Or, so they thought.

With each passing day after the arrival of the new neighbors, there was trouble. It turned out that the man who had come knocking on their door was married and had sons of his own, though Greg doesn't know how many because they never socialized with anyone else in the area. That was fine with Greg and his family and everyone else in what used to be their peaceful little haven in the mountains.

If the new neighbors had just been anti-social, there would never have been any issues among the other residents, but they were also malcontents. They took issue with everyone and everything. If a dog barked, they would be pounding on the door to complain. If children made too much noise when they were playing, one of the new neighbors would come running after them threatening to shut them up if they didn't get inside and be quiet.

Nothing was fun for Greg and his brothers anymore. They didn't dare play outside for fear of being chased back into the house by an angry man wielding a stick, a rock, a pellet gun or whatever he happened to have in his hand at the time. They didn't go hunting or fishing anymore. The new neighbors had laid claim to all of the fishing holes and as for hunting--Greg and his brothers were afraid that they would be shot "accidentally" by one of the strange people who had invaded their serene world.

The unwarranted hostility wasn't the only thing that set the new neighbors apart from the rest. They exhibited some other odd behaviors that had people talking. For one thing, they were night owls. Greg remembers seeing them outside dancing around a fire barrel on more nights than he can count. They would be singing loudly and throwing their arms in the air. Greg and his brothers would sit at the window and watch them, laughing the whole time at how silly they looked prancing around in the firelight.

Another thing that struck people as odd was the fact that no one in the house seemed to work. They almost never left their property. No one could figure out how they could afford to live. They didn't look rich by any means, although they owned several cars. One of the strangest things, although superficial, was that although the patriarch of the family was not someone anyone would describe as attractive, his wife was said to be quite beautiful. Even so, she behaved in the same manner as her husband. She, too, was standoffish and always looking for a fight.

Greg's family, along with the other neighbors, did their best to stay out of their surly neighbor's way. They didn't like it, but it seemed to be the only way to keep the peace. Things went along in this manner for years until one tragic day when an accident would unleash a vengefulness that Greg thought only existed in fairy tales. It began with, of all things, a driving lesson.

One of Greg's brothers was about to turn sixteen and his father was giving him driving lessons on the dirt road that ran between their house and that of the neighborhood bullies. They had been practicing for weeks without a hitch. Greg's father was always careful to make sure they stayed away from the neighbor's property line. They were on the road, perfectly within the boundaries. They were doing nothing wrong.

Greg's brother had put the car into reverse and had begun backing up when they heard a thud. Greg's father told him to put it in park as he got out to see if they had hit something. He was horrified when he saw what lay on the road behind the car. It was one of the neighbor's sons. He was conscious and sitting up, but screaming as though he would die.

Greg had been in the yard at the time and he swears to this day that the boy, who was around eleven or so, had purposely hit the back of the car. The boy had only a scrape on his leg that hadn't even drawn blood. All the same, he continued to wail as Greg's father offered to take him to the hospital.

All of the commotion soon roused the rest of the neighbors. The boy's father came charging out of the house, but rather than attending to his son, he stormed up to Greg's dad and butted him in the chest. He then proceeded to yell at both Greg's father and his brother. He was threatening to sue them for everything they had. He told them that he would see them in court.

Greg's father was at his breaking point. It had been an accident. He told the man that he would let the sheriff settle it. The man's face was red and his eyes blazing as he warned Greg's father that if he called the law it would be the last thing he ever did.

With that, Greg's father got back in the car and told his son to go park in the driveway. Before pulling away, he told the neighbor to send him any medical bills. That was all he said, but it made the neighbor even more furious. He continued to yell obscenities at Greg's father and his brother as they headed for the safety of home.

After that incident, even though no medical bills ever arrived, Greg and his family came to a consensus: they were going to sell their home and move away. The stress and uncertainty that had been put upon them since these neighbors had invaded their lives was too much. They had come to hate a place they once loved. They would put the house on the market right away and leave it, and the nightmare that lived across the street, behind for good.

The house sold relatively quickly, probably due to the fact that they listed it well below its fair market value. They didn't care about the money. Greg's parents had truly begun to worry for the safety for their family. No amount of money could bring back one of their boys if the neighbor ever decided to follow through on his endless threats.

On the day that the moving vans arrived to help pack up all of the family's possessions, Greg's family would receive one last visit from the neighbors who had, effectively, driven them out of their home. As Greg's dad was lifting boxes into one of the trucks, the man who had warned Greg's dad on countless occasions not to cross him, walked up and stretched out his hand. Greg was also helping to load boxes, as were his brothers.

It was too little too late, but Greg's father shook the man's hand. As he did, the man pulled him in close and told him that he wanted to give him something to remember him by. With that, he went on to lay a curse upon Greg and his brothers and any children they would ever have and any children their children's children would have and so on. No member of the family would live, from that moment on, past the age of twenty-one. For the first time since he had known of him, Greg says that the man had a smile on his face as he let go of Greg's father's hand and walked back across the way to his own yard.

The neighbor spent the rest of the day standing in his yard watching the family as they moved their possessions out of the house. He was still standing there at nightfall when they drove away for the last time. He had not stopped smiling all day.

Even though he hadn't mentioned it to him at the time, Greg heard what the man had said to his father. He didn't believe in curses and was sure that his dad didn't either. Greg figured that it was just one last jab from someone who got pleasure out of bullying other people. The family forgot all about it and left those bad memories behind. That is, until a year and a half later when Greg's brother, David, died only a few days before his twenty-first birthday.

David was an insulin dependent diabetic who required two shots a day to maintain his levels. He had always been carefully monitored and had no major health issues related to his diabetes. That was why it had come as such a shock to the family when he had suddenly taken ill and had been rushed to the emergency room the night before he passed away.

For reasons still unclear to Greg, David's heart had failed. His organs shut down and he died the day after being admitted to the hospital. The family was devastated. Just when they were starting their lives anew, everything came crashing down.

Greg made no connection at the time with the curse that the neighbor had placed on the family. Why would he? It was nonsense, or so he believed.

Eight months after David's death, Greg's brother Gary was killed, along with his best friend, in an automobile accident. Theirs had been the only car involved. For reasons only they knew, their car had left the roadway and careened into a tree as they were leaving a soccer practice.

Two deaths in less than a year rocked the family to its core. They were crippled by grief. Greg's father could no longer work. His mental state had deteriorated to the point that his wife had to help him dress himself. He just didn't seem able to do anything anymore. Losing his sons had broken him.

The deaths would keep coming over the next few years, Greg's brother Ryan died in a car crash under suspicious circumstances. Other cars in the area reported that an unknown vehicle had been blinding drivers with its headlights and then trying to force them off of the road. No one could get the make of the car or the license number. Whatever happened that night, Ryan died after his car ran off the road and over a steep embankment. He was nineteen years old.

Greg's father died of a massive stroke shortly after Ryan's death. Curtis, Greg's only remaining sibling, took his own life. He, too, had been only nineteen. Curtis had been the most sensitive of the boys and all of the deaths and hardships the family had endured over the years had been more than he could handle. He ended his life in the woods using his hunting rifle.

Although his brain told him that curses aren't real, Greg couldn't overlook all that had happened to his family since the day the neighbor had damned them. All of his brothers were now gone. Not one of them reached the age of twenty-one. Greg knew that it could all just be a macabre coincidence, but what were the odds? How could four boys from one family all die so young in a relatively short span of time?

In addition to the loss of his brothers, his father had seemed to change almost overnight after the neighbor had shaken his hand. This man, who had always been strong and hardworking had become a shell of himself in the months before his death. Greg and his mother seemed to be the only ones who, for some reason, had escaped the curse.

Greg was past twenty-one. He had lived beyond the age of the curse, but why? His only explanation is that, on one occasion, he had helped the neighbor bring in his animals when a storm was coming. The man had been almost civil to Greg that day and had even thanked him. It was the one and only time anyone in their family had experienced a decent moment with the neighbor.

Even today, Greg wonders if the nighttime fire rituals that the neighbors participated in had anything to do with the bad luck that had befallen his family. Had the neighbors possessed some sort of power that regular people couldn't understand? He wasn't sure, but there had always been something sinister about the neighbors that went far beyond their hateful nature.

In the end, all we can do is speculate as to what really caused this bizarre chain of events. Maybe it was all a terrible series of coincidences that decimated Greg's family. Perhaps the man cursing them and the events that followed were all just happenstance. Whatever the answer, Greg made a conscious decision to do whatever he could to make sure that the curse, if it does exist, dies with him.

Greg is now fifty-three years old. He has been married twice and has led a life that most people would envy. He is a successful entrepreneur, has a beautiful home, and has traveled the world. The one thing he has not allowed himself to have is children. For Greg, carrying on the family name is out of the question. He doesn't want to run the risk of bringing a child into the world only to have it taken away before reaching its twenty-first birthday. Some may find the notion ridiculous, but Greg remembers the words that the neighbor spoke that day when he condemned Greg's family and the way he smiled at them as they drove away. It was a smile of satisfaction. He had won after all.

Chapter 58:
To Hell And Back

Personal accounts from people who claim to have had near-death experiences can be found far and wide. They usually involve a white light, a feeling of peacefulness and a desire, by most, to stay on the other side. For some reason, they are persuaded to return to the land of the living for the time being to attend to some unfinished business.

Now and then, a story will fly in the face of all that we have heard before. The following tale of one man's glimpse into the afterlife is not filled with benevolence and serenity. His experience was not one of being welcomed by loved ones who had gone before. This unfortunate man had looked into the terrifying window of the most nightmarish of places for he had visited what he believed to be Hell.

For much of his life, George Workman had kept to himself. He had never felt the need to surround himself with people. He hadn't thought of himself as a mean person, he just didn't care for those around him and they seemed to feel the same way about him.

George had worked as a postal carrier for over twenty years before a heart condition had forced him into early retirement. He had loved his job. It had allowed him to earn a good living while rarely having to deal with his customers or co-workers. Even though he missed his job, he soon settled into a life of leisure. He spent his days reading and gardening. Life was good.

One thing that George had zero tolerance for was religion. His wrath would rain down on any poor soul who made the mistake of ringing his doorbell with the intention of ministering to him. He would rail against them and everything they believed in. George even went so far as to put a sign up next to his front door warning 'religious fanatics' to stay off of his property.

The only group that George held more disdain for than the pious, was children. He couldn't stand how noisy they were. When they road their bicycles up and down the street, he would sit on his porch and watch them, just waiting for one to get too close to his yard so he could chase them away. Although George didn't think of himself as a mean old man, everyone else did.

George had no family to speak of. His parents were both long dead. He had a sister who lived close by, but they had fallen out years earlier and were not on speaking terms. He had dated only a couple of women in his life. Nothing serious ever came of his brief relationships. George had never come close to marrying and was satisfied to live his life out as a bachelor.

Besides books and gardening, George can't really think of many things that he did like in those days. He never cared for animals, they were just another nuisance. He had trapped many a stray cat and taken the animal, cage and all, to the river and submerged it until the cat had drowned. He did the same thing with raccoons and possums. Anything he could trap, he would dispose of in this cruel manner. At the time, he thought nothing of it. They were just animals, after all.

It was at the age of sixty-two that George Workman's life would be changed forever. This was when he suffered three heart attacks in one day. That he lived through such trauma is a miracle in itself, but it's the story that he tells of his time between life and death that makes this so incredible.

When George had his first heart attack on that fateful day in September, he knew immediately what was happening. His left arm had gone completely numb as he was working in his garden. When he tried to stand up, he had no strength. He couldn't catch his breath and sweat was pouring off of him even though it was a cool day.

George couldn't stand so he crawled across his yard in an effort to reach the back door. If he could get that far, he figured he could make it to the telephone. It was not to be, the last thing he remembers is looking up at the sun and then laying his head down in the grass. It was then that his nightmare began.

He didn't know it at the time, but one of his neighbors had seen George sprawled face down in his yard. The neighbor had called 911 and had waited with George for an ambulance to arrive. By the time the emergency responders got there, George had no vital signs. They worked on him right there in the yard until they had a heartbeat, only then did they load him into the ambulance and rush him to the hospital.

George would suffer two more heart attacks that day while in surgery. He died on the operating table and had to be resuscitated. He had no way of knowing what was happening to his body, but George can relate exactly what his soul was experiencing and it was something out of a horror movie.

George remembers waking up, still on the lawn. The sun had gone down and dark clouds filled the sky. He felt fine so he got up and tried to walk to his house, but something was holding him back. All around him he could see dark figures. They were faceless masses whose only recognizable features were arms and legs.

As he attempted to walk, the figures that surrounded him grabbed his legs and pulled him back down to the ground. He would stand up and they would pull him down again. George began to shout at them to let him go, but even though they had no faces that he could see, they were laughing at him.

The figures began to scratch at George as he lay on the ground. The scene around George began to change. Even though he had been lying in the grass when he had first woken up; he now found himself on jagged rocks that were cutting into his skin. He could no longer see his house. The sky was completely black, but somehow he could still see everything around him.

The dark figures were now taking on a more distinctive form. George could clearly see that they had elongated faces and sharp teeth. Their eyes, which blazed like fire, were also visible to him now.

George remembers feeling fear like none he had ever experienced. This was no dream, this was real. He could feel everything that was happening to him. His skin burned from all of the wounds they had inflicted on him. He knew he had to run or they would kill him. When they finally let him stand up, he took off into the darkness hoping to find someone who could help him get back home.

He ran until he couldn't run another step only to find that he was in exactly the same place he had started from. There was no way out, every road led back to the jagged rocks and the terrifying creatures that seemed to exist only to torment anyone they encountered. In this case, that was George.

The dark figures that George now felt sure were demons, descended on him. They were beating him mercilessly, and yet he remained conscious. The pain was so excruciating that he actually hoped that he would die so that it would end. Finally giving up, George dropped to his knees and did something he had never done before in his life: he prayed.

As the demons continued to pummel George, he prayed for forgiveness from Jesus. He begged for a second chance. He made every promise to do good that he could think of. He would be a different person if he was allowed to return to his home. He would change. The longer George prayed, the fewer demons he saw. He doesn't know how much time went by, minutes or hours, but eventually, all of the demons disappeared.

As the last ones faded from his view, the sun was again visible in the sky. He could see its bright light shining down on him. The next thing he remembers is someone calling out his name. He opened his eyes and found that he was in the hospital, lying on a gurney. A bright light was shining down onto his face.

George was in the recovery room following his harrowing experiences on the operating table. Surgeons had managed to pull him back from the brink of death. Although he had suffered damage to his heart that should have ended his life, George was more alive than he had ever been.

The hospital staff marveled at George's progress. He recovered much faster than they thought possible. George was determined to get better and make good on the promises he had made. He would prove that his had been a life worth saving. He would make a difference in the world.

Following his release from the hospital, George began attending a local church twice a week. He eventually became a deacon. George also volunteered his time ministering at a homeless shelter. He would go anywhere he thought he could spread the word of God. He had a story to tell and he shared it freely with anyone who would listen.

George believes, beyond a shadow of a doubt, that he had been made to experience a taste of Hell so that he could turn his life around before it was too late. There are many who don't believe him and he accepts that without judgment. He knows what he knows.

Whatever happened to George that day, he's a better man for it. No longer a miserable curmudgeon, he is now everyone's friend. He would give the shirt off of his back to anyone in need, no questions asked. He's kind to children and animals. He married a woman he met at church and they adopted two cats from the local animal shelter.

If George didn't visit Hell that day, what else could explain his sudden change of heart about the world and everyone in it? Did he just experience a vivid nightmare while under anesthesia that caused him to conjure up so many frightening images? If so, why would he assume that praying would banish his tormenters since he had never believed in such a thing? George can't explain why anything happened the way it did. He accepts it for what it was for him: a new lease on life.

Chapter 59:
The Broach

Objects, like people, hold energy. The owner of a particularly cherished piece of jewelry, for example, can remain so attached to it that they follow it wherever it goes even after they have passed on. Problems only seem to manifest when the beloved bauble ends up in the wrong hands, this is when the rightful owner feels the need to make their presence known. Such is the case in the story you are about to read.

Before Kim Sanders' paternal grandmother passed away, she left instructions that all of her worldly possessions were to be divided up among her survivors. That consisted of her son, who was Kim's father, her two daughters and her eight grandchildren. Only a handful of her belongings had been specifically willed to individuals. One of those earmarked items was a broach that had been in the family for several generations.

The broach was a work of art. It consisted of pearls surrounded by tiny diamonds all resting in a platinum shell. Kim's grandmother had rarely worn it, it was too precious. Instead, she kept it wrapped in tissue paper and secreted away in a drawer in her jewelry cabinet. The broach only made appearances on special occasions like weddings and funerals.

Everyone in the family knew that the grandchild who was most favored by Kim's grandmother had been her cousin Hanna. From the moment the child had been born, Hanna held a special place in her grandmother's heart. It came as no surprise that she would be the person who would be gifted the broach. Even so, bickering erupted almost immediately among the other grandchildren. They felt that the broach should be sold and the proceeds split eight ways.

Kim didn't give her opinion one way or the other. She understood why her grandmother left the broach to Hanna and wasn't going to squabble about it. Hanna balked at the notion of selling the broach. She wanted it to stay in the family as it had done for decades. In her mind, they would be doing a disservice to her grandmother's memory if they sold her most prized possession.

Even though Hanna had every right to keep the broach, she compromised with her cousins. She would buy each one of them out of what they thought should be their share of the value of the broach. All of the grandchildren had received a significant amount of cash from the estate, but it still wouldn't be enough to satisfy her rather greedy relatives. They agreed that the broach would stay with a neutral party, Kim's father who didn't want the broach, until Hanna had paid off the cousins.

Almost immediately, the grandmother began making her displeasure known. Kim's father, Bob, recalls how strange things began to happen in his house soon after he took possession of the broach. It had never happened before, but now, day and night, the silence would be broken by the violent slamming of doors. It was as though someone was walking up and down the hallway shutting every bedroom door as hard as they could. Bob lived alone so there was no possibility that someone else was there with him. Even so, he would do a thorough search of the house only to turn up nothing.

Besides the phantom door slamming, Bob also noticed that things began disappearing. He had to purchase new eyeglasses because the ones he wore every day and only took off when he was sleeping had gone missing from his nightstand.

He also had to have a new lock put on the front door after he came home one day and found that his key would no longer open the door. The key still fit, but it wouldn't move the tumbler. The locksmith who installed the new lock could find no reason as to why the key wouldn't work. It was as though Bob was being barred from his own house.

Bob was also surprised one day to find his refrigerator door standing wide open even though he had not been home and was certain that it had been shut when he left that morning. As a result, he ended up throwing away the groceries he had purchased only two days earlier.

Thinking that he might have a prankster or a burglar who was making themselves at home when he wasn't there, Bob set up a video camera in his living room hoping to catch the culprit on film. When he played back the footage each day it showed nothing out of the ordinary, except for one time when he saw something he couldn't explain.

On one segment of the footage, Bob could clearly see a shadow moving from the living room into the hallway. Immediately after the dark vision was out of sight, doors could be heard slamming. When Bob showed the tape to Kim she thought the same thing that he did. He had a ghost in the house and they both had a sneaking suspicion that they knew who it might be.

What convinced them beyond any doubt that their grandmother had returned to pay them a visit was what happened when Kim's cousin Brenda announced that she was getting married. She had one request for the family and that was that she be allowed to wear the broach as her 'something old' during the ceremony. Everyone, Hanna included, agreed that this would be fine.

As soon as Brenda took possession of the broach, all of the energy that had been whirling around Bob's house and causing mischief, shifted to Brenda. She reported that doors were slamming at her house now. She also said that her expensive wedding gown had developed a smell that made it impossible for her to wear. Although it had been perfect when it was purchased, now the gown reeked of what seemed to be cat urine. Brenda didn't have a cat or any other animals for that matter. To make matters worse, the bridal shop refused to take it back. Brenda would have to wear it, stench and all.

Things went from bad to worse for poor Brenda. She suffered a nasty bout of food poisoning only days before her wedding. She was getting next to no sleep due to the noises that seemed to come from nowhere all night long. If doors weren't slamming, a steady humming would fill her bedroom until she thought she would go mad. When she confided in Kim about all of the bizarre occurrences, her cousin told her that similar things had happened at her father's house. She also told her how to make it stop: get rid of the broach. As soon as it had changed hands from Bob to Brenda, his house had gone back to normal. She needed to get rid of it as soon as possible for her own sake.

Brenda, Kim and the other cousins all got together and agreed that they had been behaving like spoiled children. Enough was enough. Clearly, their grandmother wanted Hanna--and only Hanna--to have the broach. They would hand it over to her, its rightful owner, and let bygones be bygones. And, so they did.

As soon as Hanna had the broach it was as though a cloud had lifted. Brenda's wedding went off without a hitch. She had walked down the aisle in her gown after all. The odor had left as mysteriously as it had appeared. And, since it was a most special occasion, Hanna had worn the broach to the ceremony just as her grandmother would have had she been living. Brenda also noted that the noises in her home ceased and life got back to normal.

Hanna has never reported having any odd occurrences since she took possession of the broach. She keeps it, just as her grandmother did, wrapped in tissue in her jewelry box where it will stay until the day she passes it on to her daughter. It will stay in the family after all just as her grandmother had intended.

Epilogue

Now that you have shared in the experiences of the contributors to this book, it is up to you to decide for yourself what is real and what is merely coincidence. Sometimes, people see what they want to see. Maybe they read more into a situation than is actually there. All the same, there are times when events occur that defy logic.

Are encounters such as the ones you've just read really possible? Can those who have passed on somehow return to coexist with the living? Can entities who have never lived on this earth as human find a way into our world in order to wreak havoc on their unsuspecting hosts?

Skeptics will say no to all of those questions. The people who experienced these events first-hand will tell you differently. As with life, for every action there is a reaction, even if it comes from a place we do not know and dare not venture--at least for now.

Acknowledgements

Thank you to all of the people who allowed me to share their stories for this book. Some of you I know well, others are virtual strangers, but you all have my undying respect.

Thank you to my daughter whom I love more than life itself. You make the world turn; never forget that.

Thank you to the readers who take time out of their lives to indulge in my writings. You can never know how humbled I am in this knowledge.

"True Stories of the Paranormal: The Complete Collection" is the sole property of its author.

No unauthorized reproduction is permitted without the express written consent of the author.

All Rights Reserved

Copyright 2017

Author: Cindy Parmiter

Cover Art Courtesy of: alga38

Printed in Great
Britain
by Amazon